AUTODESK®
REVIT® ARCHITECTURE 2012

ESSENTIALS

AUTODESK OFFICIAL TRAINING GUIDE

AUTODESK®
REVIT® ARCHITECTURE 2012
ESSENTIALS
AUTODESK OFFICIAL TRAINING GUIDE

Phil Read

Eddy Krygiel

James Vandezande

WILEY

Wiley Publishing, Inc.

Senior Acquisitions Editor: Willem Knibbe
Development Editor: Laurene Sorensen
Technical Editor: Adam Thomas
Production Editor: Dassi Zeidel
Copy Editor: Liz Welch
Editorial Manager: Pete Gaughan
Production Manager: Tim Tate
Vice President and Executive Group Publisher: Richard Swadley
Vice President and Publisher: Neil Edde
Book Designer: Happenstance Type-O-Rama
Compositor: Craig W. Johnson, Happenstance Type-O-Rama
Proofreader: Publication Services, Inc.
Indexer: Ted Laux
Project Coordinator, Cover: Katie Crocker
Cover Designer: Ryan Sneed
Cover Image: _spacegroup

For general information on our other products and services or to obtain technical support, please contact our Customer Care Department within the U.S. at (877) 762-2974, outside the U.S. at (317) 572-3993 or fax (317) 572-4002.

Wiley also publishes its books in a variety of electronic formats. Some content that appears in print may not be available in electronic books.

Library of Congress Cataloging-in-Publication Data

Read, Phil, 1965–
    Autodesk Revit architecture essentials / Phil Read, Eddy Krygiel, James Vandezande. — 1st ed.
       p. cm.
    ISBN 978-1-118-01683-1 (pbk.)
    ISBN: 978-1-118-09732-8 (ebk.)
    ISBN: 978-1-118-09734-2 (ebk.)
    ISBN: 978-1-118-09733-5 (ebk.)
    1. Architectural drawing—Computer-aided design. 2. Architectural design—Data processing. 3. Autodesk Revit. I. Krygiel, Eddy, 1972- II. Vandezande, James, 1972- III. Title.
    NA2728.R39 2011
    720.28'40285536—dc22
                        2011008887

10 9 8 7 6 5 4 3 2 1

Dear Reader,

Thank you for choosing *Autodesk Revit Architecture 2012 Essentials*. This book is part of a family of premium-quality Sybex books, all of which are written by outstanding authors who combine practical experience with a gift for teaching.

Sybex was founded in 1976. More than 30 years later, we're still committed to producing consistently exceptional books. With each of our titles, we're working hard to set a new standard for the industry. From the paper we print on, to the authors we work with, our goal is to bring you the best books available.

I hope you see all that reflected in these pages. I'd be very interested to hear your comments and get your feedback on how we're doing. Feel free to let me know what you think about this or any other Sybex book by sending me an email at nedde@wiley.com. If you think you've found a technical error in this book, please visit **http://sybex.custhelp.com**. Customer feedback is critical to our efforts at Sybex.

Best regards,

NEIL EDDE
Vice President and Publisher
Sybex, an Imprint of Wiley

To Justine: Thanks again for letting me work with Eddy and James. I promise not to blow all my earnings (like I did last year) at the Mix Lounge in Vegas. I had no idea that a round of drinks would require a second mortgage.

To Harrison: You've come a long way this year and you're braver than you know. If you'll go pick up the Legos strewn all over your bedroom floor, I'll make you a hot chocolate.

To Millicent: The world is a tough place, but especially for a girl. Don't trust everyone. Be honest, fair, strong, and nice. But not too nice.

To Jasper: You're capable of the best Mr. Hankey, Conky, and Gumby impersonations I know. It's seems silly, but it means you're capable of careful observation. Please keep up the great work at school and keep writing those books.

To everyone else: Choose meaning over money. Don't ever work for someone that you can't deeply respect; especially when he's sharply-dressed, sharply-elbowed, sharply-tongued, but not sharply-minded. You're holding back human progress.

—Phil

Small monkeys. It's good to have you around. You've seen that life is a lot of work and can be full of challenges. I'm proud of you for rising to meet them. It's a hard thing to do.

—Eddy

For my late father-in-law, Bill. You are missed every day and I know you would appreciate—but not necessarily understand—these books we're writing.

—James

ACKNOWLEDGMENTS

Ah, acknowledgments. While all the glory of writing a book is consumed by the authoring team, it takes so many more people than the three of us to make this book happen. Just like building design, the process of writing and publishing a book is truly a team sport and without the hard work, dedication, and willingness to put up with the authoring team, this book would never have happened.

First, we'd like to thank all the fine folks at Autodesk Revit because without their excellent software we wouldn't have a topic to write about. While it's not possible to name them all, the work of the product designers, quality assurance team, and all the others doesn't go unrecognized or unappreciated. Thank you, gals and guys, for taking a tough job and doing it with a great attitude. Thank you to the development team for putting up with all of our continued requests to make the product better.

Second, a big thanks to our technical team. They dot our i's, cross our t's, and berate us every time we turn in something late. Their work and effort makes sure that we as authors can produce something that you the reader can actually comprehend. Thank you to Laurene, Liz, Dassi, and the rest of our editing team for translating our sentence fragments into the Queen's English and not allowing us to use words like "this" and "they" and "it" as regular nouns; Pete, for keeping time; Adam, the guy who checks all of our Revit work; and our excellent support team at Sybex, who helped us develop and focus the content. As always, a special thanks to Willem Knibbe, for his continually positive attitude in the face of deadlines, misspellings, and the general chaos that comes with working on any of our projects.

—Phil Read, Eddy Krygiel, and James Vandenzande

About the Authors

 *Phil Read* is the founder of Arch | Tech as well as one of the driving forces behind the original Revit software. He's also a blogger, a speaker, and a popular presenter at Autodesk University. After working in both civil engineering and architecture, he downloaded Revit version 1.0 (at the suggestion of an ArchiCAD reseller) and was hooked. Less than a year later, he began working for Revit Technology and then Autodesk as a project implementation specialist, where he had the honor and pleasure of working with some of the most remarkable people and design firms around the world. He's a regular speaker, blogger, and Tweeter and relishes the role of change agent as long as it makes sound business sense. Phil holds degrees in communications and architecture, as well as a master's degree in architecture.

 *Eddy Krygiel* is a senior project architect, a LEED Accredited Professional, and an Autodesk Authorized Author at HNTB Architects headquartered in Kansas City, Missouri. He has been using Revit since version 5.1 to complete projects ranging from single-family residences and historic remodels to 1.12-million-square-foot office buildings. Eddy is responsible for implementing BIM at his firm and also consults for other architecture and contracting firms around the country looking to implement BIM. For the last four years, he has been teaching Revit to practicing architects and architectural students in the Kansas City area and has lectured around the nation on the use of BIM in the construction industry. Eddy also coauthored *Mastering Autodesk Revit Architecture 2011* with Phil Read and James Vandezande (Sybex, 2010).

 *James Vandezande* is a registered architect and a senior associate at HOK in New York City, where he is a member of the firm-wide BIM leadership and is managing their buildingSMART initiatives. After graduating from the New York Institute of Technology in 1995, he worked in residential and small commercial architecture firms performing services ranging from estimating to computer modeling to construction administration. In 1999, he landed at SOM and transformed his technology skills into a 10-year span as a digital design manager. In this capacity, he pioneered the implementation of BIM on such projects as One World Trade Center, a.k.a. Freedom Tower. James has been using Revit since version 3.1 and has lectured at many industry events, including Autodesk University, VisMasters Conference, CMAA BIM Conference, McGraw_Hill Construction, and the AIANYS Convention. He is a cofounder and president of the NYC Revit Users Group and is an adjunct lecturing professor at the NYU School for Continuing and Professional Studies as well as the Polytechnic Institute of NYU.

Contents at a Glance

Contents

CHAPTER 3   **Walls and Curtain Walls**   **53**

CHAPTER 4	**Floors, Roofs, and Ceilings**	**87**

CHAPTER 5	**Stairs, Ramps, and Railings**	**115**

CHAPTER 9 Rooms and Color Fill Plans 209

CHAPTER 10 Worksharing 229

CHAPTER 14   Tips, Tricks, and Troubleshooting   331

APPENDIX   Revit Certification   345

INTRODUCTION

Welcome to Autodesk Revit Architecture 2012 Essentials, based on the Revit Architecture 2012 release.

What you are holding in your hands is the first Revit book in a new series. When we authors first sat down to learn Revit (eons ago), each of us was put into a room with a trainer, and over the course of four days, we clicked through all the buttons and functionality to learn the software. Once initiated, we walked away with some answers, some questions, and a general understanding of what Revit does and how we could use it to leverage building design, documentation, and construction.

Our aim with this book is to replicate that training experience. The book is divided into training "days" with the idea that each chapter should take you a couple of hours to complete and four chapters equal a full day of training. Once you've made it through the book, in the final two chapters we offer a half day's worth of tips and tricks to help you leverage those skills on real projects.

When we sat down to plan this book, we looked to serve the needs of individuals who were fresh to Revit as well as those who had taken training so long ago they needed a solid refresher. We hope you will find that our efforts to meet that need were successful. We designed the book in a nonlinear fashion with the intention that the chapters would be freestanding, so the reader could take almost any chapter and learn its topics rather than having to work through the book from beginning to end.

We wanted to write a book that is as much about architectural design and practice as it is about software. Architecture is a way of looking at the world and the methods that inspire creatively solving the problems of the built world. The book follows real-life workflows and scenarios and is full of practical examples that explain how to leverage the tools within Revit. We hope you'll agree that we've succeeded.

Who Should Read This Book

This book is written for architects, designers, students, and anyone else who needs their first exposure to Revit or has had an initial introduction and wants a refresher on the program's core features and functionality. It's for architects (and those who'd like to be) of any generation—you don't need to be a computer wizard to understand or appreciate the content. We've designed the book to follow real project workflows and processes to help make the tools easy to follow, and the chapters are full of handy tips to make Revit easy to leverage. This book

Certification Objective

can also be used to help prepare for Autodesk's Certified Associate and Certified Professional exams. For more information on certification, please visit **www .autodesk.com/certification**.

What You Will Learn

This book is designed to help you grasp the basics of Revit using real-world examples and techniques you'll use in everyday design and documentation. We'll explain the Revit interface and help you find the tools you need as well as help you understand how the application is structured. From there we'll show you how to create and modify the primary components in a building design. We'll show you how to take a preliminary model and add layers of intelligence to help analyze and augment your designs. We'll demonstrate how to create robust and accurate documentation, and then guide you through the construction process.

As you are already aware, BIM is more than just a change in software; it's a change in architectural workflow and culture. To take full advantage of both BIM and Revit in your office structure, you'll have to make some changes to your practice. We've designed the book around an ideal, integrated workflow to aid in this transition.

Once you've mastered the content in each chapter, we include a section called "The Essentials and Beyond" where you can continue to hone your skills by taking on more challenging exercises.

What You Need

To leverage the full capacity of this book, we highly recommend that you have a copy of Revit installed on a computer strong enough to handle it. To download the trial version of Revit Architecture, go to **www.autodesk.com/ revitarchitecture**, where you'll also find complete system requirements for running Revit.

From a software standpoint, the exercises in this book are designed to be lightweight and not computationally intensive. This way, you avoid long wait times to open and save files and perform certain tasks. That said, keep in mind that the Autodesk-recommended computer specs for Revit are far more than what you need to do the exercises in this book but are *exactly* what you need to work on an architectural project using Revit.

If you're working from a 32-bit OS, you'll need the following:

> ▶ Microsoft Windows 7 32-bit Enterprise, Ultimate, Professional, or Home Premium; Microsoft Windows Vista 32-bit (SP2 or later) Enterprise, Ultimate, Business, or Home Premium; or Microsoft Windows XP (SP2 or later) Professional or Home

▶ Intel Pentium 4 or AMD Athlon dual core, 3.0 GHz (or higher) with SSE2 technology for Microsoft Windows 7 32-bit or Microsoft Windows Vista 32-bit (SP2 or later). Intel Pentium 4 or AMD Athlon dual core, 1.6 GHz (or higher) with SSE2 technology for Microsoft Windows XP (SP2 or later)

▶ 3 GB of RAM

▶ 5 GB of free disk space

▶ 1280 × 1024 monitor with true color

▶ Display adapter capable of 24-bit color for basic graphics; 256 MB DirectX 9–capable graphics card with Shader Model 3 for advanced graphics

▶ Microsoft Internet Explorer 7.0 (or later)

▶ Microsoft Mouse–compliant pointing device

▶ Download or installation from DVD

▶ Internet connectivity for license registration

If you're working from a 64-bit version (which is preferred for project work due to how much RAM you can leverage), you'll need the following:

▶ Microsoft Windows 7 64-bit Enterprise, Ultimate, Professional, or Home Premium; Microsoft Windows Vista 64-bit (SP2 or later) Enterprise, Ultimate, Business, or Home Premium; or Microsoft Windows XP Professional x64 edition (SP2 or later)

▶ Intel Pentium 4 or AMD Athlon dual core, 3.0 GHz (or higher) with SSE2 technology for Microsoft Windows 7 64-bit or Microsoft Windows Vista 64-bit (SP2 or later). Intel Pentium 4 or AMD Athlon dual core, 1.6 GHz (or higher) with SSE2 technology for Microsoft Windows XP Professional x64 edition (SP2 or later)

▶ 3 GB of RAM

▶ 5 GB of free disk space

▶ 1280 × 1024 monitor with true color

▶ Display adapter capable of 24-bit color for basic graphics; 256 MB DirectX 9–capable graphics card with Shader Model 3 for advanced graphics

- ▶ Microsoft Internet Explorer 7.0 (or later)

- ▶ Microsoft Mouse–compliant pointing device

- ▶ Download or installation from DVD

- ▶ Internet connectivity for license registration

What Is Covered in This Book

Revit is a building information modeling (BIM) application that has quickly emerged as the forerunner in the design industry. Revit is as much a change in workflow (if you come from a 2D or CAD environment) as it is a change in software. In this book, we'll focus on using real-world workflows and examples to guide you through learning the basics of Revit 2012—the *Essentials*.

Autodesk Revit Architecture 2012 Essentials is organized to provide you with the knowledge needed to gain experience in many different facets of the software. The book is broken down into 14 chapters, which represent the content you would cover if you were to attend a 3–4 day training class.

Day 1

This section is designed to be an introduction to the software, the user interface, and the basic components that you will use every day.

Chapter 1, "Introducing Revit and the User Interface," introduces to you the user interface and gets you acquainted with the tools and technology—the workflow—behind the software.

Chapter 2, "Schematic Design," introduces you to situations that would happen on a real project; say, a designer has given you a sketch and now you need to take this basic building design and model it.

Chapter 3, "Walls and Curtain Walls," helps you build on that initial learning by establishing some of the basic building blocks in architecture: walls.

Chapter 4, "Floors, Roofs, and Ceilings," rounds out the first day of training by introducing you to the other basic building blocks: floors, roofs, and ceilings. By the end of the first four chapters, you will know how easy it is to create a building form; apply walls, floors, roofs, and ceilings to that form; and easily quantify how much space and area are in your designs.

Day 2

With the basic building forms established, you spend Day 2 of training augmenting that form with components that help building form interact with reality. These components are what we interact with every day—things like stairs, windows, doors—and help establish the design.

Chapter 5, "Stairs, Ramps, and Railings," begins by explaining the basics of stairs, ramps, and railings. These core components are versatile and using them can be a bit tricky, so we'll guide you through the process of creating several types of stairs and railings.

Chapter 6, "Adding Families," shows you how to add a core element to your project: families. You use families to create most of your content, and Revit by default comes with a robust supply.

Chapter 7, "Modifying Families," shows you how to take these families, modify them, or create your own, making the library of your content limitless.

Finally, in Chapter 8, "Groups and Phasing," you'll learn techniques for taking families and repeating them in the model in ways you can use to augment your design.

Day 3

With two days of training under your belt, you'll have most of the tools you need to create building designs in Revit. What we will focus on for the next four chapters is taking that design and documenting it so you can share the building design with owners, contractors, or anyone on your project team.

Chapter 9, "Rooms and Color Fill Plans," shows you how to add room elements to your spaces, assign information to them, and create colorful diagrams based on space, department, or any other variable you need.

Chapter 10, "Worksharing," discusses how to take your Revit file into a multiperson working environment. Worksharing allows several people within your office or project team to work on the same Revit file simultaneously.

In Chapter 11, "Details and Annotations," we focus on adding annotation to explain your designs. You'll learn how to add detail to your model in the form of dimensions, text, keynotes, and tags, and how to embellish your 3D model with additional detailing.

Chapter 12, "Creating Drawing Sets," shows you how to take all this information and place those drawings and views onto sheets so they can be printed and distributed to your project stakeholders.

Day 4

The final two chapters in this book are designed to build on the skills you have just learned and give you some additional resources to leverage your new talent.

Chapter 13, "Workflow and Other Revit Essentials," provides the basics on how to take your office from a CAD environment to one that works with BIM. This chapter explores tools for every level of the project team—from the new staff to project managers. Understanding the process and workflow will be key to the success of your first Revit project.

The final chapter, Chapter 14, "Tips, Tricks, and Troubleshooting," is chock-full of useful tips and tricks, and you'll learn how to troubleshoot your Revit project.

The *Essentials* Series

The *Essentials* series from Sybex provides outstanding instruction for readers who are just beginning to develop their professional skills. Every *Essentials* book includes these features:

▶ Skill-based instruction with chapters organized around projects rather than abstract concepts or subjects

▶ Suggestions for additional exercises at the end of each chapter, where you can practice and extend your skills

▶ Digital files (via download) so you can work through the project tutorials yourself. Please check the book's web page at **www.sybex.com/go/revit2012essentials** for the companion downloads.

Contacting the Authors

We welcome your feedback and comments. You can find the three of us on our blog, **www.architecture-tech.com**, or email us at **MasteringRevit@architecture-tech.com**. We hope you enjoy the book.

CHAPTER 1

Introducing Revit and the User Interface

After one decade in the architecture, engineering, and construction (AEC) space, Autodesk Revit Architecture continues to be unique in its holistic building information modeling (BIM) approach to design integration. Sure, there are other BIM-ish tools that allow you to design in 3D. And 10 years ago, 3D might have been a differentiator, but today 3D is a commodity!

Revit provides the unique ability to design, manage, and document your project information from within a single file, something that no other BIM tool will allow you to do. Because all your data resides in a single project file, you can work in virtually any view to edit your model—plan, section, elevation, 3D, sheets, details, and even a schedule. To begin the journey in learning Revit, we will help you become comfortable with the user interface and the basic principles of a Revit project.

In this chapter, you learn the following skills:

▶ **Understanding the Revit interface**

▶ **Understanding the interface workflow**

▶ **Using common modifying tools**

Understanding the Revit Interface

The user interface (UI) of Revit is similar to other Autodesk products such as AutoCAD, Inventor, and 3ds Max. You might also notice that it is similar to other Windows-based applications such as Microsoft Word or Mindjet's MindManager. All of these applications are based on the "ribbon" concept—where a set of toolbars are placed on tabs in a tab bar, or *ribbon*, and are contextually updated based on the content on which you're working. We will cover the most critical aspects of the UI in this section, but we will not provide an exhaustive review of all toolbars and commands. You will gain experience with the common tools as you read through the chapters and exercises in this book.

Figure 1.1 shows the Revit Architecture 2012 UI. To illustrate some different project views, we've tiled four different view windows: Plan, Elevation, 3D, and Camera.

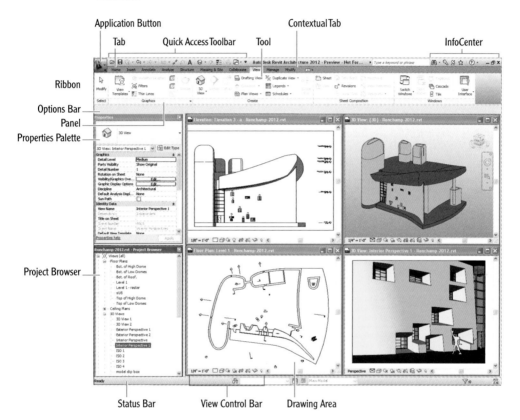

FIGURE 1.1 Revit 2011 User Interface

Let's begin by examining just a few important parts of the UI. As you progress through the remaining chapters in this book, you'll gradually become more familiar with the other basic parts of the UI.

Properties Palette

The Properties palette is a floating palette that can remain open while you work within the model. The palette can be docked on either side of your screen, or it can be moved to a second monitor. You can open the Properties palette in one of three ways:

▶ Clicking the Properties icon in the Properties panel of the Modify tab in the ribbon

▶ Selecting Properties from the right-click context menu

▶ Pressing Ctrl+1 on your keyboard, as you would in AutoCAD

Ctrl-1

As shown in Figure 1.2, the Properties palette contains the Type Selector at the top of the palette. When you are placing elements or swapping types of elements you've already placed in the model, the palette must be open to access the Type Selector.

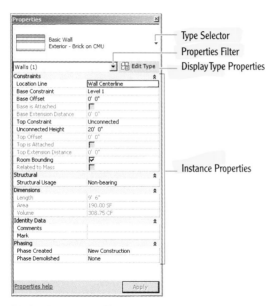

Type Selector
Properties Filter
Display Type Properties

Instance Properties

FIGURE 1.2 **The Properties palette allows you to set instance parameters for building elements and views.**

When no elements are selected, the Properties palette displays the properties of the active view. If you need to change settings for the current view, simply make the changes in the Properties palette and the view will be updated. For views, you may not even need to use the Apply button to submit the changes.

w/o selection

Finally, you can also use the Properties palette as a filtering method for selected elements. When you select a large number of disparate objects, the drop-down list below the Type Selector will display the total number of selected elements. Open the list and you will see the elements listed per category, as shown in Figure 1.3. Select one of the categories to modify the parameters for the respective elements. This is different from the Filter tool in that the entire selection set is maintained, allowing you to perform multiple modifying actions without reselecting elements.

FIGURE 1.3 Use the Properties palette to filter selection sets.

Project Browser

The Project Browser (Figure 1.4) is a virtual folder tree of all of the views, legends, schedules, sheets, families, groups, and links in your Revit project. You can collapse and expand the tree by selecting the + or – icon. Open any view listed in the Project Browser simply by double-clicking on it.

FIGURE 1.4
Project Browser

The Project Browser can also be filtered and grouped into folders based on any combination of user-defined parameters. To access the type properties of the Project Browser, right-click on Views at the top of the tree, and select Type Properties. Select any of the items in the Type drop-down list or duplicate one to create your own.

Status Bar

The status bar provides useful information about commands and selected elements (Figure 1.5). In addition to the worksets and design options toolbars, the status bar displays information about keyboard shortcut commands or simply lists what object you have selected. It is also particularly useful for identifying when you are about to select a chain of elements.

FIGURE 1.5 The status bar is located at the bottom of the Revit application window.

View Control Bar

The View Control Bar is at the bottom of every view and will have different icons depending on the type of view in which you are working (Figure 1.6).

Certification
Objective

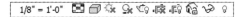

FIGURE 1.6 The View Control Bar gives
you quick access to commonly used view properties.

From left to right you have Scale, Detail Level, Visual Style, Sun Path (On/Off), Shadows (On/Off), Rendering Show/Hide (only in 3D Views), Crop On/Off, Show/Hide Crop, Lock 3D View (only in 3D views), Temporary Hide/Isolate, and Reveal Hidden Elements. Note that some of these buttons will access view properties you can also set in the Properties palette.

ViewCube

As one of several navigation aids in Revit, you'll find the ViewCube in 3D views. You can orbit your model by clicking and dragging anywhere on the ViewCube. You can also click on any face, corner, or edge of the ViewCube to orient your view.

Hovering over the ViewCube will reveal the Home option (the little "house" above the ViewCube), which will bring you back to your home view. Right-clicking the ViewCube will open a menu that will allow you to set, recall, and orient your view, as shown in Figure 1.7.

FIGURE 1.7 Right-click on the ViewCube to access more view orientation options.

Options Bar

The Options Bar is a context-sensitive area that gives you feedback as you create and modify content. This is an important UI feature when you are creating model content. For example, when you use the Wall command, the Options Bar displays settings for the height, the location line, offset, and chain modeling options, as shown in Figure 1.8. Even when you place annotations, the Options Bar provides you with choices for leaders and other additional context.

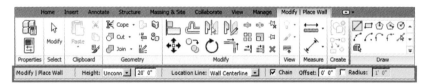

FIGURE 1.8 The Options Bar provides immediate input of options related to a selected object or command.

Understanding the Interface Workflow

In this section we will dive into the workflow of the Revit interface with some basic modeling exercises. These lessons can be applied to just about every tool and function throughout the program.

Activating a command in Revit is a simple and repeatable process that takes you from a tool in the ribbon to options and properties and into the drawing window to begin placing an element. In the following exercise, you will create a simple layout of walls using some critical components of the UI as well as a few common modifying tools.

Creating a Simple Layout

Begin by downloading the file c01-Interface.rvt or c01-Interface-Metric.rvt from this book's companion web page: **www.sybex.com/go/revit2012essentials**. You can open a Revit project file by dragging it directly into the application or by using the Open command from the Application menu. You can even double-click on a Revit file, but be aware that if you have more than one version of Revit installed on your computer, the file will open in the last version of Revit you used.

Once the project file is open, you will notice in the Project Browser that the active view is {3D}. This is the default 3D view, which you can always access by clicking the icon in the Quick Access toolbar (QAT) (which looks like a little house). Note that the view name of the active view is always shown as bold in the Project Browser. Let's begin by placing some walls on some predetermined points in a plan view:

1. In the Project Browser, locate the Floor Plans category, expand it, and double-click on Level 1. This will open the Level 1 floor plan view.

2. From the ribbon, select the Home tab and click the Wall tool.

3. In the Options Bar located just below the ribbon, change the Height to Level 2 and set Location Line to Finish Face: Exterior. Also make sure the Chain option is checked.

4. At the top of the Properties palette, you will see the Type Selector. Click on it to change the wall type to Basic Wall: Exterior - Brick on Mtl. Stud. Also find the parameter named Top Offset and change the value to 3´-0˝ [1000 mm].

    Before you begin modeling, notice the Draw panel in the ribbon (Figure 1.9). You can choose from a variety of geometry options as you create 3D and 2D elements in the drawing area.

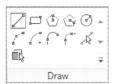

FIGURE 1.9
Select geometry options
from the Draw panel in
the ribbon.

5. You are now ready to begin modeling wall segments. In the drawing area, click through each of the layout markers from 1 through 6.

Note how you can use automatic snapping to accurately locate the start and end of each segment. At point 3, place your mouse pointer near the middle of the circle to use the center snap point.

6. After you click the last wall segment at point 6, press the Esc key once to stop adding new walls. You will notice that the Wall command is still active and you can continue adding new walls if you choose. You can even change the wall type, options, and properties before continuing.

7. Press the Esc key again to return to the Modify state. You can also click the Modify button at the left end of the ribbon.

   Your layout of walls should look like the image shown in Figure 1.10.

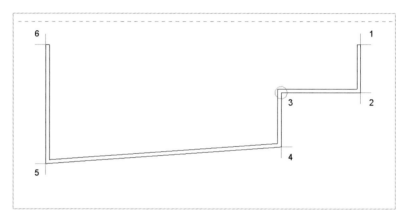

FIGURE 1.10 Your first layout of walls in a plan view

Using Filter, Mirror, and Trim/Extend

As we continue the exercise, you will use a few common modifying tools to further develop the layout of walls. You will also learn how to select and filter elements in the model. Let's begin by mirroring part of the layout and connecting the corners with the Trim tool.

1. Using the mouse pointer, click and drag a window from the lower left to the upper right to select only the wall segments running east-west, as shown in Figure 1.11.

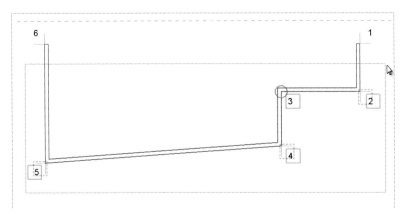

FIGURE 1.11 Drag the cursor from left to right to select some of the walls.

2. You'll probably have more than just walls when you use this method of selection. To reduce the selection to only walls, click the Filter button in the ribbon and clear all the check boxes except for Walls, as shown in Figure 1.12.

FIGURE 1.12 Filter your selection to only include walls.

3. From the Modify tab in the ribbon, click the Mirror – Pick Axis tool and then click on the dashed line representing the reference plane in the plan view. Mirrored copies of the selected walls will appear opposite the reference plane, as shown in Figure 1.13.

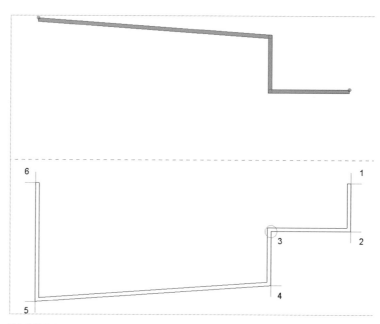

FIGURE 1.13 Mirrored copies of the selected walls

TR

4. Again from the Modify tab in the ribbon, click the Trim/Extend To Corner tool. In the plan view, pick on each of the north-south walls and then the respective wall that was mirrored in the previous step. The resulting closed perimeter wall should look like the image in Figure 1.14.

5. Save your project file before continuing to the next exercise.

Adjusting Datums

Building Elevation (shown in parentheses) is a type of elevation view. You can create more view types for elevations, sections, details, and other views as necessary.

In Revit, project datums consist of reference planes, grids, and levels. These elements are usually only visible in a 2D view, but they establish control of all model elements within your file. In the next exercise, you will examine how levels affect the modeled elements and how you can adjust their graphic representation in a 2D view:

1. In the Project Browser, locate the Elevations (Building Elevation) category and double-click on the South view. You may need to click the + symbol to expand the tree.

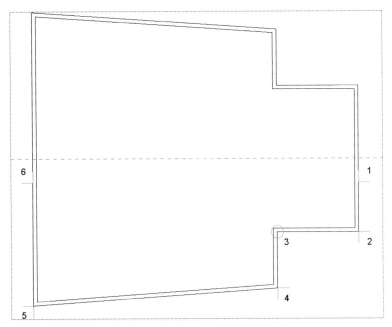

FIGURE 1.14 Use the Trim/Extend To Corner tool to complete the perimeter walls.

2. Zoom in to the right side of the view and you will see the graphic representation of the levels that are defined in this project (Level 1 and Level 2). Select the level line and you will notice that both the name of the level and the elevation turn blue. This indicates that they can be directly edited.

> You might also notice the top offset is maintained relative to the changes of the level. This value can be found in the Properties palette.

3. Click on the elevation value for Level 2 and change it from 10′-0″ [3000 mm] to 15′-0″ [4500 mm]. Notice how the walls you created in the first exercise maintain their relationship with Level 2 because you specified that datum in the Options Bar before placing the walls.

Let's suppose you want to modify the design and add a third level along with a roof. You will need to add two more levels and adjust the heights of the exterior walls. We will show you two different methods for creating new levels.   *2 methods*

4. Go to the Home tab in the ribbon and find the Datum panel. Click on the Level command and make sure the Make Plan View box is checked *KNOW* in the Options Bar. Click in the elevation view exactly 10′-0″ [3000 mm]

Remember you can zoom and pan with the mouse while other commands are active. You might need to do this to complete the level command.

▶

▶

You can also start the Copy tool first, pick the level, and then press Enter to complete the selection process and start the command.

above the left end of Level 2 using the temporary dimension as a guide. Notice the end of the new level will snap into alignment with the end of the existing level. Click the end of the level above the right end of Level 2 to complete the command.

If you need to adjust the elevation or the name of the level you just created, select the level, click on the elevation value, change it to 25′-0″ [7500 mm], and make sure the name is Level 3. Next you will create another level by copying an existing one.

5. Select Level 3 in the elevation view and click the Copy tool on the Modify tab in the ribbon. Click anywhere in the elevation to specify a start point for the copy command and place the mouse pointer in the upward (90°) direction. Type **12′-0″ [3600 mm]** and then press Enter to complete the command. Note that you can also press and hold the Shift key to force copy or move commands to operate in 90 degree increments.

6. Select the newest level and change the name to **Roof**. Also make sure the elevation value is 37′-0″ [11100 mm].

Note that when you copied the last level, a corresponding floor plan was not created. This is indicated by the graphic level symbol being black instead of blue. You can double-click on the blue level markers to activate the associated plan view of that level. In addition, you can double-click on any blue view symbol such as a section, elevation, or callout.

7. From the View tab in the ribbon, find the Create panel, click Plan Views, and then click Floor Plan (Figure 1.15). By default, you will only see levels that don't already have floor plans created. In this case you will see Roof. Select Roof from the list and click OK.

The new floor plan for the Roof level will be activated so you will need to switch back to another view to continue the exercises. Go to the View tab in the ribbon, locate the Windows panel, and then click Switch Windows, as shown in Figure 1.16.

▶

The Switch Windows tool is used so often that it is also located in the QAT by default.

8. Save your project file before continuing to the next exercise.

You might notice as you continue to work through the chapter exercises in this book that many views will be opened as you activate plans, sections, elevations, schedules, and so on. Having too many windows open at one time may affect Revit's performance, so be sure to close some view windows when you don't need them anymore. There is also a command in the View tab of the ribbon and the QAT called Close Hidden Windows. Use this command to close all but the active window. If you have more than one project open, this command will leave open only one view from each project.

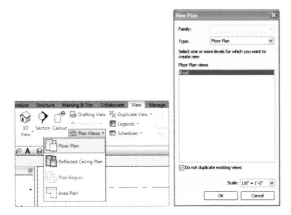

FIGURE 1.15 Use the View tab in the ribbon to create new floor plans.

FIGURE 1.16 Use the Switch Windows command to see what views you have activated.

Changing Element Types

Next you will change the properties for some of the elements you've already created using the Properties palette. You will also change some walls from one type to another. In the previous exercise, you created additional levels, thus increasing the overall desired height of your building. In the following steps, you will adjust the top constraint of the exterior walls and swap a few walls for a curtain wall type:

1. Activate the default 3D view. Remember, you can click the Default 3D View in the QAT or double-click the {3D} view in the Project Browser.

2. Click the Close Hidden Views button in the QAT and then activate the South view under Elevations (Building Elevation) in the Project Browser.

3. From the View tab in the ribbon, locate the Windows panel and then click the Tile button. The two active views (default 3D view and South elevation) should now be seen side by side.

4. In either view, find the Navigation bar, click the drop-down arrow under the Zoom icon, and then click Zoom All To Fit, as shown in Figure 1.17.

FIGURE 1.17 Use Zoom All
To Fit when you are using tiled windows.

In the 3D view, you will need to select all of the walls to change the properties. To do this you must use the *chain-select* method.

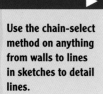

Use the chain-select method on anything from walls to lines in sketches to detail lines.

5. Place and hold the mouse pointer over one of the walls. Press the Tab key once. The status bar should indicate "Chain of walls or lines." Click to select the chain of walls. You should see an indication that 8 walls have been selected in the Properties palette, as shown in Figure 1.18.

FIGURE 1.18 The number of selected items can be seen in the Properties palette.

6. In the Properties palette, find the parameter Top Constraint. Change the value to Up To Level: Roof and then click Apply. Notice how the walls all change height in both the 3D view and the elevation view. Also note how the offset is maintained relative to the level of the top constraint (Figure 1.19).

   In the final steps of this exercise, you will change a few wall segments from one wall type to another. Making these kinds of changes in Revit is similar to changing the font of a sentence in Microsoft Word where you would select the sentence and choose a different font from the font selector.

7. In the 3D view, select the wall at the west (left) side of the layout. Press and hold the Ctrl key and select the wall segment at the east (right) side as well (Figure 1.20).

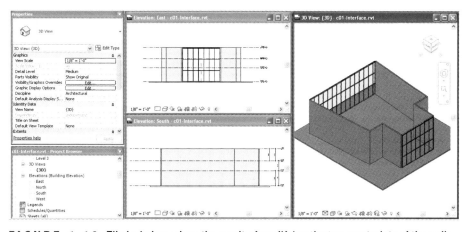

FIGURE 1.19 Tiled windows show the result of modifying the top constraints of the walls.

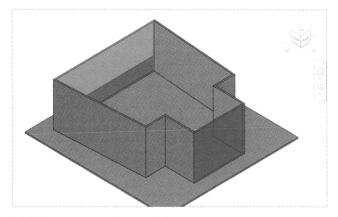

FIGURE 1.20 Use the Ctrl key to manually select multiple items in your model.

8. At the top of the Properties palette is the Type Selector. Click it to open the list of available wall types within the project. Scroll down to the bottom of the list and select the type Curtain Wall: Exterior Glazing. You may get a warning when you make this change; if so, just select Unjoin Walls or whatever the recommended action is. Your result should look like the image in Figure 1.21.

9. Remember to save your project file before continuing with subsequent lessons.

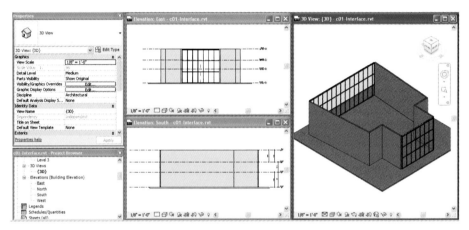

FIGURE 1.21 Wall segments have been changed to a different type.

Using Common Modifying Tools

Now that you have been introduced to the basic workflow of the Revit user interface, we will examine some common tools used to modify your designs. These exercises will not expose you to every available tool; rather, they are designed to introduce you to the ones you will most likely use every day.

You will be guided through a series of exercises in creating a simple interior layout, continuing use of the project file from the previous section. In these exercises you will learn how to effectively copy, move, and rotate elements as well as create basic constraints to preserve design intent. You will also learn how to use dimension strings not just as annotation, but as interactive modifying tools.

Using Dimensions for Modifying Designs

In your first exercise, you will create a simple layout of interior partitions to explore the use of dimensions in establishing and preserving your design intent.

1. Activate the Level 1 Interior floor plan from the Project Browser.

2. From the Home tab in the ribbon, click the Wall tool and then change the wall type to Interior - Partition Type A2.

3. In the Options Bar, set the Location Line to Finish Face: Interior. In the Properties palette, make sure Top Offset is set to 0.

4. In the Draw panel in the ribbon, click the Pick Lines icon, as shown in Figure 1.22, and then click on each of the red lines indicated in the floor plan.

The Function parameter of a wall helps define its default height options. For example, an Interior wall defaults to the level above whereas an Exterior wall is set to unconnected height.

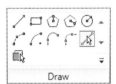

FIGURE 1.22 Use the Pick Lines mode to add walls using layout lines or other guiding elements.

5. With the Wall command still active, change the Location Line to Wall Centerline and switch the Draw mode back to Line.

6. Draw two walls inside the area at the right of the layout, as shown in Figure 1.23. Note you may need to press the Esc key once at the end of each segment to continue the command for the next segment. Don't worry about exact placement of these walls; you'll get to that next.

7. From the Annotate tab in the ribbon, locate the Dimension panel and click the Aligned tool. In the Options Bar, notice that the default placement is Wall Centerlines. You can change the default placement anytime you use a dimension tool; however, we will need multiple placement methods in the next step, so just leave it as is.

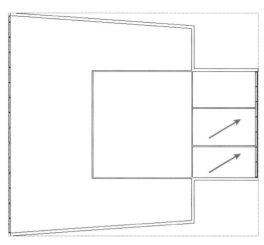

FIGURE 1.23 Add wall segments as shown.

8. In the plan view, click on each of the two interior walls you just created. You will see one dimension appear between the two walls, but
the command is still active. Keep going to the next step.

9. Hover the mouse pointer over one of the two exterior walls and you
will notice that the centerline of the wall is the default reference.
Press the Tab key until you see the inside face of the wall highlight,
as shown in Figure 1.24, and then click to add the dimension. Repeat
this process for the exterior wall on the other side.

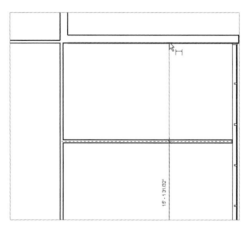

FIGURE 1.24 Use the Tab key to toggle between
wall references before you place a dimension.

10. When you have selected all four walls and you want to complete the
dimension command, click in the view window where you'd like

the dimension string to be placed. It is important that you don't click on another model object or press the Esc key.

11. After the dimension string has been placed, press the Esc key to exit the command and select the dimension you just created. You will see an EQ symbol with a slash indicating that the dimensions along the string are not equal. Click this symbol, and the dimensions—along with the wall spacing—will become equal.

Try moving one or both of the exterior walls to which the dimension string is referencing. You will see that the interior walls will remain equally spaced as long as the dimension string retains its EQ constraint.

12. Select the dimension string again and click the EQ symbol to remove the equality constraint.

13. Select one of the two interior walls and you will see that the dimension values to either side turn blue. Click the dimension between the interior wall and the exterior wall and change the value to 12´-0˝ [3.6 m]. Repeat this process for the other side.

14. With the dimension string selected, click the lock symbol below each 12´-0˝ [3.6 m] dimension to establish a constraint, as shown in Figure 1.25.

If you want to see the actual dimension values instead of "EQ" in your dimension strings, right-click on the string and select EQ Display to toggle between the two settings.

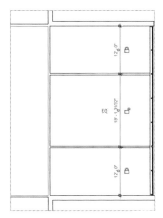

FIGURE 1.25 Lock dimensions along a string to preserve design intent.

Now try moving each of the exterior walls again. Observe how the constrained dimensions are preserving your intent to keep the outer rooms at their defined dimension.

Aligning Elements

In the following exercise, you will use dimensions to precisely place two more walls. You will then learn how to use the Align tool to preserve a dimensional relationship between two model elements. The Align tool can be used in just about any situation in Revit and is therefore a valuable addition to your common toolbox.

To begin this exercise, you will use temporary dimensions to place a wall segment. Elements in Revit can be initially placed in specific places using temporary dimensions or you can place them and then modify their positions using temporary or permanent dimensions as you learned in the previous exercise.

Before you begin this exercise, you will need to adjust the settings for temporary dimensions. Switch to the Manage tab in the ribbon and click Other Settings and then Temporary Dimensions. Change the setting for Walls to Faces and the setting for Doors And Windows to Openings, as shown in Figure 1.26.

ERROR
ADDITIONAL *
SETTINGS

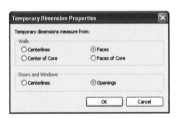

FIGURE 1.26 Modifying the settings
for temporary dimensions

1. Add a wall using Interior - Partition Type A2 to the main layout area. Continue to use the Finish Face: Interior location line option; however, use a temporary dimension to place each wall exactly 8´-0˝ [2.5 m] from the nearest wall intersection, as shown in Figure 1.27. Repeat this process for the opposite side.

2. Press the Esc key or click the Modify button in the ribbon to exit the Wall command. Select one of the walls you created in step 1. You will see a string of temporary dimensions appear. Drag the grip on the far left of the dimension string so that it aligns with the outside edge of the other wall, as shown in Figure 1.28.

3. Click the dimension icon just below the length shown in the temporary dimension to convert it into a regular dimension string. Select the dimension string and click the lock symbol to establish a constraint, as shown in Figure 1.29.

AL   4. Zoom out so you can see both new interior wall segments. From the Modify tab in the ribbon, select the Align tool.

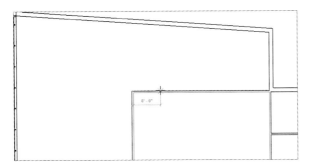

FIGURE 1.27 Place an interior wall using temporary dimensions.

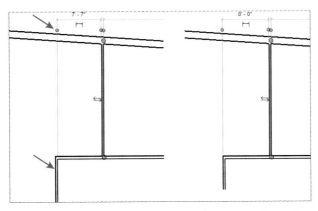

FIGURE 1.28 Adjust references of temporary dimensions by dragging grips.

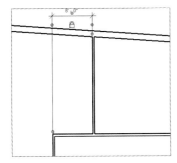

FIGURE 1.29 A temporary dimension has been converted and locked.

5. As illustrated in Figure 1.30, click the face of the wall that has been constrained in step 3 (a), click the corresponding face of the other new wall (b), and then click the lock to constrain the alignment (c).

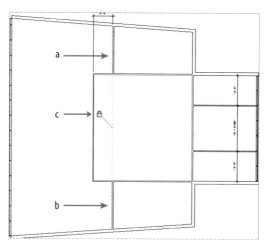

FIGURE 1.30 Use the Align tool to create an alignment and constrain the relationship.

Once you have completed this exercise, try moving the central interior wall to see how the two flanking walls maintain their dimensional and aligned relationships. Note that the constrained dimension can be deleted while preserving the constraint, as shown in Figure 1.31.

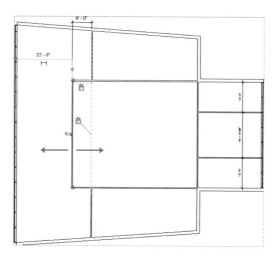

FIGURE 1.31 Try moving the main wall to observe how the flanking walls behave.

Rotating, Grouping, and Arraying

Out of all the other basic modifying tools we could address in this chapter, the Rotate tool is perhaps the most unique. Rotating elements in Revit is not quite the same as in other applications like AutoCAD. For that reason, we will step through a simple exercise to explore the various ways of rotating content.

1. Activate the Level 1 Furniture floor plan from the Project Browser.

2. From the Home tab in the ribbon, click the Door tool. Place a few doors within walls in a variety of places throughout the interior layout. Use the spacebar to flip the rotation of the doors before you place them.

   Note that you can disable automatic door tagging by clicking the Tag On Placement button in the contextual tab of the ribbon when the Door command is active.

3. From the Home tab in the ribbon, click the Component tool and select Desk: Type D1 from the Type Selector.

4. In the floor plan, place one desk in the main central space. Press the spacebar once to rotate the desk and place another desk in one of the spaces in the east wing, as shown in Figure 1.32.

Try using the temporary dimensions to specify distances between doors and nearby walls before you place them.

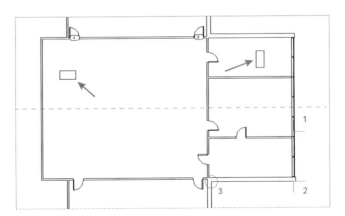

FIGURE 1.32 Place two desks in the layout as shown.

5. Use the Component tool again and choose Chair-Desk from the Type Selector. Press the spacebar until the chair orients properly with the desk (Figure 1.33).

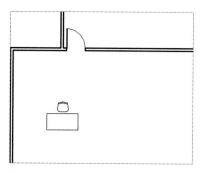

FIGURE 1.33 Place a chair with the desk in the main space.

6. Repeat this process for the desk in the east wing, but add two additional chairs on the opposite side of the desk (Figure 1.34).

7. Select the desk and chair in the main space and click the Create Group command in the Create panel of the contextual ribbon. Name the group **Desk-Chair-1**.

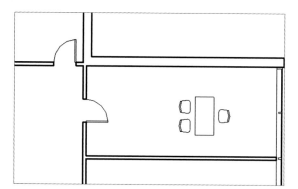

FIGURE 1.34 Place three chairs with the desk in the east wing.

8. Repeat the process for the desk and chairs in the east wing. Name the group **Desk-Chair-3**.

9. Select the group Desk-Chair-3 and click the Copy command in the ribbon. Set the Constrain and Multiple options in the Options Bar and begin to copy the group into each of the three spaces in the east wing.

10. With the Copy command still active, uncheck the Constrain option and place a copy of the group in the space at the north side of the layout. Your copied furniture should look like the image in Figure 1.35.

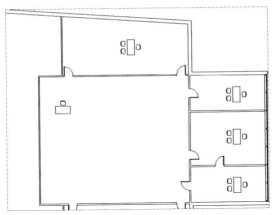

FIGURE 1.35 Create copies of the group with multiple chairs.

11. Select the last copied group and click the Rotate tool in the Modify panel of the ribbon.

12. Drag the rotation center icon to the lower-right corner of the desk.

13. Point the mouse pointer in the east direction and click. This is the reference angle.

14. Move the mouse pointer to the south direction (Figure 1.36) and click. This is the final rotation.

◄

Remember to use the Esc key or click the Modify button in the ribbon to complete a command and select an object.

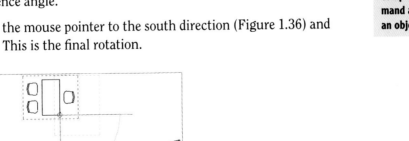

FIGURE 1.36 Use the Rotate tool to modify the last copy of the Desk-Chair-3 group.

15. Select the Desk-Chair-1 group in the main space and click the Array tool in the Modify panel of the ribbon. In the Options Bar, uncheck the option for Group And Associate and set the Number to 4.

16. In the plan view click somewhere near the group, point the mouse pointer in the east direction and then enter 8´-0˝[2.5 m]. You will see four copies of the group.

17. Use any combination of copy, array, and rotate to complete the layout of the desk-chair groups, as shown in Figure 1.37.

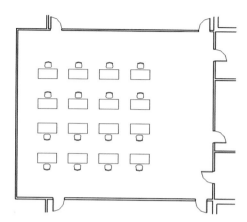

FIGURE 1.37 Complete the finished layout on your own.

In this exercise, you created a simple group of furniture elements. Groups can be a powerful tool for managing repeatable layouts within a design, but they can cause adverse performance if they are abused. There are far too many opinions and best practices for using groups to be listed in this chapter; however, there are just a few important tips to be aware of. Groups should be kept as simple as possible and they shouldn't be mirrored. You should also avoid putting hosted elements in groups—but you'll learn more about these types of elements throughout this book.

Aligned Copying and Group Editing

One powerful and essential tool in Revit is the copy-to-clipboard command known as Paste Aligned. As you've seen throughout this chapter so far, this is yet another tool that can be used on just about any kind of model or drafting element. In the following exercises, you will take the interior content you developed in the previous exercises and replicate it on other levels within the building.

1. Activate the Level 1 Furniture floor plan from the Project Browser.

2. Select all the interior walls, doors, and furniture seen in the floor plan.

3. In the Clipboard panel of the ribbon, click the Copy To Clipboard tool. You could also press Ctrl+C on your keyboard.

Certification Objective

4. Also in the Clipboard panel of the ribbon, click the Paste drop-down button and select Aligned To Selected Views. You will be prompted with a dialog box to select levels to which the selected content will be

copied in exactly the same position (Figure 1.38). Select Level 2 and
Level 3 using the Ctrl key to make multiple selections.

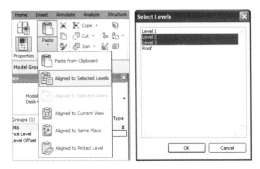

FIGURE 1.38 Use Paste Aligned To Selected Levels
to create duplicate floor layouts.

5. Activate the view 3D Cutaway from the Project Browser to view the
results of the aligned copying (Figure 1.39).

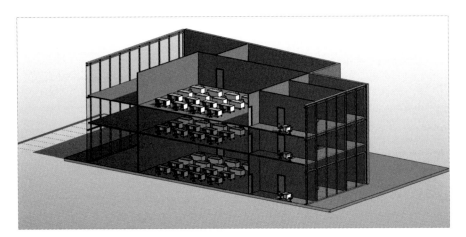

FIGURE 1.39 The 3D Cutaway view uses a section box to display the inside of a building.

Now that you have created many copies of the furniture group on several levels,
you can harness the power of the group by making changes to the group and
observing how the overall design is updated.

1. Activate the Level 2 floor plan from the Project Browser.

2. Select one of the Desk-Chair-1 furniture groups in the main space.
Click on the Edit Group button from the contextual ribbon. The view
window will turn a light shade of yellow and a temporary toolbar will
appear at the upper left of the view area.

3. Select the chair in the group and from the Type Selector, change it to Chair-Executive.

4. Rotate the chair 20 degrees using the Rotate tool (Figure 1.40).

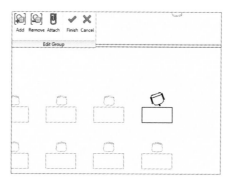

FIGURE 1.40 The view window will enter a temporary group editing mode.

5. Click the Finish button in the Edit Group toolbar and observe how the changes you made are propagated to all the group instances on all levels. Once you've saved your changes, activate the Level 1 and Level 3 floor plans to see the extent of the changes.

THE ESSENTIALS AND BEYOND

The Revit interface is organized in a logical manner that enforces repetition and therefore increases predictability. Almost every command can be executed by selecting a view from the Project Browser, choosing a tool from the ribbon, specifying settings in the Options Bar, and then placing an element in the drawing window. Although we only covered the most basic tools in the preceding exercises, you will be able to apply what you've learned in this chapter to the many exercises exploring other tools in subsequent chapters.

ADDITIONAL EXERCISES

▶ Use the Window and Door tools to place some hosted elements in the walls.

▶ Create copies of these elements on other levels using the copy-paste aligned tools.

▶ Experiment with various ways to organize the Revit interface that support your preferred working method. Try tiling windows and undocking the Properties palette or the Project Browser.

▶ Try a radial array of furniture by changing the Array tool settings in the Options Bar.

CHAPTER 2

Schematic Design

Design inspiration comes from many sources. For example, some designers still like to sketch by hand, but the sketch needs to align with the building program. Many of our modern sketches now happen digitally to make this transition easier.

When you begin migrating your conceptual design from the sketch to the computer, don't start with building elements (walls, floors, and so forth). Start with more primal elements, a process called *massing* in Revit, to make sure your program is correct. Once you've confirmed that the mass contains the required building program, you'll be able to start placing building elements with far more confidence. While massing is capable of much more complex form-making than you'll see in this chapter, it's a great starting point for learning Revit.

In this chapter, you learn the following skills:

▶ **Working from a sketch**

▶ **Modeling in-place masses**

▶ **Creating mass floors**

▶ **Scheduling mass floors**

▶ **Updating the massing study**

Working from a Sketch

Sketches can be a great source for starting design massing in Revit. In certain cases, hand drawings can be scanned from physical pen and paper drawings. In some design workflows, sketching directly within a computer application is becoming increasingly common. To support this digital workflow, in 2010 Autodesk released a tool for Apple's iPad called SketchBook Pro (Figure 2.1) that allows you to sketch directly on the iPad or iPhone using a stylus or even your finger.

The sketch in Figure 2.1 was created on the iPad, but this example will work for any scanned sketch design—even one on tracing paper. In our sample scenario for this chapter, the designer has created sketches of a proposed building form and would like you to import each of the orientations into Revit and use them as context for a quick massing study. The building program allows a maximum building height of about 800′ [244 m] and requires a gross area of 3.5 million square feet [325,000 square meters].

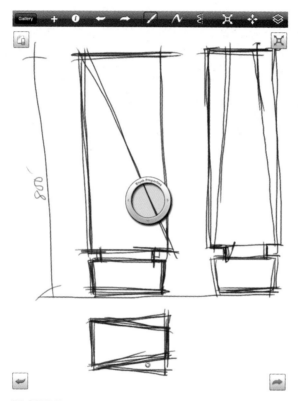

FIGURE 2.1 A hand sketch from Autodesk's SketchBook Pro for the iPad.

Importing Background Images

Let's look at how you can combine the design's sketches with Revit's massing tools to help deliver preliminary feedback about the design. When you open Revit for the first time, you'll find yourself at the Revit home screen. This screen keeps a graphic history of the recent projects and families that you've worked on.

1. From the home screen, select New to open the default Revit template. Open the South elevation by double-clicking on it in the Project Browser.

2. On the Insert tab, select the Import panel and click the Image tool (Figure 2.2).

FIGURE 2.2 Select the Image tool on the Import panel.

3. Select the Ch 2 Massing Sketch.png file from the Chapter 2 folder on this book's web page (**www.sybex.com/go/revit2012essentials**). Once you select the image, you will be put back in the South elevation view.

4. You'll see a large, empty-looking box with an X through it. This is the Image Placement tool. Place the image as shown in Figure 2.3 so that the base of the building sketch roughly aligns with Level 1.

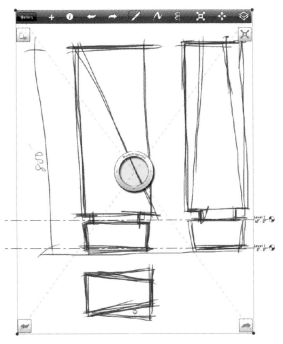

FIGURE 2.3 The placed image. Note the location of the levels relative to the base of the image.

As you can tell from Figure 2.3, the scale of the sketch doesn't relate to the real-world units of Revit. To remedy this, let's quickly scale the imported image.

Accurately Scaling Images

 Select the Measure tool from the Quick Access toolbar (QAT) located at the top of the screen. When the tool is active, pick between the two points, as shown in Figure 2.4. As you can see, the real-world distance in our image is about 70′ [52 m]. Depending on how you inserted your image, it might vary a bit. That's fine; your next step is to learn how to scale these images.

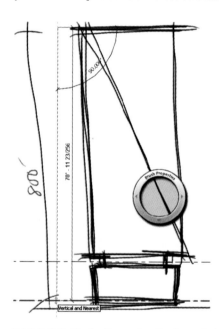

FIGURE 2.4 Measuring the imported image

You know the desired distance is 800′ [243 m] between the two points you just measured. One way to change the image size is to select the image and manually enlarge it by dragging the corner grips until the distance is correct—and in many cases this might be close enough. However, we'll show you a more precise method:

1. Select the image and look at the Properties palette on the left. Notice the current dimension for the Height field is 85′-4″ [26 m] in our example. To modify the image size, you need to increase the Height value with regard to the desired and actual dimensions.

2. To determine this value, first divide 800' [243 m] (the desired height) by 70' [52 m] (the measured distance). Then multiply the result by 85'-4" [26 m] (the current height) and enter the quotient. Using Revit's built-in database functionality, you can do the math right in the Properties palette!

3. Type the formula shown in Figure 2.5. Be sure to add the = sign at the beginning of the formula. The height of the image will increase significantly (over 975' [2,735 m]). But now the imported image has proportionally increased the correct amount.

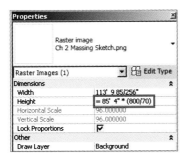

FIGURE 2.5 A formula for adjusting the image height

4. Move the lower edge of the sketch to align with Level 1 again. Also, increase the scale of the view to 1" = 30'-0" [1:500] so that the level's symbols are more visible (Figure 2.6).

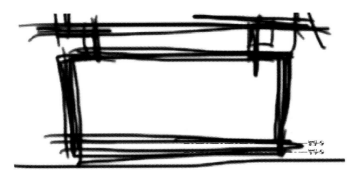

FIGURE 2.6 The resulting image

Reference Planes and Levels

Reference planes are one of the most useful tools in Revit. The planes are represented in Revit as green dashed lines, and they will display in any view perpendicular to the reference plane. They don't print in your drawing sheets, but they are handy as a tool to align elements that are coplanar. Think of them as levels and grids except that you don't need to show them on your sheets.

In our example, it's important to use reference planes as guides to help you create the masses in other views since the image you imported will only be visible in the imported view. Reference planes are like guidelines that can be seen across many views. They will be extremely helpful when you line up the sketch in the South elevation and then in the North elevation or plan view.

To begin, click the Home tab, and on the Work Plane panel, select the Ref Plane tool. Next, create reference lines that correspond with the edges of the sketch by tracing over the edges. The dimensions in Figure 2.7 have been added as a reference for you. You don't need to add dimensions—just add the reference planes as shown. We also adjusted the scale of the view so that the level symbols are easy to read.

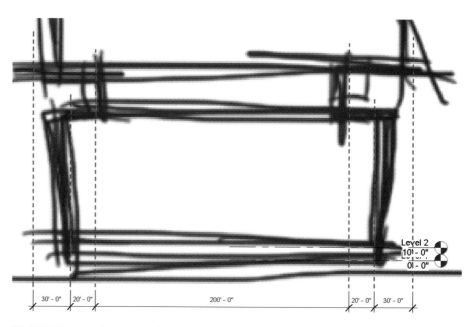

FIGURE 2.7 Dimensioned reference planes

Now let's add some levels to the sketch that will be useful for determining the limit of the three masses you'll add:

1. Move Level 2 to 20'-0" [6 m] by selecting the 10'-0" [3 m] value and typing in the new elevation, as shown in Figure 2.8.

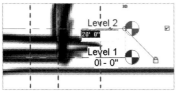

FIGURE 2.8 Enter the new elevation.

2. To add levels, select the Home tab and then choose the Level tool from the Datum panel. By clicking and dragging your cursor from left to right, you will create a level that also creates a corresponding floor plan. Place Level 3 at 35'-0" [10 m].

3. You can also create levels by copying an existing level. To try this, use the Copy tool to create Levels 4–10, as shown in Figure 2.9. Start by selecting the level you wish to copy, and when the Modify tab appears at the top of the screen, click the Copy tool.

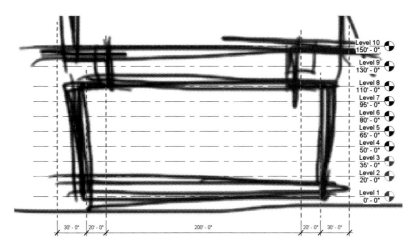

FIGURE 2.9 View vs. reference levels

Using the Copy tool will not create a corresponding floor plan. Rather, it creates what Revit calls a *reference level*. Reference levels are not "hyperlinked" and show black instead of blue. Levels that have corresponding floor plan views are blue, and when you double-click the blue level marker they link to those associated views.

In Figure 2.9, Levels 1–3 have corresponding floor plan or level views, whereas Levels 4–10 are reference levels only. Reference levels can be turned into view levels, but during the design process (and later in documentation) you'll find it helpful to create levels that don't necessarily need to be views. Having 100 or more view levels would create a lot of clutter in Revit and your drawing set.

Now let's create the rest of the levels, as shown in Figure 2.9, by arraying Level 10:

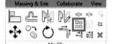

1. First, select Level 10. The Modify | Levels menu becomes active. Select the Array tool from the Modify panel.

2. Since Level 10 is at an elevation of 150'-0" [45 m], you need to create an array with the options shown in Figure 2.10. These options can be adjusted in the Options Bar below the context menu. The Options Bar will dynamically change based on the tools you have selected.

FIGURE 2.10 Array options

3. Select the second Move To option in the Options Bar, and pick a location that is directly 12'-0" [3.6 m] above Level 10. Change the value of the Number field to 55. Once you click to place the 5th level, the additional 55 levels at 12'-0" [3.6 m] will be created, and your final level (Level 64) appears at 798'-0" [243 m]. That's pretty close to our goal of 800'-0" [243 m]!

The final step before creating the mass is to add the sketched image to the East elevation and Level 1, which you'll do in a moment. Before you add the final elevation, let's discuss a change management tip. No design work is ever static (it's always changing), so it's important to understand how to keep up with those iterations in Revit. In this case, you want to be able to manage the ability to update the images in case the designer gives you some new sketches. Keep in mind that if the image changes in size or shape, you'd probably want all the images to change as well. Here is where groups come in handy. A group is similar to what in AutoCAD is called a *block* or in MicroStation, a *cell*. Groups are collections of Revit elements that you want to move or repeat as a single unit, but you want to have the ability to subdivide or "ungroup" if needed. Let's explore a few uses for groups, and then add our final elevation.

Creating and Placing Groups

In this exercise, we're going to create a group and explore potential uses for the Group command.

Create

1. Select the image you inserted earlier in the South elevation and then select the Group tool from the Create panel on the Modify tab.

2. When the Create Detail Group dialog opens, name the group **Massing Sketch 1**, as shown in Figure 2.11, and click OK.

FIGURE 2.11 Create Detail Group dialog

3. In the Project Browser, click Groups and then Detail to see the group that you just created (Figure 2.12). By clicking and dragging this group into your project window, you can add the detail group to other views in your project.

**FIGURE 2.12
Finding your new group
in the Project Browser**

4. Open your East elevation and drag a copy of the detail group from the Project Browser into the view. Then create some more reference planes as shown in Figure 2.13 to form guides that will be visible in other views.

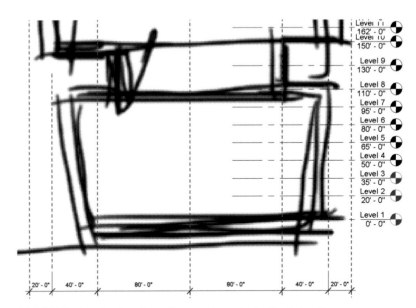

Level 11
162' - 0"
Level 10
150' - 0"

Level 9
130' - 0"

Level 8
110' - 0"
Level 7
95' - 0"
Level 6
80' - 0"
Level 5
65' - 0"
Level 4
50' - 0"
Level 3
35' - 0"
Level 2
20' - 0"

Level 1
0' - 0"

20' - 0"   40' - 0"   80' - 0"   80' - 0"   40' - 0"   20' - 0"

FIGURE 2.13 Creating reference planes in the East elevation

5. Drag a final copy of the detail group into your Level 1 view and center it within the South and East view reference planes you created,
as shown in Figure 2.14. Now you have the three views necessary for
massing the building.

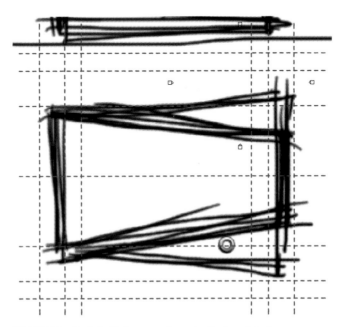

FIGURE 2.14 Reference planes in the Level 1 view

IMAGES AND GROUPS

Each image that you import in Revit can only be seen in the view that it is placed within. In other words, an image placed in the South elevation view will only be seen in that elevation view. In our example, we're trying to assemble a 3D context for modeling geometry and we'll need to place the image in multiple views.

When you change the scale or proportion of one of the images, you'll likely want to change all of them. Groups are used in Revit to maintain relationships between collections of elements. When one group changes, all the groups change. This is very helpful for collections of components that are compiled into units, such as like furniture layouts, hotel rooms, and apartment types.

Modeling In-Place Masses

Now that you've imported the designer's sketch and drawn the appropriate reference planes for added context, you can start creating the massing elements that will represent the building. You will do so using a tool called In-Place Masses. Consider masses as families in Revit that are created directly within the project. This tool allows you to model within the context of the project you're actively working in.

Modeling the Base Mass

To model the base mass, follow these steps:

1. Open your Level 1 floor plan view by double-clicking Level 1 in the Project Browser.

2. Select the Massing & Site tab on the ribbon and select the In-Place Mass tool.

3. Revit displays a dialog telling you that it has now enabled the Show Mass option in the current view. Click Close.

4. The Name dialog appears. For this exercise, let's use the default name, which is Mass 1 (see Figure 2.15). Click OK.

FIGURE 2.15 Use the default mass name.

5. Now you're in a special, in-place editor for creating masses in Revit. You'll notice the menu options have changed. Select the Rectangle tool.

6. Using the Rectangle tool, sketch lines as shown in Figure 2.16. These lines should cover the form and be placed along the reference planes you created earlier.

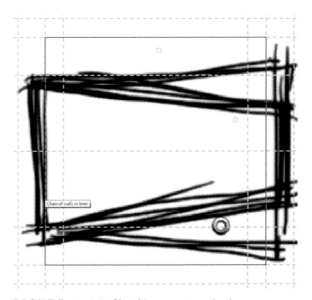

FIGURE 2.16 Sketching a rectangular form

7. Select the lines and then select the Create Form tool from the Form panel.

The results aren't immediately obvious since you're looking at a solid form in plan. To view the results from another angle, return to the South elevation. Select the top of the form by clicking on it and use the grip arrows, as shown in Figure 2.17, to increase the form's height until it aligns with Level 8. The edge of the forms will "stick" to the level when you're close and snap itself into place.

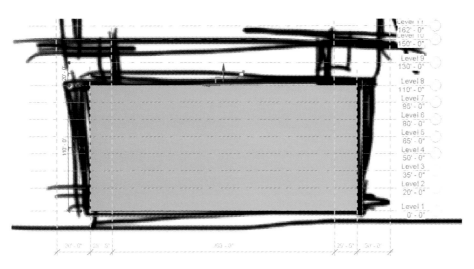

FIGURE 2.17 Increasing the height of the mass

SKETCHING MASSES

The type of mass that you're creating in this exercise is called an *extrusion*. There are many other configurations of masses, including blends, sweeps, swept blends, and revolves. After you've created the initial mass, it's possible to edit the form dramatically; you can even use voids to "carve" away at your initial form.

We don't have the space to go into that level of complexity. But modeling more complex masses is something that you'll likely want to learn. Check out **http://au.autodesk.com/?nd=class_listing**.

Modeling the Middle Mass

The next step is to model the middle mass form:

1. Return to the Level 1 plan view. Set the view to Wireframe, as shown in Figure 2.18 (so you can see through the mass you've just created). The Wireframe button is located in the View Control Bar at the bottom of the screen.

FIGURE 2.18 Setting View to Wireframe

2. Using the same workflow, sketch another rectangle as shown in Figure 2.19. Then select the rectangle and click Create Form.

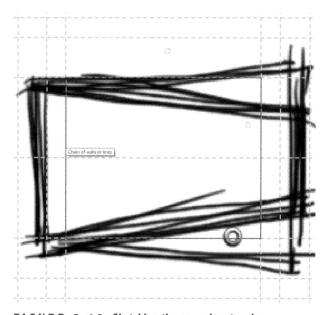

FIGURE 2.19 Sketching the second rectangle

3. Once again, open the South elevation and use the grip arrows to move the second mass form so that the upper face aligns with Level 10 and the lower face aligns with Level 8, as shown in Figure 2.20. Don't forget that you can set the view display to Wireframe if you need to see through the first mass to the second mass. Changes to one view won't be reflected in every view.

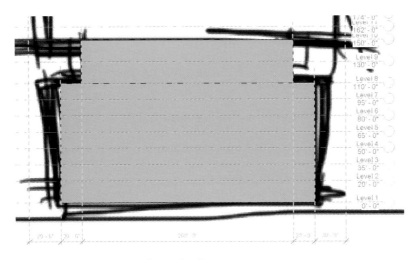

FIGURE 2.20 Second mass in place

Modeling the Upper Mass

The process of creating the third (and uppermost) mass starts the same as for the first two masses:

1. Return to Level 1 and create a rectangular sketch that connects the outermost reference planes, as shown in Figure 2.21. Then select the lines and click Create Solid. Extend the upper and lower faces to align with Levels 64 and 10, respectively.

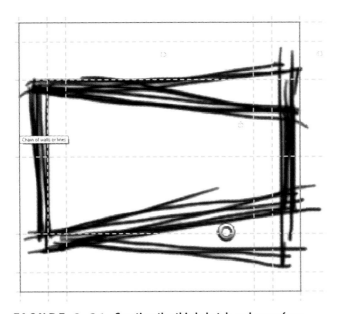

FIGURE 2.21 Creating the third sketch and mass form

   2. Return to the South elevation and use the grip arrows to extend the top and bottom of the form.

You could continue to work in 2D views, but it'll be more helpful if you can see what you're doing in 3D.

Working in 3D

 Select the Default 3D View icon from the QAT. Doing so allows you to see the working mass more completely, as shown in Figure 2.22.

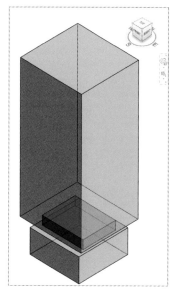

FIGURE 2.22 Default 3D view
of the completed mass

You likely noticed from the imported sketches that the East façade of the mass should taper in elevation. The base and the top are different widths. By adding an edge to each face (both North and South), you'll be able to adjust the upper form appropriately:

   1. First, hover over the South face of the upper form and select the face by clicking on it. Doing so activates the Add Edge tool on the Form Element panel.

   2. The Add Edge tool divides one plane on the mass by adding another edge that can be adjusted independently of the other edges. Add the edge at the front, lower corner of the upper mass, as shown in Figure 2.23.

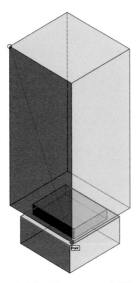

FIGURE 2.23 Adding
the South face edge

3. Rotate the model to expose the North face. Do so by selecting the
   intersection of the ViewCube between the right, back, and top sides.
   The model will spin around, zoom extents, and center.

4. Select the North or Right face to add an edge.

5. Open the East elevation from the Project Browser. Use the grip
   arrows to adjust this face of the upper mass. As you hover your
   mouse pointer over the intersection, a vertex control will appear
   as a purple dot at the upper-right corner where you added a face
   (Figure 2.24).

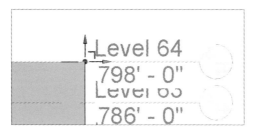

FIGURE 2.24 Selecting the vertex

6. Select this control and then use the grip arrows to move it to the intersection of the uppermost level and right reference plane. Next, do the same thing to the west side of the mass. The result will resemble Figure 2.25.

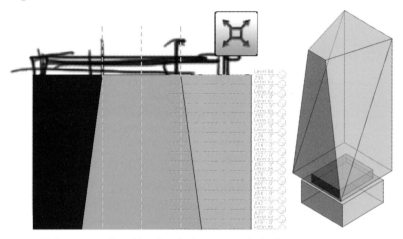

FIGURE 2.25 Resulting South elevation and 3D view

7. Your mass is nearly complete, but first you need to join all the mass geometry together. From the Modify tab select the Join tool on the Modify panel. Then select the lower and middle forms to join them. Repeat this process for the middle and upper forms.

8. Now that the forms have been joined together, select the Finish Mass tool from the In-Place Editor panel. It's the big, green check mark , meaning you're done!

Congratulations! You've just created your first massing study!

JOINING MASSES

Each mass is an independent object. Masses can even be scheduled independently from each other. You'll find this functionality helpful for creating separate masses for programming purposes (such as convention space or meeting rooms). But be careful if you have overlapping masses.

If overlapping masses are not properly joined, Revit will create overlapping mass floors and your schedules will be incorrect. Furthermore, if you create real floors from the mass floors, the floors will overlap rather than create a single element.

Creating Mass Floors

Floor area faces are incredibly useful for getting a sense of the gross area of a building mass at any intersecting level. Furthermore, the results can be quickly and easily scheduled. Any changes to the massing study will update the schedules and all views in real time.

Select the completed mass and then click the Mass Floors tool in the Model panel. You'll be given the option to select all the levels in your project. You want to select them all, but rather than select them one at a time, select Level 1, and then scroll down. While pressing Shift, select Level 64. Now all of the levels are selected. Check any box, and all of the boxes will automatically be checked. Click OK.

Your mass has now been bisected with mass floors (faces with no geometry), as shown in Figure 2.26.

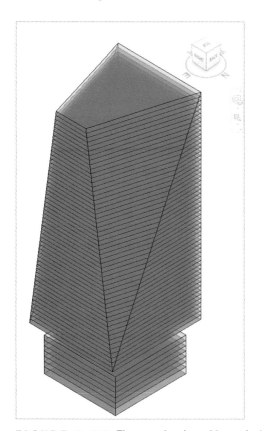

FIGURE 2.26 The mass has been bisected with mass floors.

Scheduling Mass Floors

Creating schedules in Revit is easy, and schedules can be used across projects (or put in your project template). Doing so allows you to understand the context and impact of your work while you work—rather than at the end of a long design process that can prove to be a waste of time. Schedules can help you not only track elements in Revit, but also assess how conceptual design work meets your program requirements.

Schedules are just like any other type of view in Revit—they show you a current, specific look at the model. These views show you this information in a spreadsheet format than geometrically, but just like the other view types, schedules dynamically update as changes are made to the model.

1. To begin the mass schedule, select the View tab from the ribbon. Then select the Schedules drop-down in the Create panel. Click Schedules/Quantities.

2. In the New Schedule dialog, select the Mass Floor option from the column on the left and leave the other fields (Schedule Name and Phase) at their default values. Click OK.

3. The next dialog contains a series of tabs. We'll step through some of these to set up the schedule. On the Fields tab, select level and floor areas by double-clicking them in the Available Fields list or by selecting a field and then clicking the Add button (Figure 2.27).

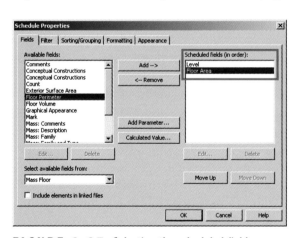

FIGURE 2.27 Selecting the scheduled fields

4. On the Sorting/Grouping tab, change Sort By to Level. Also, choose Title, Count, And Totals from the drop-down next to Grand Totals, as shown in Figure 2.28.

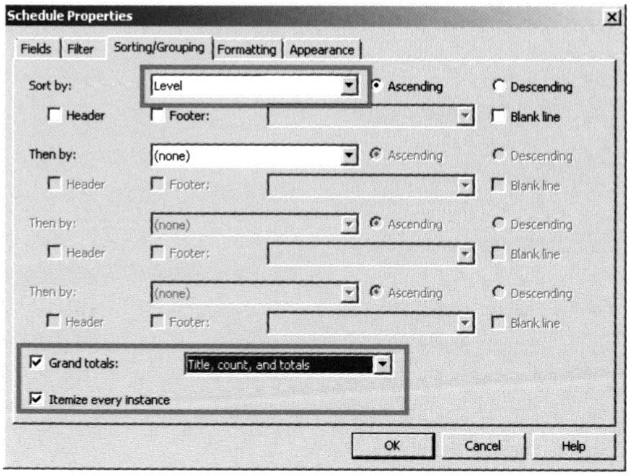

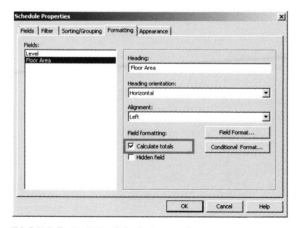

FIGURE 2.28 Selecting the Sorting/Grouping fields

5. On the Formatting tab, select the Floor Area field and then click the Calculate Totals option (Figure 2.29). Click OK.

FIGURE 2.29 Calculating totals

Figure 2.30 shows the resulting schedule. With a total of 63 floor levels, Revit is calculating a gross floor area of just over 4.5 million square feet [418,000 square meters].

Level 59	61769 SF
Level 60	60852 SF
Level 61	59917 SF
Level 62	58963 SF
Level 63	57661 SF
Grand total: 63	4530617 SF

FIGURE 2.30
Gross floor area

Unfortunately, we know from the program (at the beginning of this section) that the gross floor area needs to be closer to 3.5 million square feet [325,000 square meters]. So let's get back to that massing study and tweak the form to get it closer to the program's results.

Updating the Massing Study

Begin by selecting the mass in the default 3D view and then clicking the Edit In-Place button on the Model panel. Doing so returns you to In-Place editing mode and allows you to have specific control over mass geometry.

You're going to modify the east and west faces, moving each face 40′-0″ [12 m] to the center. Hovering over and selecting the east face of the upper mass displays a temporary dimension and the shape handles.

Select this dimension and, by clicking on the blue text, change the value from 300′-0″ [91 m] to 260′-0″ [80 m]. Do the same for the middle and lower east faces. Now the gross floor area is closer to 3.25 million square feet (Figure 2.31), or about 302,000 square meters. We quickly and easily got the program where it needs to be.

Level 56	47232 SF
Level 57	46601 SF
Level 58	45956 SF
Level 59	45297 SF
Level 60	44625 SF
Level 61	43939 SF
Level 62	43240 SF
Level 63	42327 SF
Grand total: 63	3287039 SF

FIGURE 2.31 Resulting gross floor area

We also need the program to be closer to 3.5 million square feet. A quick discussion with the designer reveals that the base of the building is meant to hold important meeting and conference spaces. So you'll extend the eastern base of the building to 300′ [91 m]. Once again, you do so by repeating the previous steps of selecting the mass and returning to In-Place editing mode. Make certain that the base element is 300′ deep and then finish the mass.

Once this is done, the mass will look like Figure 2.32 and the gross floor area will be within the required program.

FIGURE 2.32 Final mass

If you would like to download the completed Revit file, you can find it in the Chapter 2 folder at the book's web page. The file is called c02 Massing Exercise.rvt.

THE ESSENTIALS AND BEYOND

Ultimately, masses can be used to host relationships to real building elements that would otherwise be nearly impossible to maintain. Mass floors can be used to control the extents of real floors. Many times this will allow you to change location of many slab edges at once by changing the mass and then updating the floors within that mass.

Masses can also host walls, curtain walls, and roofs. This allows you to create (and modify) complex design forms that would be nearly impracticable to assemble bit by bit. The idea is that you're working from general to specific: Get the big ideas down first (as masses) and then go back and assign real building elements to those faces to build the building.

THE ESSENTIALS AND BEYOND *(Continued)*

But keep in mind that it's unlikely you'll only be able to use one mass to host all of your building elements. You may need one mass to host floors and control slab edges, another to host roofs, and even another to host walls and curtain wall systems. Don't be afraid to use overlapping masses in these situations to control different host elements. More specific control will often require overlapping masses. But for initial design/programming purposes, using a single mass to resolve gross floor areas is often sufficient!

ADDITIONAL EXERCISES

▶ After you've created your mass and mass floors, use the Floor By Face tool to assign real floors to the mass floors.

▶ Modify the mass and remake the geometric floors that you created in the previous item.

▶ Experiment with walls and curtain walls by using the Pick Face tool to assign walls to the face of the mass.

▶ Modify the mass and remake the walls and curtain walls created in the previous item.

▶ Explain what you would do if you wanted to control floors and walls with a mass but the floors and the walls didn't always align. For example, what would you do if the floors were set back or deviated from the face of the mass?

CHAPTER 3

Walls and Curtain Walls

Walls in Revit can range a great deal in complexity. Early in the design process, walls and curtain walls can be more generic, vertical containers for space and function. But they can also be associated to masses in order to create incredibly complex shapes. As the design progresses, these generic walls and curtain walls can be swapped out for more specific vertically compound walls that indicate a range of materials as well as geometric sweeps and reveals.

In this chapter, you learn the following skills:

▶ **Creating generic walls**

▶ **Creating numerous wall configurations**

▶ **Modifying walls**

▶ **Creating curtain walls**

▶ **Modifying curtain walls**

▶ **Understanding basic wall parts and parameters**

Creating Generic Walls

Certification Objective

The first thing you want to do is understand how walls generally work and how you should modify them. The challenge is that during the design process there's a lot that is not known (and probably can't be known), which can lead to a lot of unnecessary confusion.

Revit uses a system of "Generic" walls that in most cases are not made of anything specific. They're simply about the right thickness for the eventual condition. We recommend using these generic walls during the design process, and then swapping out these walls for more specific geometry later.

By default, the generic walls that have no specific structure are visually identical to walls that contain structure and finish layers. So it's a great idea to make your design walls visually unique. This way, you'll know what has to be swapped out for more specificity later. And there are also some more advantages, such as giving your walls transparency, that will help you quickly and easily visualize your design.

Let's start by giving our generic walls a material assignment that can be used to distinguish them from more specific wall types:

1. Go to the Home tab on the ribbon and select the Wall tool from the Build panel (Figure 3.1).

FIGURE 3.1 Choose the Wall tool from the Build panel.

2. Now select Basic Wall Generic – 6″ from the Properties menu (Figure 3.2) and sketch a west to east 20′-0″ (6.1 meters) portion of a wall. Don't worry about any of the other settings for the time being. When you're done, go to the Default 3D View, from the Quick Access toolbar.

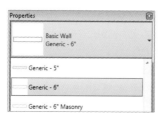

FIGURE 3.2 Generic 6″ wall from the menu and the wall in 3D

3. Select the wall and look at the properties. As you can see, there are a lot of values that apply to this particular piece of wall. You can change its height, constraints, and many other values (we'll get to most of them later). For now, let's create a unique Type property for the wall's material.

4. Select the Edit Type option to open the Type Properties dialog box for the wall. To the right of the Structure label, click the Edit button. Select the <By Category> field, as shown in Figure 3.3.

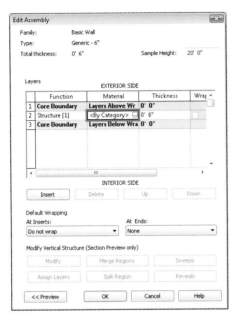

FIGURE 3.3 Select the Material Field.

5. Rather than create a material from scratch, let's duplicate something that is close and then modify it. Scroll down to the Default Wall material and then select the Duplicate option, as shown in Figure 3.4. Name the Material **Generic Material** and then click OK.

FIGURE 3.4 Duplicating the wall material

Certification
Objective

6. Once you click OK, you will have a new material that you'll be able to replace with other rendered and shaded values. Click the Replace button on the Render Appearance tab. On the Graphics tab, set the Shading value as shown on the left in Figure 3.5 by selecting the colored panel. Then select the Appearance tab in Figure 3.5 to assign a newly rendered material, as shown on the right in Figure 3.5. This material will be useful for any design elements (floors, ceilings, roofs, etc.) that are used to resolve the design intent when you're not sure of the specific design content.

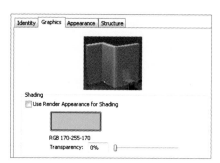

F I G U R E 3 . 5 Assigning the material

Designing Generic Elements

Generic elements play a large part in Revit. When you're creating your design, it's not practical to use lines to represent ideas when you can use content. But if you select something that's too specific, you might become frustrated. A design that is too specific too early has the tendency to be "exactly wrong."

"Design" elements and materials help convey the intent of your design with the added benefit of scheduling, so that the data about a project is headed in the right direction without distracting anyone. They'll help you emphasize "where" something is as well as some of "what" something is without getting into the detail of how it's supposed to be assembled—until the time is right. Most of the frustration in design comes from working specifically to generally, rather than the other way around. Design elements will help you avoid this trap.

The Shading and Rendered values don't need to be the same. And in this case it's really helpful if they're not. When you use a white rendered material, you'll get a neutral, matte rendering. But changing the Shading value will help you quickly distinguish between design intent and more specific resolved elements.

Click OK in all open dialog boxes until you're back in the project environment. Set the view to Shaded With Edges, as shown in Figure 3.6. Now you can quickly and easily tell your design elements from more specific selections.

FIGURE 3.6 Shaded With Edges

Creating Numerous Wall Configurations

Now let's return to our Level 1 Floor Plan view and start creating a number of wall configurations. Pick the Wall command and you'll notice that a number of configurations are available for creating walls (Figure 3.7).

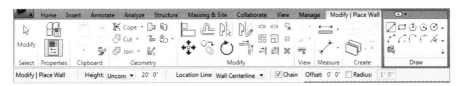

FIGURE 3.7 Configuring walls

Sketching Walls

Walls are sketched by drawing the various configurations. These options are available in Figure 3.8. Take a moment to go through each of the sketching and editing options so that you become familiar with the results—particularly when drawing curved sections. The option to keep concentric is very important. Creating tangent arcs takes particular care as well.

FIGURE 3.8 Wall configurations that can be sketched

CREATING ELLIPTICAL WALLS

Since creating elliptical walls often comes up, we'll get it out of the way and give you the answer in two parts. First, elliptical walls can't be sketched as a singular element. And second (more importantly), they can be created via other workarounds (like creating elliptical masses and then picking the face of the mass to create elliptical walls).

The reason is that documenting the elliptical walls is difficult. There's no center to locate, and the arcs are continually changing in plan.

So what's a better way? Create the ellipse from a series of tangent arcs. Doing so will give you an approximation that is indistinguishable from an actual ellipse, and you'll be able to guide a more exact construction.

And if you don't know how to create an ellipse, just look around the office and ask for the person who used to design buildings with pencils. And after they tell you how, expect them to walk away snickering a bit at your expense.

Picking Walls

You can also create walls by picking lines. This approach is helpful if you have a CAD file that needs to be converted to a BIM model, or if the designer has created a single line design in another tool (like SketchUp) and expects you to use the exported results to start from in Revit.

Start by creating a few model lines. Click the Model Line tool, as shown in Figure 3.9.

FIGURE 3.9 Picking model lines

Now draw a series of lines that resembles Figure 3.10. Now that you have a few lines in your project, you can create walls using these lines with the Pick Lines tool (highlighted in Figure 3.10).

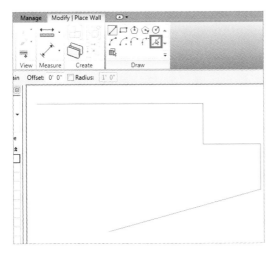

FIGURE 3.10 Sketching model lines

You have two options. You can create walls by picking single lines one at a time. Or, you can hover over one line and then press and release the Tab key. Doing so will highlight the chain of lines, as shown in Figure 3.11. Now you can pick the entire chain of lines to create a chain of walls.

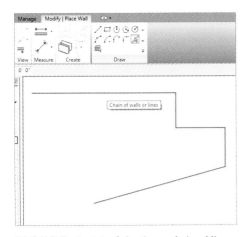

FIGURE 3.11 Selecting a chain of lines

Hosting Elements in Walls

Walls can host elements that are meant to create openings. As long as the walls exist, the elements they are hosting will exist as well. Doors and windows are two common hosted elements.

Placing a door in a wall is very easy and can be done in plan, elevation, or 3D views. In this exercise, you'll place doors from the Level 1 view. You'll use the very first wall that you created at the beginning of this chapter. From the Home tab, select the Door tool from the Build panel.

As you hover over walls, you'll notice that you're able to place doors in them. You're also shown temporary dimensions that will help you place the door closer to its correct location. Go ahead and place two doors as shown in Figure 3.12. Notice that by default Revit will tag the door number for you.

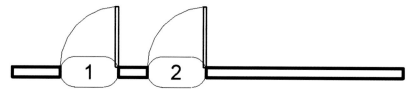

FIGURE 3.12 Hosting Doors in Walls

As mentioned earlier, walls can also host windows. Start by selecting the Window tool from the Home tab on the Build panel. Hover over the same wall and place a window as shown. As with any hosted elements, you'll only be able to place them within a host (Figure 3.13).

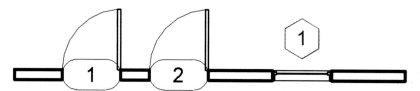

FIGURE 3.13 Hosted window

Containing Spaces

Walls (and a few other elements) may also contain space. This is essential for creating space plans and tracking other room information in your project. But first the walls will have to be organized so that they can contain a space:

1. Sketch additional walls to add to the walls that you created in the previous section so that the series of walls resembles Figure 3.14.

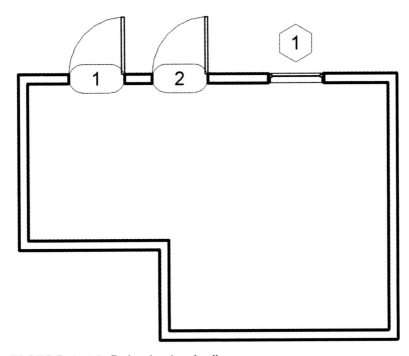

FIGURE 3.14 **Enclosed series of walls**

2. Now that you have a series of walls, you can select the Room function from the Room & Area panel shown in Figure 3.15. Doing so allows you to add spaces to enclosed areas.

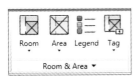

FIGURE 3.15
Selecting the Room function

3. Select Room Tag With Area from the Properties menu and then hover over the enclosed space. The extents of the space will highlight along with a room tag. Select the room tag and change to one

that indicates the area. Then place the room and tag in the space (Figure 3.16).

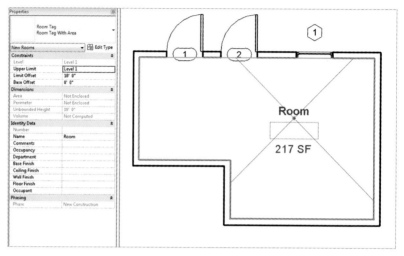

FIGURE 3.16 Placing the room and room tag

What's really great is that when the shape of the room changes, the area reported will immediately update to reflect the new space. Return to the Wall tool and use the Fillet Arc tool to fillet the lower-right intersection of the walls. The room area will update as shown in Figure 3.17.

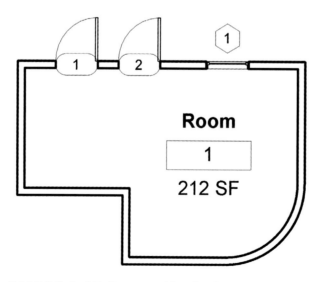

FIGURE 3.17 Room tag with updated area

Modifying Walls

Now that you've created a few wall configurations, it's important to understand how you can modify them. Sometimes this is done simply by selecting the wall and dragging a wall end or a shape handle to a new position. In other cases, you want to be more exact and assign a specific value.

Your approach depends on where you are in the design process. Just remember that you can update design decisions and all your views, schedules, tagging, and so forth will update. So don't get too concerned with being too "exact" early in your design.

Start by sketching another straight segment of a wall, but this time as you draw the wall, type 40 (or 12 meters). Depending on the default units, typing 40 will create a 40´ segment. Notice that you didn't have to indicate the units "feet." If you wanted to indicate "inches," you'd only have to put a space between the first and second values. So 40´-6˝ can easily be entered as "40(space)6".

To modify the length, select the wall. You'll notice there are three options (Figure 3.18). You can type in a new value by selecting the temporary dimension, or you can simply drag either wall end to a new location.

FIGURE 3.18 Modifying the wall length

Now let's go to the Default 3D View and look at some other options. The highlighted areas of Figure 3.19 are called shape handles. You can press and drag them to adjust the top and bottom locations of a wall. As you drag the shape handle, the new location will be shown, whereas the existing location will be "ghosted" until you release the Shape Handle.

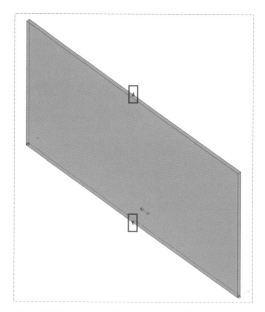

FIGURE 3.19 Wall shape handles

Instance Parameters

In many cases you'll want to enter more exact values, or just have more specific control over a particular wall instance. You can do this through the Instance Parameters menu (Figure 3.20). Select the wall and look at the properties.

Location Line   The location line is the "origin" of the wall, and if you swap one wall for another, the location line will be maintained.

Base Constraint   The base constraint is the bottom of the wall. Be careful! Deleting a constraint (in this case Level 1) also deletes what is associated to the constraint!

Base Offset   The base offset is the value above or below the base constraint. So if you wanted a wall associated to Level 1 but 3´-0˝ (1 meter) below, the value would be –3´-0˝.

Base Is Attached   The Base Is Attached value will allow you to automatically attach the bottom of a wall to the top of another wall, floor or roof.

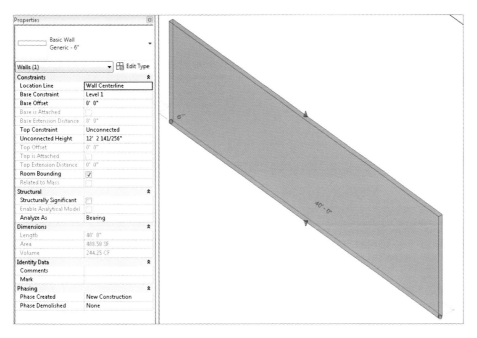

FIGURE 3.20 Instance Parameters

Unconnected Height   The Unconnected Height value is the height of the wall. You can type in a specific value, but in this case the value is pretty irregular because we've manually dragged the shape handle to the new position.

Top Constraint   The top constraint is presently shown as Unconnected. It can also be associated to Level 2, for example. This way, the wall will move vertically up or down if the level moves. For example, setting the Top Constraint to Level 2, the Unconnected Height will immediately reset to that value.

Top Is Attached   Top Is Attached allows you to automatically attach the top of the wall to the underside of a wall, floor, or roof.

Room Bounding   The last value you should be aware of is the Room Bounding option. Walls often are meant to contain space and remain space aware. This is what happened when you placed the Room tag in a previous exercise. But if you have a situation where you don't want walls to define a space, you can deselect this option and the Room tag will ignore the walls.

Editing and Resetting Profiles

Of course not all walls are rectilinear in elevation. For these situations you can edit the profile of a wall. Note that you'll only be able to edit the profile of a straight wall, not curved walls.

1. Start by selecting the 40′ wall and selecting Edit Profile from the Modify | Walls tab (Figure 3.21).

FIGURE 3.21 Editing the profile for walls

2. From a South Elevation view, create the internal sketch as shown in Figure 3.22. Don't worry about dimensioning the sketch. We're just showing the dimensions for reference. Now delete the top line and fillet the two side sketch lines (Figure 3.22). Note that the reference lines indicating the extents of the original wall will remain.

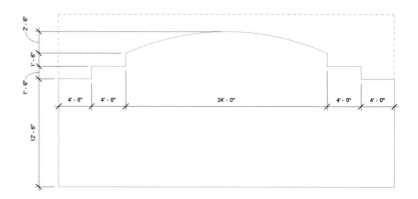

FIGURE 3.22 Adding new sketch lines

3. When you are done, click Finish Sketch Mode.

Attaching and Detaching Top and Base

We've previously attached the top of a wall to a roof. But walls can also be attached to the top or bottom of other walls. Let's do this with a copy of the wall from the edit elevation example.

Certification
Objective

1. Copy the wall off to the side, select it, and then click Edit Profile. Modify the exterior sketch as shown in Figure 3.23. Don't forget to trim and delete unnecessary sketch lines. Then finish the sketch.

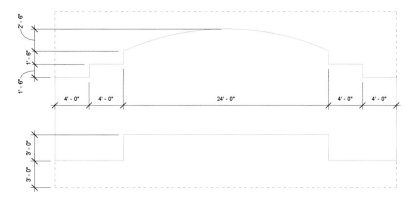

FIGURE 3.23 Edited wall profile

2. Now return to your Level 1 Plan View and sketch another wall right on top of the same location of the wall you just edited. But in this case, use a Generic 12″ wall. The walls will overlap and that's okay.

3. Select the lower 12″ wall and then click Attach Top/Base (Figure 3.24). Now select the wall with the profile that we just edited. This will attach the top of the 12″ wall to the underside of the other wall, as shown on the right side of the figure.

The great thing about this technique is that relationships between the two walls are maintained if you edit the elevation profile of the upper wall. Performing these steps is a lot faster than having to edit the elevation profile of both walls!

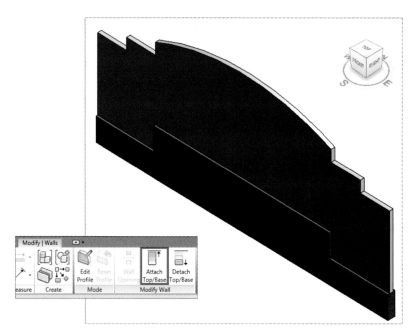

FIGURE 3.24   Attach Top/Base

Resetting Profiles

One last thing about editing wall profiles: If you need to remove the edited condition, don't reenter Edit Profile mode and manually remove the sketches. Select the wall and click Reset Profile in the Mode panel on the Modify | Walls tab. Doing so will reset the extents and remove any interior sketches.

Cutting Openings

Openings can be cut in both straight and curved walls. But the command tends to get used in curved walls because you already have the option to edit the elevation profile in straight walls. And when you cut an opening, you're not able to sketch beyond the extents of the wall boundary or create shapes that are not rectilinear. Here are the steps to create a rectilinear opening in a curved wall:

1. Start by creating a curved wall segment and then go to your Default 3D View and select the wall.

2. The Wall Opening option will then appear on the Modify | Walls tab, as shown in Figure 3.25 on the left. Select this command and then

hover over the wall; you'll be prompted to create a rectilinear open-ing, as shown on Figure 3.25 on the right. To delete an opening, hover over the opening, select it, and then press the Delete key.

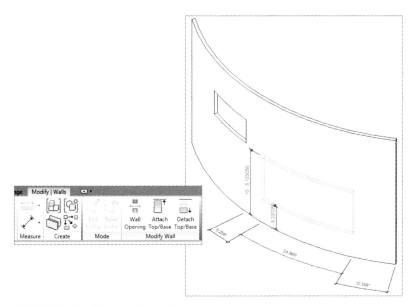

FIGURE 3.25 Creating wall openings

Splitting Walls

Sometimes after you've created walls you realize that you don't need an inner segment—or you need to change a segment to another wall type. Having to delete and re-create walls would be tedious. Revit allows you to split walls, effectively breaking them up into smaller pieces. This can be done along both horizontally and vertical edges of either curved or straight walls.

Let's experiment with this technique by creating a plan configuration of walls, as shown in Figure 3.26. The dimensions are shown for reference.

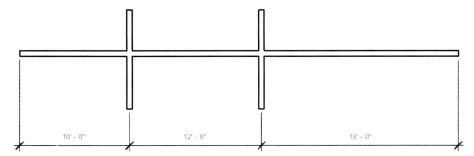

FIGURE 3.26 Configuration of walls

In this case the section of wall between the two parallel walls is not needed. But rather than delete the wall and create three new walls, let's split the wall twice and delete the inner wall.

1. Select the Split Element command from the Modify tab.

2. Hover over the location of the wall that you intend to split. You'll be prompted with a reference line that helps indicate to you which wall you're splitting. Split the wall twice at each intersection.

3. Delete the inner segment. Your wall will now resemble Figure 3.27.

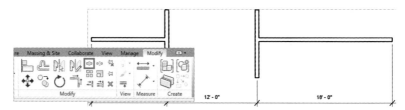

FIGURE 3.27 Using the Split Element command

Swapping Walls

Swapping walls keeps you from having to delete them and start over. You can do the same thing when changing walls from one type to another. Doing so is as easy as selecting a wall and then selecting the new type from the Properties palette.

1. We'll use the wall from the section, "Attaching and Detaching Top and Base." Select the lower wall and then associate it to a new type.

2. Change the lower wall to Generic – 12″ Masonry. Once you select the new wall type, the result will resemble the wall in Figure 3.28. Note that the patterns of the individual CMU courses are shown on the new wall's surface.

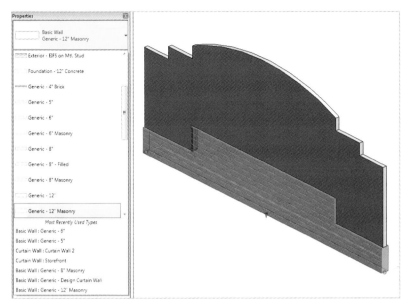

FIGURE 3.28 Selecting a new wall type

Creating Curtain Walls

Curtain walls are created in much the same way as regular walls: by selecting the type of curtain wall and then sketching the desired shape. But the available parameters are rather different. Let's start by creating a 40´-0˝ (12 meter) section, using Curtain Wall 1 as the wall type.

*Certification
Objective*

Grid Lines

Before adding mullions, we need to add grid lines to the curtain panel to which the mullions can associate.

1. Select the Curtain Grid tool from the Build panel (Figure 3.29).

FIGURE 3.29 Curtain Grid tool

2. As you hover over the edge of the curtain panel, Revit will prompt you with a dashed line that indicates the grid location. Also notice that the grid location gets kind of "sticky" at the ½ and ⅓ lengths along the edge

3. Place two evenly spaced grid lines in the horizon and vertical edge. When you're finished, the curtain panel will look like Figure 3.30.

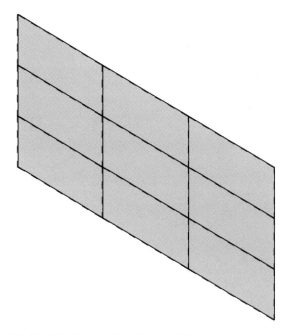

FIGURE 3.30 Completed grid lines

Adding Mullions

Now that you've added grid lines, you can add mullions to the curtain panel:

1. Select the Mullion tool from the Build panel. You'll be given three different options to place those mullions: You can place a mullion continuously along a grid line, a segment of a grid line, or even on all empty grids on a panel (including the boundary). Let's select the third option (Figure 3.31).

FIGURE 3.31 Selecting the Mullion tool

The default mullion is fine for this exercise, but note that there are several mullions in the default template. You can even create mullions with user-defined profiles.

2. Hover over the curtain panel and left-click, and the mullion will be assigned to all empty grids.

3. To modify an element in the curtain panel, hover over the location and press and release the Tab key (don't just hold the Tab key down). Doing so will sequentially select the mullion, the grid line, the nearest panel, or the entire curtain system.

4. Selecting the grid line and temporary dimensions allows you to enter exact values (or even press and drag to move the grid), as shown in Figure 3.32.

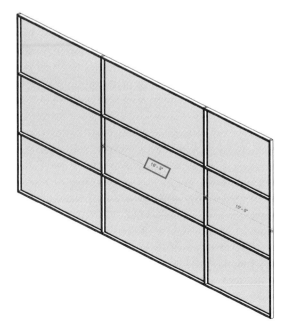

FIGURE 3.32 Moving the grid line

CURVED CURTAIN PANELS

Curved curtain wall panels that you create will appear "flat" until you add the vertical grid lines. But specifying exact grid locations during the design process is often tedious—and difficult to correct. You can create a "design" panel from a specially created wall that is very thin and transparent. Use this wall to figure out the design, and then swap it out for a curtain wall later. The wall can even have a pattern file associated to it that will visually help it to read as a curtain panel. Don't worry—we'll put a sample in the file that will be available at the end of the chapter.

Embedding Curtain Walls

Curtain walls can also be embedded in walls. Follow these steps:

1. Create a 40′-0″ section (12 meters) of a Generic 6″ Wall.

2. Sketch a 30′-0″ (9 meters) section of a Storefront type curtain wall inside the wall. This curtain wall type has grid and mullion definitions as part of the wall (see Figure 3.33).

As you can see, the curtain wall will automatically imbed itself in the generic wall.

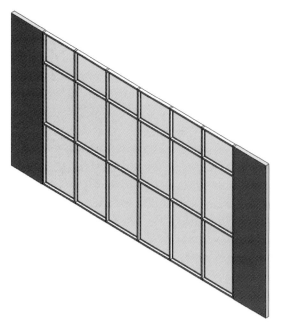

FIGURE 3.33 Embedding curtain walls

Modifying Curtain Walls

It's very seldom that our design ends up exactly where we started. So let's experiment with modifying our embedded curtain wall. This is a very important step not only in grasping how certain functionality works in Revit, but also in understanding the flexibility in your workflow and how Revit will accommodate it.

Editing the Elevation Profile

Complete the following steps to modify the elevation profile of a curtain system—even one embedded in a wall:

1. Select the entire system by hovering over the outer edge of the curtain panel and selecting it. Now you can modify the elevation profile.

2. Click Edit Profile and modify the sketch of the curtain wall as shown in Figure 3.34.

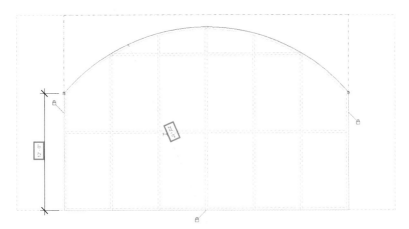

FIGURE 3.34 Modifying the sketch lines

3. Trim the side sketch lines and delete the top sketch line before finishing the sketch. Then click OK.

4. When you attempt to finish the sketch, Revit will warn you that some of the mullions in the original system can't be maintained. This is fine, because some of the mullions are outside the sketch area. Click Delete Elements to continue.

Revit has already "healed" the outer generic wall to match the new boundary condition.

Adding and Modifying Grids and Mullions

Now let's add some additional grids that are not part of this defined system:

1. First, select the grid tool and hover over the curtain system, as shown in Figure 3.35.

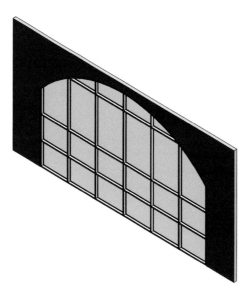

FIGURE 3.35 Adding a new grid and mullion

2. When the grid line is evenly spaced between the upper and lower mullions, place the new grid line, which will resemble the one in Figure 3.35.

   Because this type of curtain system already has a defined mullion, Revit will automatically add the mullion when you place the grid line.

Unpinning and Toggling Mullions

Now we need to exchange a door for one of the panels. Let's start by deleting one of the added mullions:

1. Zoom into the curtain system and hover over the mullion. When it highlights, select the mullion.

2. Notice the "pin" icon just above the mullion in Figure 3.36. The mullion is "pinned" because it's part of a defined system (in the type properties of the curtain panel).

3. You need to "unpin" the mullion before you can delete it. Select the pin icon and it will "unlock."

4. Now unpin and delete the mullion below the previous one. This gives you room for our curtain wall door.

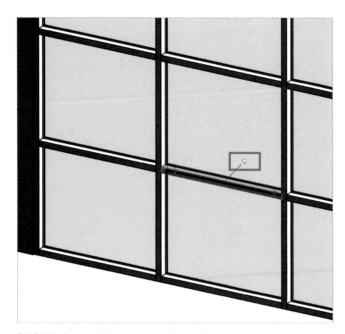

FIGURE 3.36   Unpinning the mullion

Adding and Modifying Panels

Before you swap out the panel for a door, you need to "weld" these two panels into a single panel. Follow these steps:

1. Hover over the intersection of the two panels and select the grid line shown in Figure 3.37.

FIGURE 3.37
Add/Remove Segments

2. Click Add/Remove Segments and then select the grid line that separates the two curtain panels.

   Now you have a single panel rather than two panels, because the two panels have been welded together.

   You can swap out the single panel with another panel; when you do so, the entire element is replaced. If you had not welded these two panels together, only the upper or lower panel would have been replaced individually.

Adding and Modifying the Curtain Panel Door

Before you swap out the glazed panel for curtain wall doors, let's load the appropriate family into the project. There's little point in getting ready to exchange the panel if you don't have the new panel ready to go!

1. From the Insert tab, select the Load Family option on the Load From Library palette. From the Doors folder, select the Curtain Wall Dbl Glass family. The family is now loaded into our project and you can exchange it for the default curtain panel.

2. You'll exchange the panel by first selecting the panel that you want to replace. Right away, you can see that the panel is also "pinned" since it's being defined by the type properties for the curtain wall system—

just like the mullions. As you'll recall, pinned elements can't be exchanged until they're unpinned. The same holds true for this panel.

3. Select the panel and unpin the panel. Now you can select a new option from the Properties pallet and replace the panel with a door, as shown in Figure 3.38.

FIGURE 3.38 Exchanging the panel for a door

The curtain panel doors automatically expand to fill the space of the entire panel that preceded it. These are special doors that are really a curtain panel category. If you want a "real" door, you can swap out the curtain panel for a wall (even a wall made only of glass), and then place the door in the wall.

Understanding Basic Wall Parts and Parameters

Without going into too much detail, let's take a moment and discuss some of the various wall types that are available in Revit. We don't think it would be a good idea to have you make all of these now. But it's good to know what is in the box so that as your design progresses you won't get the sense that you'll be backed into a corner. The idea is that once you get the basics down, you'll want to begin experimenting with more complex wall types.

There are basically three types of walls in Revit: basic, stacked, and curtain walls. Let's discuss each of these types in a bit more detail.

Basic Walls

Many basic walls have no defined vertical information. They'll be monolithic—
like the generic wall type that we've been using for most of these exercises. But
in some cases they'll be specific types of monolithic walls. In these cases, the
structural region is defined.

Select the Generic – 8″ Masonry wall type and then open the wall's type properties. Click Preview and select the Section view type. In Figure 3.39, the structural region of this wall is defined by a diagonal crosshatch pattern. This is a
basic wall with only one pattern defining the wall's material.

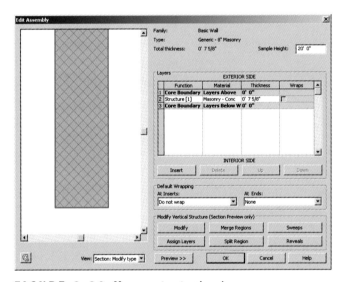

F I G U R E 3 . 3 9 Masonry structural region

However, basic walls may show far more vertical information and detail.
Select the wall type Exterior - Brick on Mtl. Stud and you'll see the difference
(Figure 3.40). Notice that there are numerous values that control the function,
material, and thickness for this wall type. These values help you coordinate your
project information across views and schedules. If the wall you select is right
anywhere, it's right *everywhere*!

Basic walls can even have profiles associated to them. Profiles can be used
to add or remove geometry in your walls. Take a look at the wall type Exterior
- Brick and CMU on MTL. Stud. Note the parapet cap at the top of the wall
(Figure 3.41). This is a profile associated to the basic wall type. So while you can

manually add profiles to walls in your project on a case-by-case basis, we think you'll find adding them to the wall definition makes creating and updating wall types easy and quick.

Certification
Objective

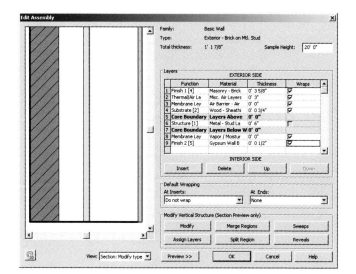

FIGURE 3.40 Vertically compound walls

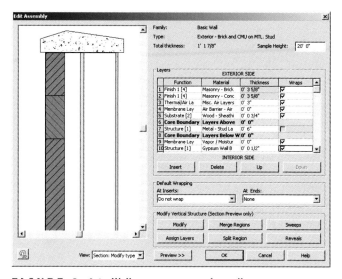

FIGURE 3.41 Wall sweep as part of a wall

Stacked Walls

**Certification
Objective**
So what are stacked walls? They're your basic wall types, but in a single defined type. So any of your basic walls can be used to create a stacked wall.

Look at the wall type Exterior - Brick Over CMU w Metal Stud, shown in Figure 3.42. It's defined by two different basic walls, but you can add more. However, you can't combine stacked walls (talk about confusing!) or curtain walls into your stacked wall.

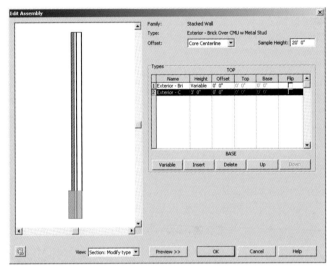

FIGURE 3.42 Stacked wall section

Curtain Wall Types

Curtain walls can have complete type definitions (Figure 3.43). The definition will include the mullion type (horizontal and vertical) for the interior and border conditions. But you can also control the horizontal and vertical spacing in the type definition as a type, which is very handy. But what's really cool is that you can also assign panel types to the curtain system type.

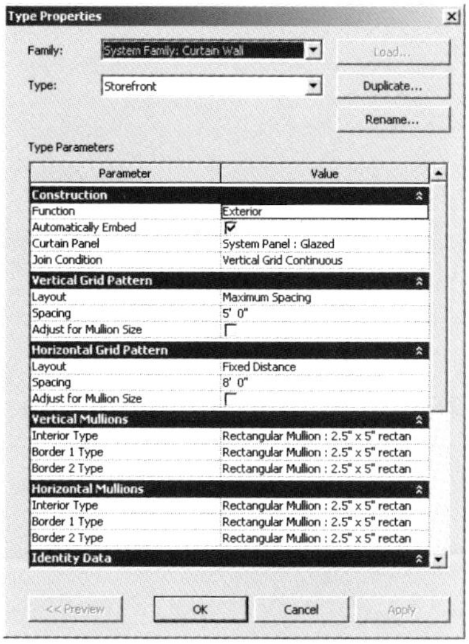

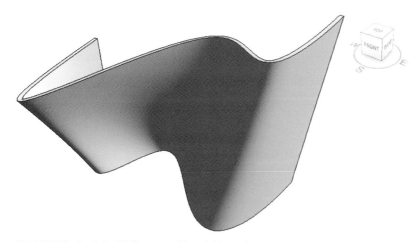

FIGURE 3.43 Curtain wall type definitions

Just One More Thing

Walls and curtain walls can be far more complex than the examples you've created in this chapter. If you want to examine all the types, go to the Chapter 3 folder at this book's web page at **www.sybex.com/go/revit2012essentials** and download 03_Walls_and_Curtainwalls.rvt.

First, there's the option to create walls by picking a face (Figure 3.44). Essentially you create a mass and then assign walls to the face of the mass. If the mass is modified, you can reassign walls to the modified faces. As you can see in Figure 3.44, the results can be complex.

FIGURE 3.44 Walls created by picking a face

Not only can you create walls in this manner, you can also create complex curtain systems. These mass-based curtain types can contain *very* complex panel configurations. In some cases, the results may not even resemble a typical glazed system (Figure 3.45).

Once again, the important thing is to understand the basics. Resolve your design intent. Don't get hung up on modeling in Revit when you can sketch. Get feedback from someone who's a Revit expert and is willing to share.

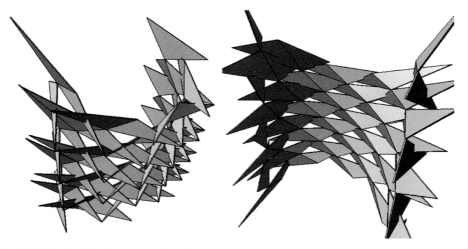

FIGURE 3.45 Curtain panel system

The Essentials and Beyond

Creating complex wall conditions is possible but takes time and patience. In more complex conditions, walls can also be embedded into other walls. But for an essential understanding of Revit, this is a great start; you've created walls of many types, added hosted elements—and even edited their profiles.

Additional Exercises

Create the following curtain wall condition. Note that the mullions are angled. You'll need to modify the Type, Instance, and Grid Layout properties to come up with the most flexible solution.

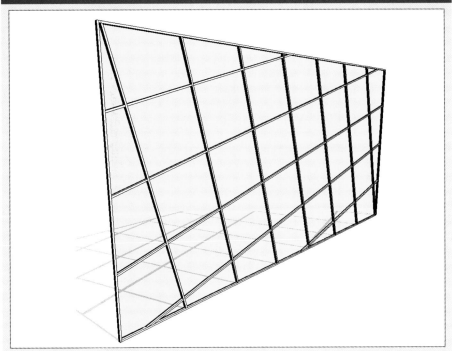

The curved wall in the next graphic has a complex star-shaped opening that is being filled by another curved wall that is star shaped (and fits exactly inside that opening). You can't create non-rectilinear openings in curved walls with the Wall Opening tool. You'll need to use an in-place family.

If you get stuck, both of these walls are in this chapter's sample Revit project at the book's web page.

CHAPTER 4

Floors, Roofs, and Ceilings

We've approached this chapter by grouping together horizontal host elements that make up your building. Although the initial creation of a floor, roof, or ceiling is somewhat different, the tools used to edit the initial design element have a lot of overlap and similarity.

In this chapter, you learn the following skills:

▶ **Creating floors**

▶ **Laying out roofs**

▶ **Adding ceilings**

Creating Floors

Certification Objective

There are quite a few ways to create floors in Revit. But we honestly don't have the space to dig deep into all these variations! Quite frankly they're not important for early design iteration.

What's important is that you understand what the various approaches to a single floor type will do and what kind of relationships they'll make. So let's get started!

Sketching

First, let's create floors by sketching the desired shape in the Level 1 floor plan view. The floor type that we'll be using is Generic – 12″. Start by selecting the Floor tool on the Build panel of the Home tab. You'll enter Sketch mode, which will allow you to create a sketch that will eventually be used to define the boundary of your floor.

Let's create a simple sketch for the floor, 15′ × 30′ [4.5 m × 9 m]. The dimensions are shown for reference only. Even though this is a simple shape, what's more important is how you'll be able to manipulate the shape.

Finish the sketch and select your default 3D view. Now select the Floor tool and your floor will resemble the one in Figure 4.1.

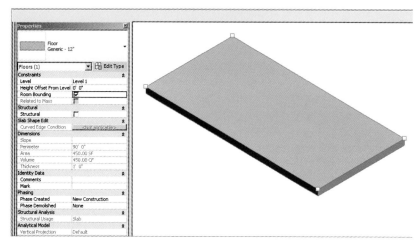

FIGURE 4.1 Our finished floor

Editing the Boundary

Note that you're able to see a couple of things right away in the instant properties: metadata about the floor (location, area, volume, etc.) as well as the ability to revise the geometry via sketching or spot elevations. Let's select Edit Boundary and return to the Level 1 floor plan.

Add additional sketch lines to generate the shape at the bottom right of Figure 4.2. Don't forget to trim back any intersecting lines.

Once this is done and there are no overlapping lines, finish the sketch by clicking the green check button. Select the floor and you'll notice that the options and metadata have already updated, as shown in Figure 4.3.

Now let's create another floor of the same type and same initial dimensions: 15' × 30' [4.5 m × 9 m], just above the first floor. Leave some space between the two floors. Offset the floor 1'-0" [300 mm] above Level 1 by entering this distance into the Properties palette. Finish the sketch to complete the floor (Figure 4.4).

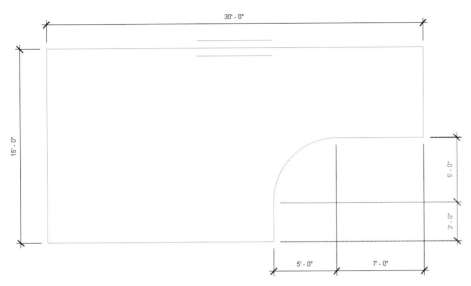

FIGURE 4.2 Modifying the floor sketch

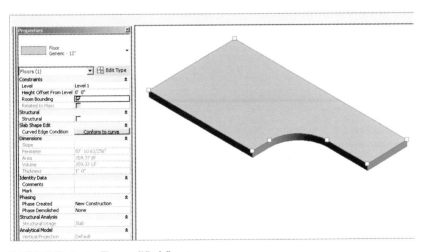

FIGURE 4.3 The modified floor

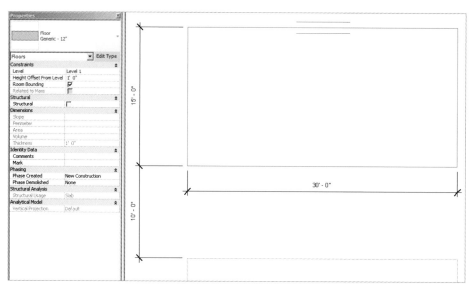

FIGURE 4.4 New floor 1'-0" above Level 1

Sloped Arrows and Floors

Not all floors are flat, and many have large openings. Let's investigate both options. We'll begin by bridging another sloped floor between the first two. Sketch another floor between the two previous floors, filling the gap between the two (Figure 4.5).

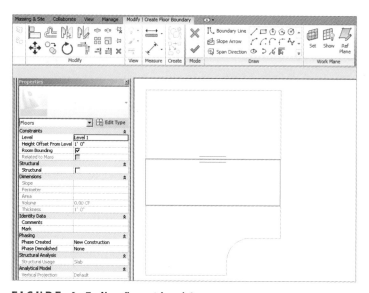

FIGURE 4.5 New floor at Level 1

If you were to finish the sketch like this, the floor wouldn't connect the upper and lower sections. You need to add a slope arrow. Do so by selecting the Slope Arrow tool on the Draw panel. Sketch the arrow as shown in Figure 4.6. The first location that you pick will be the tail of the arrow; the second location is the head.

FIGURE 4.6 Slope arrow constraints

Once you create the slope arrow, select it and modify the parameters as shown in Figure 4.6 so that they match the location of the upper and lower floors. Be sure to specify the heights of the tail and head. Finish the sketch and return to your default 3D view (Figure 4.7), which shows the finished condition. Now the sloped floor connects the lower and upper floors.

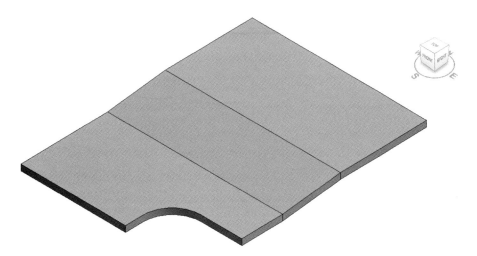

FIGURE 4.7 Completed sloped floor

Sloped Floors via Shape Editing

Slightly sloped floors and depressions could be created with slope arrows and separate floors—but this approach is probably too complex since you'd have to create a lot of separate pieces of geometry. For these kinds of conditions, you have the Shape Editing tools.

Let's start by returning to Level 1 and selecting the upper floor. Now you can see the Shape Editing tools in the Shape Editing panel. Let's suppose that this entire floor is at the right level, except for one small portion that needs to be slightly depressed in order to accommodate a loading area.

First, let's define the upper and lower boundaries of this depressed area by selecting the Add Split Line option from the Shape Editing panel. Add the spline lines as shown in Figure 4.8. Dimensions are shown for reference.

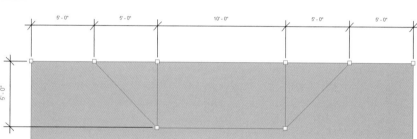

FIGURE 4.8 Adding split lines

Now that you've added the proper locations to break the slope, you'll modify the points at the ends of the lines to change the slope of the floor. Start by returning to your Default 3D View.

As you hover over the endpoint of the line, Revit highlights the shape handles. Press the Tab key to highlight a specific handle and then select it (Figure 4.9). Now you can adjust the elevation of the shape handle. In this case we're depressing the floor, so the value will have to be negative. But you could also increase the elevation in a small area by using a positive value.

Change the value as shown in Figure 4.9. Then do the same for the shape handle to the right. When you're done, the depressed area will resemble Figure 4.10.

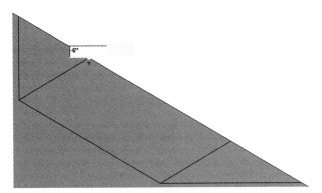

FIGURE 4.9 Editing the shape handle

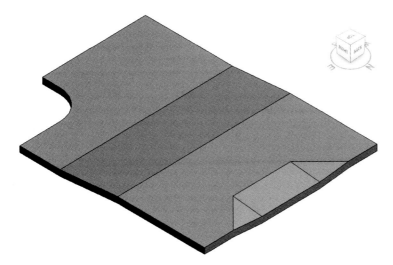

FIGURE 4.10 The finished depression

Creating Openings by Sketching

For the occasional or irregular opening in a floor, it's easy to add a secondary opening using the Opening tool.

From the Home tab, select the By Face tool from the Opening panel. Then select an edge of the sloped floor slab you created to enter Sketch mode. Now sketch an opening 10′ × 3′ [3 m × 1 m] in the center floor panel.

When you finish the sketch, the result will resemble Figure 4.11. There's no limit to the number of interior sketches that you can create. You can also edit sketches previously created.

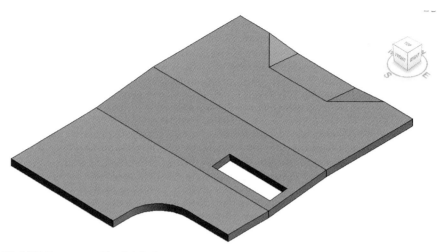

FIGURE 4.11   The finished opening

An opening of this type will remain perpendicular to the floor, roof, or ceiling. On the other hand, a vertical opening will remain perpendicular to the level that it was created on. Select the same slab and sketch a new opening of the same size and dimensions to the right of the first one. The result will resemble Figure 4.12.

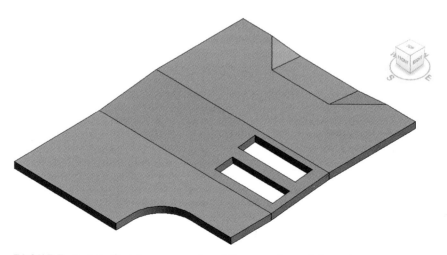

FIGURE 4.12   Sketch a new opening of the same size and dimensions.

The differences are subtle but very important. By creating a section through both openings, you can see the difference in an opening that remains perpendicular to the floor compared to one that remains perpendicular to the level (Figure 4.13).

FIGURE 4.13 Finished parallel and perpendicular openings

Keep in mind that from a project management standpoint, if you have a number of openings that are predictably shaped (circular, rectilinear, etc.) and *highly* repetitive, you'd be better off creating a host- or face-based opening (with parameters for options) as a family component and then loading it for use in your project.

Creating Openings with Shafts

For openings that occur from level to level with vertical regularity (like a shaft or elevator core), you can use the Shaft tool. This tool allows you to create an opening in numerous floors, roofs, and ceilings quickly and easily. Start by adding a few more levels to your project so that you have 10 levels that are evenly spaced.

Select all three floors on Level 1 and copy them by pressing Ctrl+C. Now the geometry is ready to be pasted to each of the levels. The best way to do this is by using the Paste tool, which allows you to select all the levels to which you intend to paste the floors. Select Paste from the Clipboard palette and then select Aligned To Selected Levels (Figure 4.14).

Now you'll be given the option to select all the levels. Select levels 2–10 (Figure 4.15). The resulting floors are shown in the same figure. Return to the Level 1 view and select the Shaft tool from the Opening panel. Once again, you'll enter Sketch mode. Create a new rectangle perpendicular to the last two you just drew. Be sure to modify the top constraint so that the shaft goes up to Level 10. Also be certain to assign a Top Offset value since the upper floor is slightly above the level (Figure 4.15).

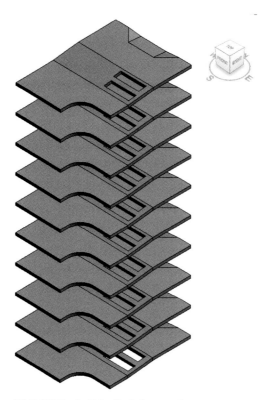

FIGURE 4.14 Pasted geometry

FIGURE 4.15 Creating a multistory shaft

Figure 4.16 shows the resulting shaft in 3D. All the floors were automatically cut. Any ceilings, roofs, and additional floors that may be added in the future will automatically be cut as well.

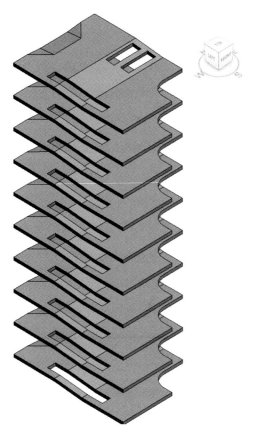

FIGURE 4.16 The finished multistory shaft

Picking Walls

Selecting walls defines a visual boundary that has been created during the design process; you can also use walls to create floors by using this boundary made by the bordering walls. Let's start by creating a series of walls on Level 1 that resembles Figure 4.17.

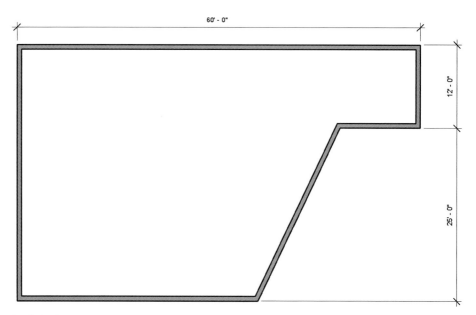

FIGURE 4.17 Creating a chain of walls

Now select the Floor tool to enter Sketch mode. But this time, you don't want to sketch the boundary of the floor manually. There's an easier way. Select the Pick Wall tool from the Draw palette. Doing so allows you to select an individual wall or an entire chain of walls.

Hover over one of the wall edges and then press and release the Tab key. Your selection will "cycle" from one wall to the series of walls. When all of the walls highlight, select them with one pick. Note that the edge of the new floor will be constructed where your mouse clicks when you pick the wall in reference to the interior or exterior of the wall. The floor goes to the outside of the wall; in order to do that, you have to pick the outside edge of the wall—otherwise, the floor aligns with the interior. The entire chain of lines will be created that correspond to all of the walls.

If you move the walls that were used to determine the floor sketch, the boundary of the floor will automatically update. This is incredibly powerful for a multistory building, where updating one floor at a time would be nearly impossible. As soon as one update would complete, the design would have likely changed, requiring you to start over.

Laying Out Roofs

You create roofs much like you do floors: from a sketch resulting from either drawn lines or picked walls. And as with floors, if you pick the exterior walls as a reference, then moving the walls will move the corresponding edges of the roof. Roofs can also be created in elevation (which we'll get to in a bit).

Roofs tend to slope, for a lot of good reasons. Let's create some roofs and investigate a few slope options.

Picking Walls

Let's start by adding a roof to the same walls you used in the previous floor exercise. First, return to your Level 1 plan view. Select the Roof tool and choose Roof By Footprint. At this point, Revit will automatically ask you to select levels this roof is going to be associated with; select Level 3.

Once again, you don't have to pick all the walls individually or sketch all the roof boundary lines. Select the Pick Walls option. Then hover over one of the exterior walls and press the Tab key to select the entire chain. When you select the entire chain of walls at once, all of the roof boundary lines will be created.

Note the icon with the double arrows. Clicking this icon will flip the boundary lines to the inside or outside of the wall face. Click this icon to move all the boundary lines to the inside of the wall's faces.

Since this will be a sloped roof, you can make the slope perpendicular to the left edge by deselecting the Defines Slope check box for all the other lines. Now define the slope of the left edge with a 1/12 rise over run (about 8 percent).

Finish the sketch and look at the project in 3D. While the roof begins at Level 3 and has the proper slope, it's immediately obvious that the walls don't extend beyond the roof.

Revit excels here at helping your team during the design process. Rather than not anticipate a potential conflict, you're able to identify conflicts earlier rather than later so you can resolve them before other design issues create circular conflicts.

Select all the walls (using the Tab key to select the entire chain) and set Top Constraint to Level 4 in the Properties palette. The results will resemble Figure 4.18.

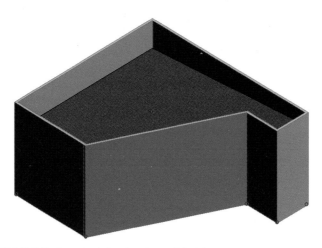

FIGURE 4.18 Adjusting the wall height

 Slope Arrow

Select the roof and reenter Sketch mode. Another option to determine the slope of a roof is using slope arrows. Slope arrows allow you to specify a slope, and they will also allow you to specify the levels of the arrow at both the head and tail.

The tail of the slope arrow must reside on the boundary of the sketch. But the head of the slope arrow may point in practically any direction! Add a slope arrow as shown in Figure 4.19. Note the Height Offset At Head value is set to 6′ [2m]. Make sure you uncheck the Define Slope option ▱ for the edges of the roof to see the full effect of using the Slope Arrow.

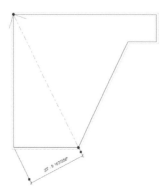

FIGURE 4.19 Sloping the roof

When you finish the sketch, you'll notice that a single slope proceeds across the roof. A single slope in this direction would be nearly impossible to specify without slope arrows.

You can create roof slopes using multiple slope arrows. This technique is incredibly helpful when you want to create sloped conditions where two perpendicular slopes must meet at exactly the same location. Again, this is something that's difficult to do without slope arrows.

Let's explore this topic by reentering Sketch mode with the previously created roof. Delete the existing slope arrow by editing the sketch. Now sketch two new slope arrows so that the heads of the arrows meet at the upper-left corner of the roof. The Slope Arrow should have the following properties:

Head Offset At Tail: 0″

Head Offset At Head: 6′ [2 m]

Make sure that Height Offset is the same for both Tails and Heads. When you finish the sketch, the results will resemble Figure 4.20.

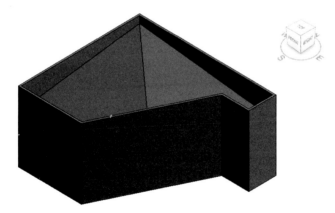

F I G U R E 4 . 2 0 Sketching two slope arrows

Another common condition in residential-styled roofs is one of multiple slopes that are perpendicular to their many edges. To create this condition, you'll reenter Sketch mode for the previously created roof and start by deleting both the slope arrows.

Now select all the lines that represent the roof sketch. You can do this by holding down Ctrl and selecting the lines individually or by clicking on one and pressing Tab to highlight the rest of the lines. Once you have them selected, in the Options Bar, enter 3′ [1 m] for the overhang. Now select the Defines Slope option for all the boundary edges from the Properties palette. Also modify the Slope property for a slope of 9/12. The roof in Sketch mode should look like Figure 4.21. Finish the sketch.

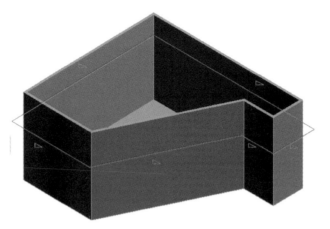

FIGURE 4.21 Offsetting the roof sketch and defining slopes

Initially the edges of the wall extend beyond the overhang of the roof. Select all the exterior walls (use the Tab key) and then select the Attach Top/Base option on the Modify | Wall tab. The result will resemble Figure 4.22.

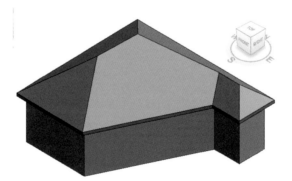

FIGURE 4.22 Attaching the walls to the roof

The great thing about attaching walls is that if the roof's angle or slopes change, the walls will automatically react to the new condition. To test this, reenter Sketch mode and remove the Defines Slope option for one of the edges.

When you finish the sketch, the results will resemble Figure 4.23. Since the walls have previously been told to attach to the roof, the gable condition is already updated.

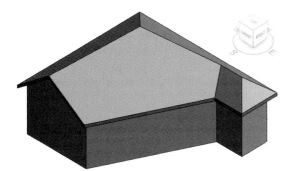

FIGURE 4.23 Removing a defined slope

Extruded Roofs

In addition to being able to create roofs in a plan or footprint orientation, you can extrude roofs from vertically planer surfaces. To do so, first select the Roof By Extrusion command from the Roof flyout on the Home tab. Once you select this command, you'll be immediately prompted by Revit to select the plane from which the extruded roof will spring. Select the face of the roof highlighted in Figure 4.24.

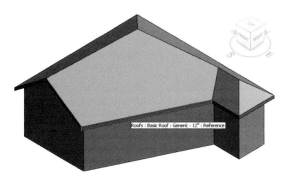

FIGURE 4.24 Defining the slopes

Now you'll be prompted to associate the roof to the appropriate level. This step is important for scheduling purposes and you can modify the value later. For now select Level 3 since it's closest to the base of the extruded roof.

Next, you'll create the sketch for the extruded roof. The sketch line will not be a closed loop. It's just a line (or series of connected lines) that defines the top of the extruded roof. For this example, you'll create an arc. Select the Arc tool from the Draw panel [图].

Now create the arc approximately as shown in Figure 4.25. The important detail is that we're going to set the Extrusion End to 20'-0" [6 m].

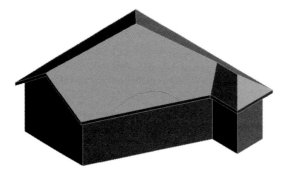

FIGURE 4.25 Creating the sketch

When you complete the sketch, the roof is springing from the arc that you created. But it's not reaching back and connecting to the roof face. This issue is easy to resolve. First, select the roof and then select the Join/Unjoin Roof option on the Geometry panel. Then, hover over the rear edge of the extruded roof, as shown in the left image of Figure 4.26. Finally, select the face of the previously created roof that you want to connect the extruded roof.

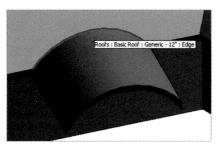 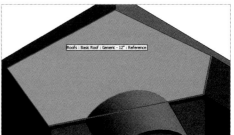

FIGURE 4.26 Attaching the Roof

The extruded roof will now extend back to meet the face of the other roof (Figure 4.27). If either roof is modified, Revit will do its best to maintain this connected relationship.

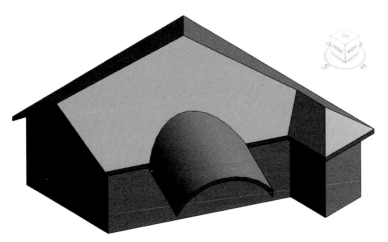

FIGURE 4.27 Joined roofs

Overall, there are so many other complex areas that we can talk about with regard to roofs, starting with point elevations and then digging into more instance and type parameters. But once again, this is beyond the space limitations for an introduction to Revit. Learning how to use Revit organically is a better approach: Start with the basics of design iteration and then build on these concepts as the need arises.

Adding Ceilings

Ceilings in Revit are easy to place as well as modify. As you move the walls, the ceiling associated to those walls will stretch to fit their new conditions.

Let's start by returning to the Level 1 floor plan of the previous exercise. Add 10'-0" [3 m] high walls and doors to create individual, shared, and open spaces (Figure 4.28).

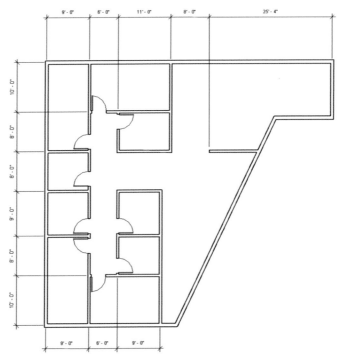

FIGURE 4.28 Level 1 with walls

Automatic Ceilings

The Ceiling tool is found on the Build palette of the Home tab. When you select the tool, the default condition is Automatic Ceiling. This means that as you hover over a space, Revit will attempt to find the boundary of walls. Let's do this for one space (Figure 4.29). As you hover over the space, Revit indicates the boundary with a broad, red line. As you can see, Revit offers four default ceiling types: one Basic type and three Compound types. Let's select the 2′ × 2′ [600 mm × 600 mm] system.

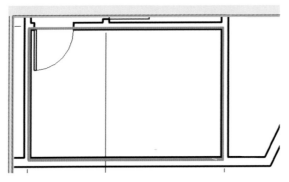

FIGURE 4.29 Placing the ceiling

As you place the first ceiling in the Floor plan view, you'll get a warning. This happens frequently and for good reason. You've placed the ceiling but you can't see it. As a rule, you should not ignore warnings. We've seen people click and click only to find that they've repeatedly placed ceilings in the same space.

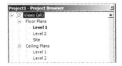

Go to the proper view in the Project Browser to see the ceiling—in this case the ceiling plan for Level 1. Now you can plainly see the ceiling that you've created. Let's automatically place the remaining ceilings as shown in Figure 4.30. Notice that Revit will center the grid based on the space that you've selected.

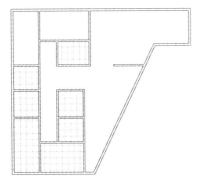

FIGURE 4.30 Resulting ceiling

Sketching Ceilings

Next, you'll place ceilings in the upper-left corner of the ceiling plan for Level 1, but this time you'll share the ceiling between the two spaces. This practice is common in interior projects. The partitions only extend to the underside of the ceiling (rather than connect to the structure above). Begin by selecting Sketch Ceiling on the Ceiling panel. Add sketch lines as shown in the first image in Figure 4.31. The result is shown in the second image.

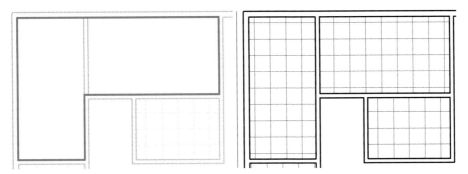

FIGURE 4.31 Sketching the ceiling

Now let's place a ceiling in the upper right of the plan, but this time you'll sketch a 2′ × 4′ [1.2 m × 600 m] system (Figure 4.32). Choose this new system from the Type Selector before you finish the sketch of the ceiling.

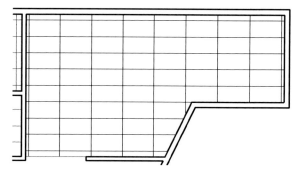

FIGURE 4.32 2′ × 4′ ceiling

And finally, create a GWB on Mtl. Stud Ceiling for the area shown in Figure 4.33.

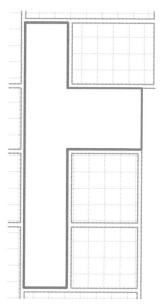

FIGURE 4.33 Creating a GWB on Mtl. Stud Ceiling

By default, the GWB material doesn't have a surface pattern. While this material would be too graphically busy for walls, it will be fine for ceilings. So let's create a new material for GWB associated to ceilings and give it a pattern.

Select an edge of the ceiling and click Edit Type. Then click the Structure button to open the Edit Assembly window. Select the Gypsum Wall Board material option and duplicate the existing material. Name the new material **Gypsum Ceiling Board**. Now associate a surface pattern called Sand to the material. Click OK until you close all the dialog boxes and return to the Ceiling plan view. The result is shown in Figure 4.34. You can now distinguish the ceiling from the open areas that have no ceiling.

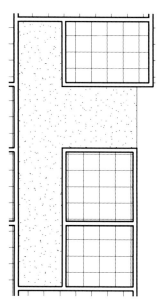

F I G U R E 4 . 3 4 Assigning materials to a ceiling

Bulkhead Conditions

Creating a bulkhead to separate two ceilings is straightforward. To begin, place the walls that will act as the bulkhead, as shown in Figure 4.35. Be sure to set the Base Offset value of the walls to 7'-9" [2.3 m] and the Unconnected Height value to 2'-3" [700 cm]. This will create two walls above head height.

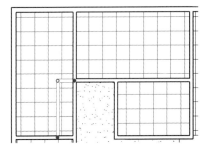

FIGURE 4.35 Creating a bulkhead

It requires a bit of finesse to delete or edit a placed ceiling. Most beginners simply select the grid. But you actually need to select the *edge* of the ceiling to edit it. Hover over the edge of the ceiling and use the Tab key to cycle through options until the edge of the ceiling is highlighted. Then select it and choose Edit Boundary. Modify the ceiling as shown in Figure 4.36. Sketch a new GWB ceiling that is 9'-0" [2.7 m] and finish the sketch. The second image in Figure 4.36 shows the finished ceiling.

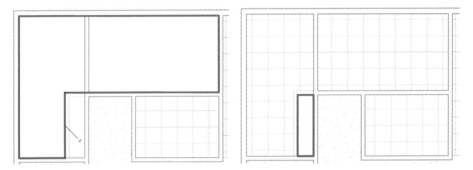

FIGURE 4.36 Editing the boundary

To get a better idea of the finished configuration in 3D, go to a 3D view and orient a section box of the Level 1 plan view. Right-click the ViewCube and from the Floor Plans flyout of the context menu, select Level 1. Use the grip arrows to pull the boundaries of the section box to resemble Figure 4.37. You'll find that working this way is helpful because having both 2D and 3D views aids in communicating the design issues.

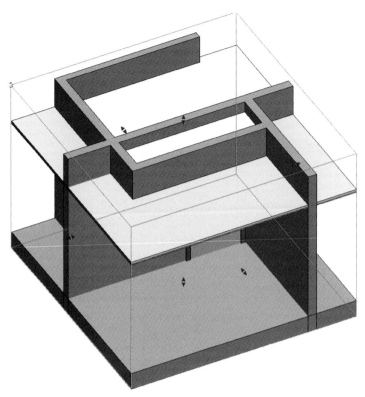

FIGURE 4.37 Orienting the section box to the 3D view

Adding Lights and Rotating the Grid

Adding lights is easy and since they're hosted by the ceiling, lights will often create openings for you. Let's begin by loading one of the lighting families.

From the Insert tab, select Load Family from the Load From Library panel. Open the Lighting Fixtures folder and double-click on the family Ceiling Light – Linear Box.rfa.

You'll be prompted to place the first family type of the family in your ceiling, but be sure to select the 2′ × 4′ type from the Type Selector. You'll place lighting fixtures into the 2′ × 4′ ceiling in the upper-right ceiling plan.

As you will notice, the insertion point for the light is the center of the light. So place the first light and then use the Align tool to get the first one into the right spot. Then copy the first light based on the intersection of the ceiling grid. All of the lights are shown in Figure 4.38 on the left. To rotate the grid, select any grid line and use the Rotate tool rotate the grid line. In this case, we specified a 10-degree angle. You'll notice the lights have rotated as well.

Now press and drag the ceiling grid lines to better center the lights in the overall space. Again, the lights have moved with the grid. This technique is incredibly helpful for maintaining design coordination. The finished condition is in Figure 4.38 on the right.

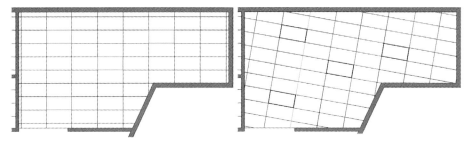

FIGURE 4.38 Placing lights and rotating the grid

Changing the Ceiling

Ceiling types often change in the design process. Again, where most beginners struggle is mistakenly selecting the ceiling grid (which is actually selecting the material). But you need to select the geometry of the ceiling, which you do by selecting the *edge* of the ceiling.

Select the edge of the ceiling and then you'll be able to pull down the Properties menu to select the GWB option for this ceiling (Figure 4.39). The result is shown in the second image in Figure 4.39.

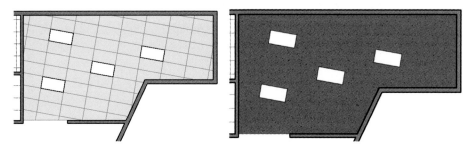

FIGURE 4.39 Selecting ceiling geometry

Sloping the Ceiling

We can even slope the ceiling by placing a slope arrow while editing the boundary of the ceiling. This is basically the same process as sloping a floor or a roof.

Select the edge of the ceiling and choose Edit Boundary. Place a slope arrow as shown in Figure 4.40. Then set the Height Offsets for the Tail and Head to 0 and 3′ [1 m], respectively. Finish the sketch. The result is shown 3D using a section box. The lights even follow the revised ceiling slope!

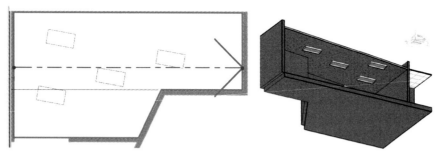

FIGURE 4.40 Adding a slope arrow to the ceiling

THE ESSENTIALS AND BEYOND

In this chapter you learned to create floors, lay out roofs, and add ceilings.

ADDITIONAL EXERCISES

▶ Create a mass and intersecting levels and then create mass floors from those levels. Use the mass floors to create a Floors By Face.

▶ Modify the mass from the previous step and then update the Floors By Face.

▶ Create a shaft opening and intersect it with all the Floors By Face from the previous step.

▶ Create a Roof or Floor and then use the Shape Editing tools to model slopes for drainage.

CHAPTER 5

Stairs, Ramps, and Railings

Revit is capable of creating wonderfully complex and elegant stairs, ramps, and railings. But to get started, you need to understand the basic functionality so that you can confidentially resolve design intent. Then once the design intent is resolved, you'll have plenty of time to go back and modify the stair and revise the entire design quickly and easily!

In this chapter, you learn the following skills:

▶ **Creating numerous stair configurations**

▶ **Designing ramps**

▶ **Building railings for level and sloped conditions**

▶ **Working with parts, parameters, and properties**

Creating Numerous Stair Configurations

Stairs contain many, many parameters, but not all of the parameter controls are going to be equally important during the design process. Design is often about the intent of what something is as well as where it is meant to go. Once the intent is resolved, it's necessary to go back and revise the specifics of how something will be carefully assembled.

Let's first simplify the default railing that is associated to the stairs. The default railing is very busy from a design standpoint. It contains lots of balusters, which are graphically distracting. It's important that you indicate the handrail and nothing more.

Creating the "Generic" Railing

Certification Objective

Open the default template and expand the Family tree in the Project Browser. As you can see, four railing definitions exist in the project: Guardrail – Pipe through Handrail – Rectangular. There are also two types of stair families in the default template: the Monolithic stair family and the 7 Max Riser 11″ Tread stair family.

Let's start by creating a railing that is useful from a design standpoint. Too much specificity too soon can cause a lot of confusion, so you'll simplify the geometry. You'll do this by duplicating a railing definition that's close to what you need and then modify it to suit your purposes.

Here are the steps to duplicating and creating your own custom handrail that you'll use for designing stairs. For these exercises, you're going to work from the c05_Stairs_Ramps_Railings.rvt file found on the book's companion web page, www.sybex.com/go/revit2012essentials.

1. Right-click on Handrail – Pipe and select Duplicate.

2. Right-click on the duplicated handrail and select Rename. Rename the duplicate handrail to **Handrail – Design**.

3. Select the handrail that you've just created and drag it into your Level 1 view. Doing so initiates the Railing command and allows you to draw a portion of the railing that you've selected.

4. Create a 24′ [7.3 m] long segment.

5. Select the Finish command and go to your 3D view. As you can see in Figure 5.1, there are balusters and rails below the handrail portion of the railing; you'll simplify this area to create your design railing.

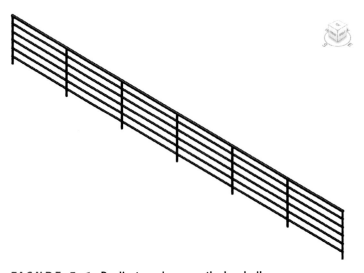

FIGURE 5.1 Duplicate and rename the handrail.

To modify the type properties of this railing, select the handrail in your drawing and choose Edit Type from the Type Selector. The Type Properties dialog box opens, which is where you'll modify the properties of the railing.

Start by editing the rail structure. Click Edit Rails in the Type Properties dialog box. In the resulting dialog box shown in Figure 5.2, delete Rail 2 through Rail 6. Leave Rail 1; it will serve as the design intent handrail for your stairs. Close the dialog box by clicking OK.

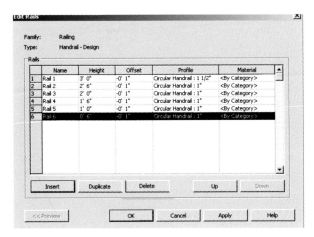

FIGURE 5.2 Deleting types

Next you'll edit the balusters. With the Type Properties dialog box open:

1. Select the Baluster Placement option and click the Edit button; doing so opens the Edit Baluster Placement dialog box, shown in Figure 5.3.

2. In the Main Pattern panel, select Regular Baluster and set its Baluster Family value to None.

3. In the Posts panel, set the Baluster Family value for the Start, Corner, and End posts to None. Then click OK to close the Edit Baluster Placement dialog box and click OK again to close the Type Properties dialog box. The image shows a railing with a handrail only, but for design purposes, this is exactly what you need in order to express design intent.

FIGURE 5.3 Edit Baluster Placement settings

Now let's start creating our "design" stair.

Creating Your Design Stair

By default, there are two types of stairs in your Revit project. Let's duplicate the 7" Max Riser 11" Tread stair family type in the Project Browser and name the duplicate **Stair-Design**. This is the stair that you'll use to create numerous configurations.

Straight Run

Let's start by creating a straight run stair. Select the Stairs tool from the Circulation panel of the Home tab on the ribbon. Or, drag the component name into the project view to activate the Stairs tool.

1. From the Level 1 plan view, pick a point to the left and then move your cursor to the right. As you do, you'll notice that Revit is telling you how many treads remain to complete a stair that starts on Level 1 through Level 2 (Figure 5.4).

FIGURE 5.4 Sketching the straight run stair

2. Select the Railings Type option in the Tools palette. Specify the Handrail – Design type that you created earlier, as shown in Figure 5.5. This will be the default handrail that Revit will use whenever you create this stair until you specify another type.

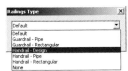

FIGURE 5.5 Specifying the railings type

3. Finish the Sketch mode. The resulting stair is shown in Figure 5.6.

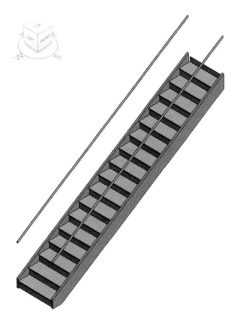

FIGURE 5.6 The resulting stair

Straight Run with Landing

What you just created is the most basic type of stair: a straight run with a pair of railings. However, it's important to understand how to create a variety of

Certification Objective

stair types, including stairs with landings. Follow these steps to start your first straight run of stairs.

1. Let's start the sketch this time from the ribbon. Choose the Home tab, and then click the Stairs button in the Circulation panel. Doing so starts your stair in Sketch mode. Begin by drawing a straight run, but stop about halfway through the run.

2. Start the second run of stairs, as shown in Figure 5.7. When you finish the second run of stairs, you'll notice that Revit creates the landing between the two runs automatically.

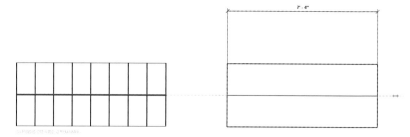

FIGURE 5.7 A second run of stairs and landing

3. Finish the sketch and the stair will resemble Figure 5.8.

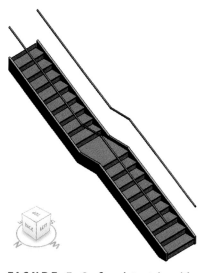

FIGURE 5.8 Complete stairs with a middle landing

Multistory Runs

For multistory runs, Revit is able to take a stair that only goes between two levels and repeat it continuously. But this will only work if all of the level-to-level heights are identical. Let's turn one of the stairs that we've created into a multistory stair. It's easy!

1. First, you need to create some additional levels. As shown in Figure 5.9, open the South elevation and click the Level tool on the Datum panel of the Home tab. Click on the elevation and drag the mouse from left to right to place the level, taking care that the heights are equally spaced.

   As discussed earlier, you can change the level heights by clicking the blue elevation text. For this example, we repeated the levels at 10'-0" [3 m] increments—up to 40'-0" [15m)]. Figure 5.9 shows several stair types, including the ones you've created.

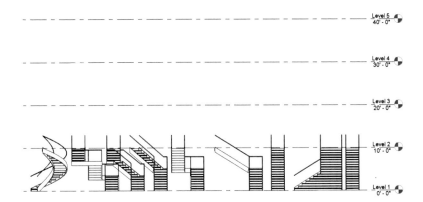

FIGURE 5.9 Adding additional levels to the model

2. Select any of the stairs you've created. Highlight one of the stair runs and look at its properties in the Properties palette. You'll see there's an option to designate the Multistory Top Level. Set it to Level 5, as shown in Figure 5.10.

FIGURE 5.10
Changing the properties
for a multistory stair

3. Once you complete the multistory stair, the stair will quickly propagate across all levels (Figure 5.11). If you edit the stair or railings associated to the multistory stair, the entire multistory configuration changes as well.

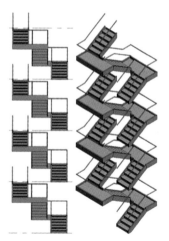

FIGURE 5.11 The completed
multistory stair

Setting the Host Function for Railings

By now you've noticed railings have special relationships to stairs. By default Revit creates railings at the same location as the boundary sketch of the stair. You can then select the railing and modify its sketch to suit a particular condition. It's important to understand that railings are hosted by stairs, and this relationship allows railings to follow the path of the stairs that host them. So let's create another stair that's a bit wider than the stairs you've created thus far. Also, let's remember to tell the railing that it is hosted by the stairs.

1. Create the stair as shown in Figure 5.12. Notice the landing as well as the extra width that will easily allow traffic in both directions. Finish the sketch by clicking the green check on the Modify tab of the ribbon.

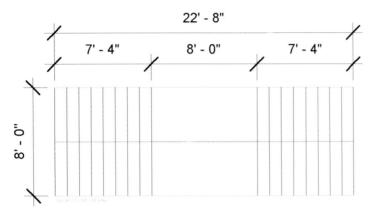

FIGURE 5.12 Stair sketch for hosting the center railing

2. Add two separate railing sketches: one for the lower run and another for the upper run. And while you're at it, you'll also include the handrail extensions.

3. Drag the Handrail – Design railing type into the project view. Revit will initiate the Railing tool for you and select the railing. Sketch the lower railing as shown in Figure 5.13. Add the extensions shown as separate sketch lines.

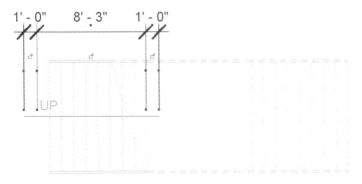

FIGURE 5.13 Lower railing sketch

Pick
New Host

4. Before you complete the sketch, be sure to set the stair as the host for the railing. Click the Pick New Host icon on the Tools palette; then select the stair. It will highlight when you hover over the stair.

5. Finish the stair and the view will resemble the left side of Figure 5.14. Now create the second sketch for the upper railing. Don't forget to extend the railing beyond the lower treads and add the extension. The results will resemble the image on the right of Figure 5.14. Don't forget to set the host each time you create a new railing!

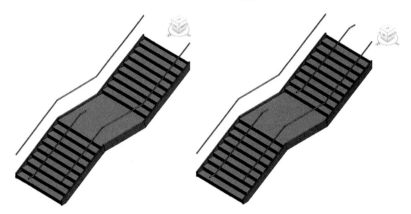

FIGURE 5.14 Handrail extensions

One final note: not only is hosting important for railings and stairs, but it's also something that you'll deal with when creating ramps as well as sloped floors.

Designing Ramps

Now that you're familiar with designing a number of stair configurations, ramps will come easy. It's the same basic process of sketching a desired shape and then completing the sketch—with one major difference: far more frequent landings and a shallower slope.

You access the Ramp tool from the Circulation panel on the Home tab or by dragging the desired ramp from the list of families in the Project Browser. For the following exercises, let's just use Ramp 1.

Keep in mind that ramps have different constraints than stairs. We'll cover some details of these constraints at the end of this chapter. For now, just understand that the maximum length of a ramp in one section is 30'-0" [9m)] and a 1:12 slope (8 percent). These parameters can be changed, but by default they correlate to common code requirements.

Straight Runs

Let's start by creating a straight run. Because we're traversing Level 1 to Level 2 (and they are 10' [3 m] apart), this will require a ramp length of 120' [36.5 m] at a maximum 1:12 slope, not including landings. You'll be limited to runs of 30' [9 m] in length. So right off the bat, you know that four runs will be required with three landings.

1. Sketch the straight runs as shown in Figure 5.15.

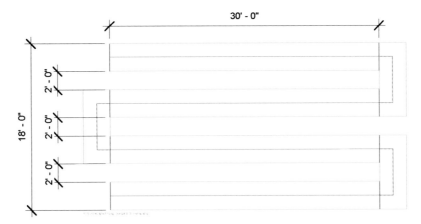

FIGURE 5.15 Straight runs of ramps

2. Note that the run lines that indicate slope versus landings are different. Blue lines indicate slope whereas black lines indicate level landings.

3. Finish the sketch. You'll see something like Figure 5.16, which displays the results in 3D.

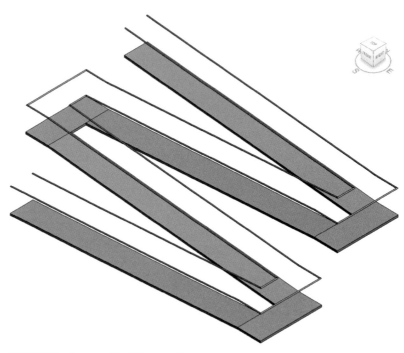

FIGURE 5.16 Straight runs of ramps

The process is the same as that for all the other stair configurations you've created. Multistory rules are permitted, and you must use the Set Host function when creating additional railings.

Editing Boundary Conditions

Editing boundary conditions of both stairs and ramps typically modify the railings associated with those elements. Let's test this now with the ramp you just created.

1. Return to Level 1, select the ramp, and enter Sketch mode.

2. Delete the boundary lines that represent the landings, as shown in Figure 5.17.

FIGURE 5.17 Straight runs of ramps

3. Select the Boundary tool and then choose the Tangent Arc tool.

4. Create the new boundaries shown in Figure 5.18 by picking one boundary edge and then the other. Then finish the sketch. The finished ramp in 3D is shown on the right in Figure 5.18. Notice that Revit has already modified the railings to accommodate the new boundary.

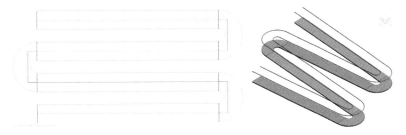

FIGURE 5.18 Modified ramp with curved boundary

Building Railings for Level and Sloped Conditions

Railings are created much like stairs and ramps; you select the tool, enter Sketch mode, create your linework, and then finish the sketch. The Railing tool can be found on the Circulation panel of the Home tab in the ribbon, or you can drag the desired railing type from the Project Browser into the project view window.

Sketches for railings can consist of a series of connected lines, but sketches with gaps or overlapping lines aren't permitted. Sketches that cross or fail to intersect properly will also produce an error message. Both sketches in shown in Figure 5.19 would not be completed.

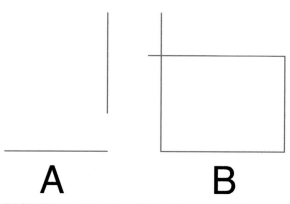

FIGURE 5.19 A doesn't join; B crosses itself.

If you attempt to complete railings like either of the ones in Figure 5.19, you'll get the warning shown in Figure 5.20.

FIGURE 5.20 You'll see this error message.

Floors can also be sloped, so let's create this condition as well.

1. Start by creating a floor as shown in Figure 5.21 from the Build panel of the Home tab. If you need to review how to create floors, please refer to Chapter 4, "Floors, Roofs, and Ceilings."

FIGURE 5.21 Creating a floor

2. Now look at the contextual menu in the ribbon. Select the Slope Arrow tool and then pick the two points, first to the left and then the right.

3. Set the Height Offset At Tail value to 0'-0".

4. Set the Height Offset At Head value to 3'-0" [1 m]. Your floor should resemble the one shown in Figure 5.22 with the associated slope arrow.

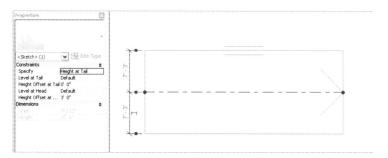

FIGURE 5.22 Adding the slope arrow

5. Finish the sketch by clicking the green check.

Set Host Function

Next let's add a curved railing that follows the slope of the floor.

1. Select the Railing tool from the Home tab, which will place you in Sketch mode.

2. Select Pick New Host and then select the floor you just created.

3. Create a curved sketch for the railing, as shown in Figure 5.23. Then finish the sketch by clicking the green check. That's all there is to it! The railing will now follow the path of the floor, even if you change the configuration of the railing sketch or the slope direction of the floor.

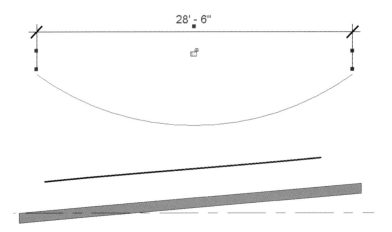

FIGURE 5.23 Curved railing sketch in elevation view

Working with Parts, Parameters, and Properties

So far you've been getting familiar with sketching various configurations for generic stairs, ramps, and railings. Now let's dig a little deeper to explore the properties of these three system families so you'll know how they affect these families. We'll begin with stairs.

Stair Parameters

Start by creating a section through the U-Shaped in our Revit file. The Section tool can be found in the QAT toolbar or in the View tab.

Open the section by double-clicking the blue section head. Adjust the section so that you can see the full flight of stairs. Select the stair and take a look at the instance parameters in the Properties palette. These are essentially self-explanatory and deal with the stair materiality, nosing overhang, and some other basic stair properties. You can try adjusting some of them to visualize the changes here in section.

Next, look at the type properties. With the stair still selected, click Edit Type to open the Type Properties dialog box for the stairs, shown in Figure 5.24. Let's step through some of the key ones and explain what you need to do to change them.

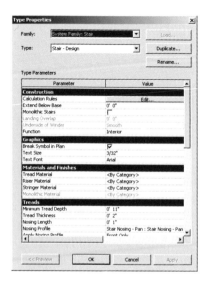

FIGURE 5.24 The stair type properties

Extend Below Base Extend Below Base will continue the structure of the Stringer below the base level of the stair. Set the value to –1'-0" [30 cm] and the results should be easy to see in section.

Monolithic Stairs Checking the Monolithic Stairs option will activate the next two options. They don't apply for this particular stair since we're only going up one level. For more information on Monolithic stairs, review the section "Creating the 'Generic' Railing," earlier in this chapter.

Function The Function option allows you to designate the stair as an interior or exterior type. It doesn't change the geometry in any way; it's more of a scheduling function.

Break Symbol The Break Symbol option controls the graphic break line. If checked, the condition on the right of Figure 5.25 is shown. If unchecked, the break symbol disappears and it is represented as a single line.

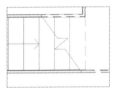

FIGURE 5.25
Break Symbol option

Text Size and Text Font   The Text Size and Text Font options refer to the "UP" or "DOWN" text. (This reports the direction of the stair.)

Material and Finishes   The Material and Finishes options control the shaded and rendered material assignments for the stairs.

Treads   Figure 5.26 indicates the corresponding dimensions from the Treads section. The Nosing Profile (if applied) is associated to the front of the tread, but can also be associated to either side, or even all three sides.

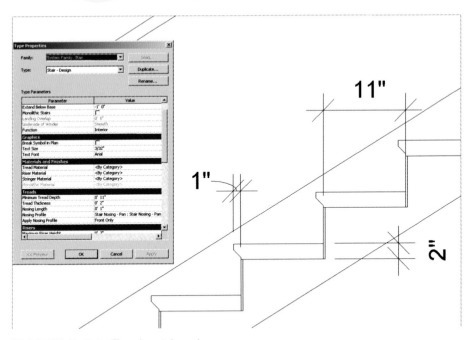

FIGURE 5.26   Changing stair nosings

Risers   The Risers function allows you to control the absence or presence of a riser, as well as what type (straight or slanted). Extending the tread under the riser will result in the image on the left of Figure 5.27, whereas extending the riser behind the tread will result in the image on the right.

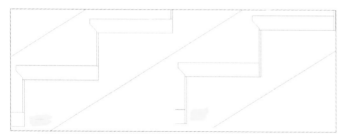

FIGURE 5.27 Extending the riser location

Stringers　Stringer properties control the properties of both left and right stringers. Stringer Height is the depth of the stringer as measured from edge to parallel edge (Figure 5.28).

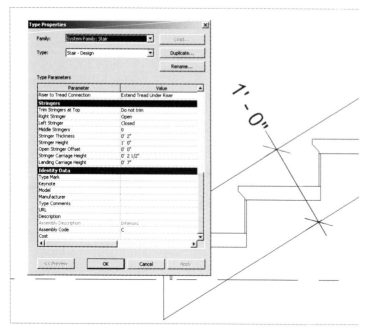

FIGURE 5.28 Stringer Height

Stair Carriages　Stair Carriages are simply the structural framing that supports the treads and landings.

Carriage Heights　Carriage Heights are dimensional clearances between the carriage to the treads and landings.

Ramp Parameters

As with stairs, the type parameters of ramps contain most of the information you'll need to set the rules of the ramp. To view the properties, follow these steps:

1. Create a section of the first ramp in the same way you created the section of the stair.

2. Open the section and select the ramp.

3. Select Type Properties from the Properties palette. The dialog box shown in Figure 5.29 appears.

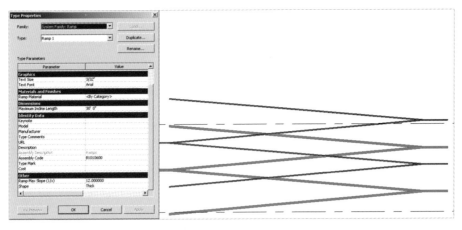

FIGURE 5.29 Type Properties for the ramp

We're most concerned with two values. The first is Maximum Incline Length. This value determines the maximum continuous length that will be allowed before you have to create a landing. The second value is Ramp Max Slope, and it is expressed as a rise-to-run ratio or percentage based on your project settings.

Railing Parameters

After stairs, railing parameters are probably the most unfamiliar part of Revit for new users, so let's investigate what the parameters control. Since many of these values don't do anything clearly noticeable for stand-along railings, we'll use the same U-Shaped stair that we used to understand important stair parameters.

First, select the inner railing and click Edit Type in the Properties palette. Look at the Rail Structure and Baluster Placement fields.

Rail Structure   The Rail Structure option controls all the horizontal sweeps that are associated with a railing. A railing can have many, many horizontal sweeps.

Balusters   The balusters are any vertical elements, and they can be specified depending on location of use. The four options that Revit gives you are Start Post and End Post, Main Baluster Pattern, and Corner Post.

Baluster Offset   The Baluster Offset value controls all baluster positions to the left or right of the sketched line that creates the baluster. It's convenient to be able to move all the balusters to the left or right from this parameter. But another reason is that there are frequently conditions where the sketched line *must* reside on a host (like on stairs or a ramp). Yet the actual baluster geometry may need to reside on the stringer or beyond the edge of the ramp.

Landing Height Adjustment   The Landing Height Adjustment value raises or lowers the height of the railing based on the value given (and whether the box is checked). Figure 5.30 shows the unchecked result.

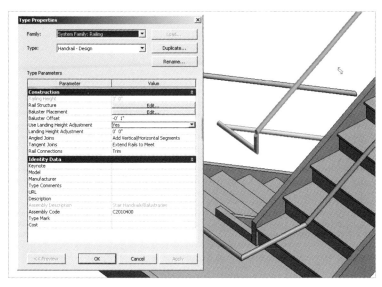

F I G U R E   5 . 3 0 No Landing Height Adjustment

Figure 5.31 shows the checked result with a value of 1'-0" [30 cm]. Notice that with the landing height adjustment selected, the railings have moved up in elevation.

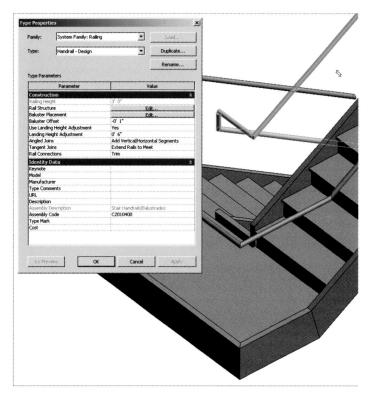

FIGURE 5.31 With Landing Height Adjustment

Angled Joins   With No Connector selected in the Angled Joins option, no vertical elements are added to maintain a continuous railing (Figure 5.32). This option affects angled joins (from a plan view) as seen with the inner railing, and either vertical or horizontal segments can be added. There are only two options: either add a vertical or horizontal segment or don't.

Tangent Joins   The outer railing illustrates a tangent join.

Rail Connections   Vertical or horizontal segments can be added to maintain a continuous railing. There are three options. The first option is Extend Rails To Meet (Figure 5.33).

The second option is Add Vertical/Horizontal Segments to complete the connection (Figure 5.34).

The third option is to choose No Connector between tangent joins (Figure 5.35).

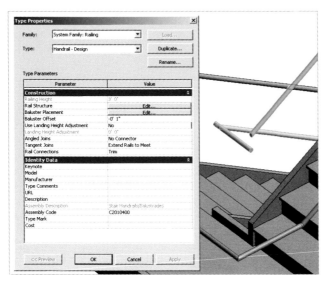

FIGURE 5.32 No Connector is selected for Angled Joins.

FIGURE 5.33 Extend Rails to Meet

FIGURE 5.34 Add Vertical/Horizontal Segments

FIGURE 5.35 No Connectors

Trimmed conditions will create vertical cuts when rails can't be mitered, as shown in Figure 5.36.

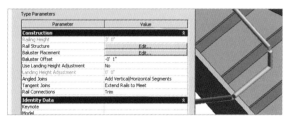

FIGURE 5.36 Trimmed railings

But if Weld is selected, Revit will try to join the railings as close as possible to a mitered condition (Figure 5.37).

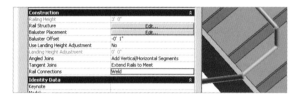

FIGURE 5.37 Welded railings

If you would like to download the completed Revit file that was created during this chapter, you can download it from the book's companion web page. The file is named c05_Stairs_Ramps_Railings.rvt.

Just One More Thing

Keep in mind that what you start with can be quickly and easily swapped out with more complex configurations and designs later. The important thing during design is that you resolve *what* something is and *where* it is. Then after the initial design is approved you can return to your intent and begin to specifically resolve the details and how it will be assembled.

Revit can be used to create incredibly complex and compelling stairs and railings! Creating these types of system families are discussed in depth in *Mastering Autodesk Revit Architecture* by Krygiel, Read, and Vandezande (Sybex 2011).

Again, don't get ahead of yourself. Concentrate on the basics. Once you have those down you'll be able to create far more detailed stairs, ramps, and railings.

Stairs and railings can not only be architectural works of art, but equally creative in Revit if you really leverage the tools available. Below is an example of what you can create if you stretch the limits of the Stairs tool. Your stairs can be elegant and versatile. The image on the bottom left is a very creative use of the stair tool—as an elevated railing system! The bollards hold up the track (which is the railing).

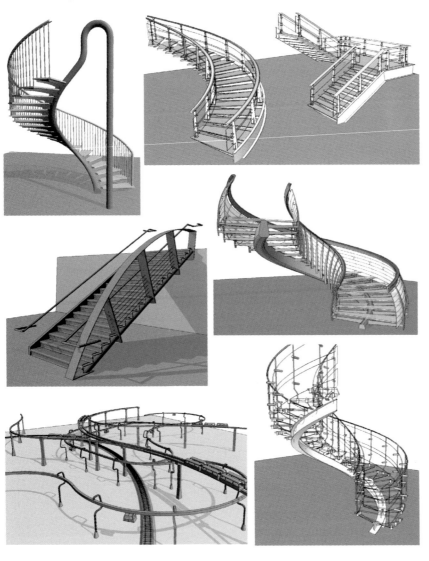

THE ESSENTIALS AND BEYOND

You can use the default Stairs, Railing, and Ramp tools to create the vast majority of your standard conditions during your early design processes. And since this is book is about "getting started," we don't want to get too far ahead of ourselves. One day at a time!

ADDITIONAL EXERCISES

▶ Try to create any of the stair configurations shown in the following graphics. Everything you need is the default file; you won't need to load any external content. Just create and modify new stair types.

▶ The stair in the first graphic is actually two separate stairs that share half a landing. But they appear to be a single stair that split at the landing. They're a combination of straight and curved sections. In some cases you'll need to sketch boundary and riser locations manually as well as reconfigure railing sketches.

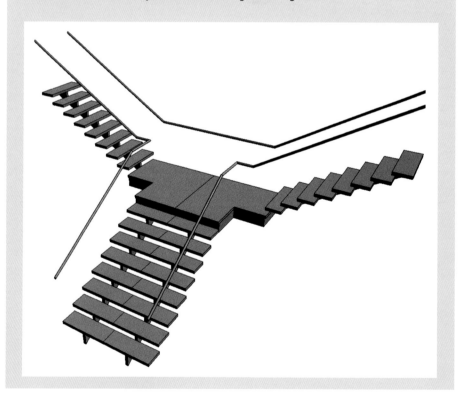

THE ESSENTIALS AND BEYOND (Continued)

▶ The stair in the second graphic is two stairs that appear to come together to join into a single stair. You'll also need to create at least part of the boundary manually. And the width of the upper run is the same with as the lower runs, so you'll have to modify the width of the default boundary.

CHAPTER 6

Adding Families

Revit includes quite a few family categories. Becoming familiar with the various categories will help you develop the right lexicon of terms and understanding. There are families in the project environment (system families) like Walls, Floors, and Roofs—basically anything that is defined and created directly in the project. But there are other families created outside the project in the Family Editor. These are referred to as *component families*. In this chapter, we'll be dealing only with component families.

In this chapter, you learn the following skills:

▶ **Understanding different family types**

▶ **Loading families**

▶ **Placing families**

Understanding Different Family Types

There are various family types and many behave somewhat similarly. In some cases you can change the family definition from one category to another. But in other cases, the behavior is unique to a family, and families can't be changed to another category.

There are only two important things to remember. First, schedules are based on family categories. So when you create a schedule, you'll be scheduling inside a single category as shown in Figure 6.1.

FIGURE 6.1 Schedule categories

Certification Objective

Second, you load families into your project based on their category. The Revit library is organized into real-world categories, so even if you've never used Revit before today, finding the right content (or at least a good placeholder during design iteration) should be straightforward (Figure 6.2).

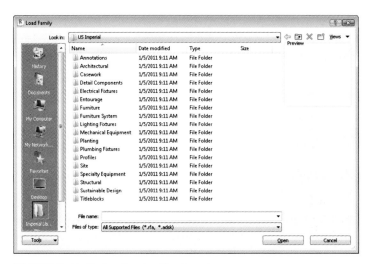

FIGURE 6.2 Loading families by category

Now let's discuss some of the family categories in Revit. We're not going to do this alphabetically (as shown in the list in Figure 6.2). We'll progress with regard to how things behave and whether they're one-, two-, or three-dimensional.

Loading Families

You load component families into your project by selecting the Insert tab, and on the Load From Library panel, clicking Load Family. If the family that you're looking for isn't in the default Revit library, don't panic. You can also try Autodesk Seek, an online repository of content in many different formats. Type your search term in the Autodesk Seek panel (Figure 6.3) or go to **http://seek.autodesk.com/**.

FIGURE 6.3 Autodesk Seek

Another great website for user-created content (Figure 6.4) is RevitCity (www .revitcity.com). Sometimes downloading a good placeholder during design is much faster than modeling it from scratch!

FIGURE 6.4 RevitCity offers user-created content.

Remember that whenever you place any content in your project (particularly from nonofficial Autodesk sources), you should take a moment to review the family components. It could be overly detailed or contain non-native Revit elements, and by using it you run the risk of slowing down your project's performance.

Placing Families

Placing families in your project is easy to do. Be aware that a family's category will determine from where it is loaded and how it can be placed. Once the family has been placed, its relationship to other elements in the model will determine how it continues to behave as your project evolves.

In this section, we'll investigate how you place families of different categories in your project.

Annotations

Annotations are graphics that are used in your project. Some are intended for use across all project disciplines, such as Area Tag, Callout Head, and Centerline. Other annotations are discipline specific to architecture, structure, mechanical, and so forth. Architecture, for example, includes Casework Tag, Ceiling Tag (with or without Height), and Stair Tag.

The default project template has many annotations preloaded (Figure 6.5). If you don't have the right annotation loaded and you try to use one, Revit prompts you to load the correct category.

F I G U R E 6 . 5 Preloaded annotations

Let's look at an example. Place the desk (one is already preloaded in the template) in your project. Then select the Tag panel on the Annotate tab and click Tag By Category.

Now select the desk. Because no furniture tag annotation has been loaded, Revit prompts you to load one from the appropriate category.

Certification Objective

To do so, first select the Annotations folder. Then select the Architectural folder and click Furniture System Tag (Figure 6.6). Click the Open button to load the tag into your project.

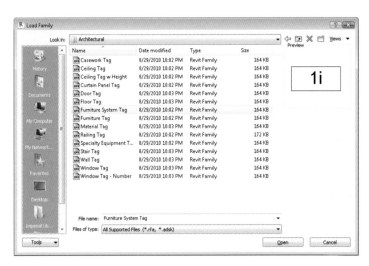

F I G U R E 6 . 6 Selecting the Furniture system tag

Now you can tag the desk with the correct annotation. You can even select a custom tag end (like an arrowhead or heavy tick). When you fill out the value of the tag, every element of the same type will be immediately updated (Figure 6.7).

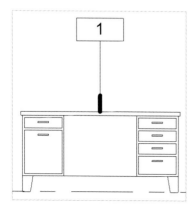

FIGURE 6.7 Tagging the desk

Don't worry when you select other views in your project and don't see the tag in those views. With few exceptions, all 2D elements, including annotations, are specific to each view.

Profiles

Many profiles are preloaded in the Revit template (Figure 6.8). These profile families are a single loop of lines that are created in 2D. Once they are loaded in a project, they can be associated with other system families.

FIGURE 6.8
Preloaded profiles

Profiles aren't used in a stand-alone fashion; they're used in combination with other components. For example, a profile family defines the cross section of a handrail. The parapet cap shown in Figure 6.9 is defined by a profile.

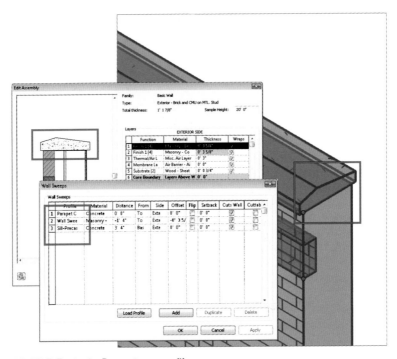

FIGURE 6.9 Parapet cap profile

Detail Components

Detail components are 2D objects that are used to complete your details.
Sometimes they're 2D representations of 3D objects, like the bond beam shown
in Figure 6.10. Go ahead and load this family into your project.

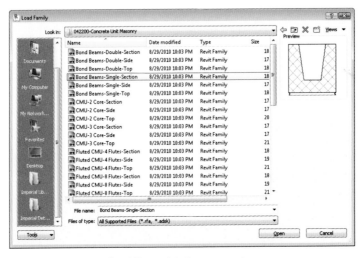

FIGURE 6.10 Bond Beam detail component

Detail components are a lot like blocks in AutoCAD. While you could draft all of your details manually, detail components help coordinate all the repetitive 2D elements that complete an assemblage. To place a detail component, click the Component button on the Detail panel of the Annotate tab.

Detail components can also be parametric, which means that a single component can have parameters that allow many types to be created from a single family (Figure 6.11). For example, once you load the Bond Beam component, you'll see that it helps you coordinate your project.

FIGURE 6.11
Parametric types

In other cases, the detail component is just a graphic element, like the break line shown in Figure 6.12. The break line is used to mask the geometry beyond the view and serves as a graphic convention that lets you know the element continues beyond the view boundaries.

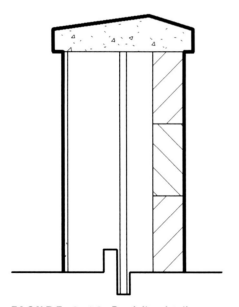

FIGURE 6.12 Break line detail component

Repeating Details

Repeating details are based on component families that are given rules to repeat based on some defined interval (Figure 6.13). Brick and mortar will repeat three times in 8″ [200mm]. A rule can be applied to this so the brick detail can be drawn like a line—lengthened and shortened while keeping a consistent pattern. The old method of doing this was to draw one brick and array it in a straight line. Changes to that line meant redoing the array, so this is much easier. You'll find repeating details on the Component flyout of the Detail panel on the Annotate tab.

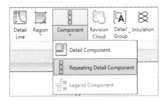

FIGURE 6.13 Selecting a repeating detail component

Rather than place a single detail component, you can sketch a linear path to define repetitive elements (Figure 6.14).

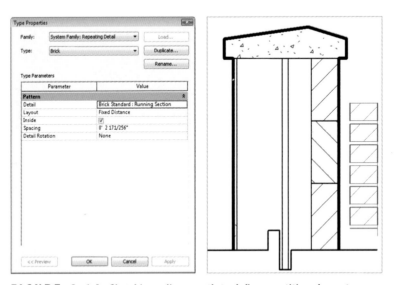

FIGURE 6.14 Sketching a linear path to define repetitive elements

Title Blocks

Title blocks are also 2D annotations. To place a title block, click the Sheet icon on the Sheet Composition panel on the View tab (Figure 6.15). Many more can be loaded from the `Title Blocks` folder in the Revit library.

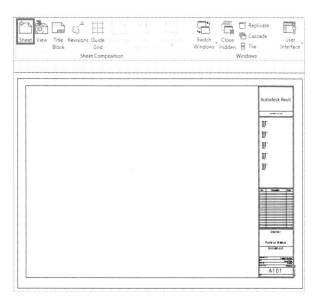

FIGURE 6.15 Title blocks

Level Based

When you place a family in your project, it usually has a relationship to something else in your project. But this is not necessarily a relationship to another piece of geometry. In many cases, the family will be constrained to the level on which it was placed. The level constraint is reflected in the instance parameters of the desk you placed earlier, as shown in Figure 6.16.

Many objects in Revit are constrained by their level. You want to be especially careful when dealing with level constraints. If you delete a constraint—in this case, the level—the objects constrained by that level will also be deleted. Revit displays the warning shown in Figure 6.17.

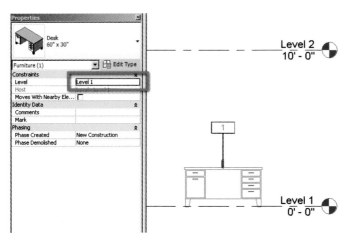

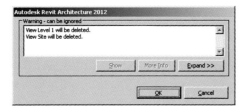

FIGURE 6.16 Level constraint for the desk

FIGURE 6.17 Warning that appears when deleting a level

So be careful when deleting elements in Revit. A stray "line" could be much more, such as the edge of a wall or the level in a project.

Face Based

Face-based families associate to any face on either a host or component family. To place a face-based family, you'll have to initially associate it to a face. You can try this by loading a simple face-based family we have created for you called c06_Face-Based_Box.rfa, which you can download from the Chapter 6 folder at this book's web page, **www.sybex.com/go/revit2012essentials**. The component is a simple 1′ × 1′ × 1′ box, but in practice it could be most anything, such as a light or a shelf.

After you load this component, place it by selecting the Placement panel on the Modify | Place Component tab and clicking the Place On Face option. You'll quickly see that a face-based component will not allow itself to be placed without a face or work plane selected as a constraint (Figure 6.18). But as you hover near a face, the component will show up in a wireframe mode, indicating the location where it's going to be placed.

FIGURE 6.18 Placing a face-based component

An interesting thing about face-based families is that if their constraint is deleted, the element remains in the project (even if the constraint is a level). When you select the component, Revit prompts you to pick a new face to associate with the element (click the Pick New button on the Work Plane panel of the Modify | Generic Models tab).

Hosted

A hosted family has a specific relationship to a specific host category, such as Floors, Walls, Roofs, or Ceilings. Without the host, the hosted family can't be placed. For example, a wall-hosted family will only allow itself to be placed in a wall.

Furthermore, if the host is removed, the hosted families are also deleted. Keep in mind that you will not be warned when the hosted elements are being deleted. Here are examples of commonly hosted relationships between system and component families:

- ▶ Walls: Windows and Doors
- ▶ Curtain Walls: Curtain Panels and Mullions
- ▶ Ceilings: Lighting Fixtures
- ▶ Railings: Balusters

You can see how this feature works by creating a 10'-0" [3 m] length of a Generic - 6" wall. Then go to your default 3D view.

Door

Select the Door tool from the Build panel of the Home tab, and you'll notice that you can't place a door until you hover over the host wall. Place a door as shown in Figure 6.19. Then place some windows in the same wall section, as shown in Figure 6.20.

FIGURE 6.19 Placing a door

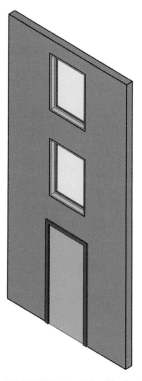

FIGURE 6.20 Placing two windows

As you can see, the hosted families automatically cut the opening in their host. If you delete the hosted family, the opening is automatically healed. As you can imagine, this is a useful feature when you need to maintain specific relationships between your family content and a host.

When you start creating your own content, remember that you can overdo hosted relationships. You wouldn't want to "overconstrain" a custom piece of furniture by making it floor hosted, only to realize that you couldn't use it during design iteration (when you may not have modeled a floor yet). For this reason, we generally recommend that hosted relationships be limited to conditions where you need to create a recess or opening in the host. If the family is likely to be hosted across multiple hosts, consider creating a face-based family.

If you'd like to download the project and content created during this chapter, go to **www.sybex.com/go/revit2012essentials** and download the project file c06_Adding_Families.rvt. You can also download the family file c06_Face-Based_Box.rfa.

THE ESSENTIALS AND BEYOND

Adding families to your project is easily done either by using the default family library that is provided with Revit or by creating your own. Now that you have a better understanding of how families work and the different family types, you can create a host of new elements for any project.

ADDITIONAL EXERCISES

▶ Open a Generic model template. Modify the family category. What are some of the categories that you cannot change the Generic model to?

▶ Create a repeating detail component from a brick section or other element.

▶ Modify the default profile of a railing or wall-hosted sweep.

▶ Create a new profile family for a handrail and assign it to an existing handrail.

CHAPTER 7

Modifying Families

Now that you have added a number of families to your Revit project and the design has progressed, you'll often find it necessary to modify the families. Sometimes swapping out a less-detailed family component for one that is more exact and correct is the best solution (and in some cases opening it and modifying it slightly). In other cases, it's simply a matter of opening the component family that you started with and tweaking the geometry to better fit your design. Either solution is viable—which you choose depends on the result that is better for your design process.

In this chapter, you learn the following skills:

▶ **Editing view display and detail level**

▶ **Changing the family category**

▶ **Modifying family geometry**

Editing View Display and Detail Level

Adding content is pretty straightforward, but learning to modify it will take a bit more time. We'll use the last exercise from Chapter 6, "Adding Families" as a starting point for the exercises in this chapter. Open your finished project file now, or download the file c06_Adding_Families.rvt from the book's web page.

To download the project and content you create during this chapter, go to **www.sybex.com/go/revit2012essentials**. From there you can download the project file c07_Modifying_Families.rvt. You can also download the family files c07_Three_Light_Fixed.rfa and c07_L_Shaped_Handrail.rvt.

One of the first things that you want to consider when loading a family into your project is the level of detail that the family displays at different orientations and scales. It's not likely that every part of a component family needs to display at all scales. It's more likely that too much detail will be confusing (particularly at smaller scales). Just a decade or so ago when we used pencils, knowing when to stop drawing detail was pretty easy. But high-resolution computer displays that give you the ability to zoom in and out as well as modern printing technologies have allowed us to create far more detail than is necessary (or meaningful). So how do you display just the right level of detail in Revit?

First, go to the South elevation of our project. Create a copy of the desk to the right of the first one. You can zoom to fit by right-clicking in the view and selecting Zoom To Fit. But this only shows you everything in your view—it doesn't give you a sense of what is going to legibly print (Figure 7.1).

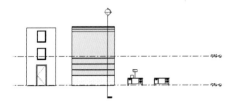

FIGURE 7.1 Zoom To Fit

A great way to tell what is going to be graphically legible when you print is to select the Zoom Sheet Size option from the Navigation bar on the right side of the view. Doing so will take the scale of the view into account when zooming in (or out). The difference is shown in Figure 7.2. If you find yourself needing to see what's important in a view (and you don't want to get too carried away with details that don't yet matter), this is a great tool.

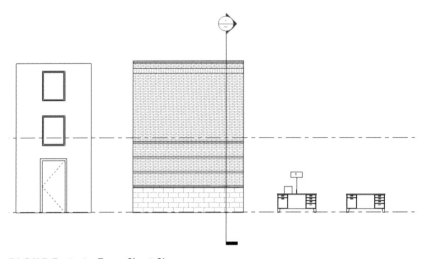

FIGURE 7.2 Zoom Sheet Size

Something that you'll notice from both of the previous figures is that the hardware on the desk is completely visible in both views—which is reasonable to expect. But let's see what happens when the view scale changes. Figure 7.3

illustrates the same desk in elevation at dramatically different scales (1′= 50′ [1:50], 1′=20′ [1:20], and 1′=10′ [1:10], respectively).

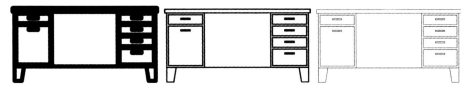

FIGURE 7.3 Elevation at different scales

View Display

As you can see, all of the geometry of the desk—drawers and hardware—is visible at all view scales. But it doesn't have to be this way. Our rule of thumb is that if two lines are overlapping to the point that they'll print like a single line, they probably don't need to be seen. Nor do you want Revit to spend processing power displaying, printing, and exporting information that isn't important. Revit has built-in settings for displaying information at different scales. You can find them in the Additional Settings option of the Settings panel on the Manage tab, as shown in Figure 7.4.

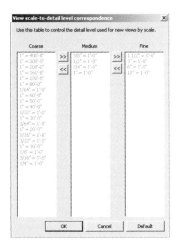

FIGURE 7.4 View Scale-to-Detail Level Correspondence settings

Based on the scale of the view, Revit will automatically display or hide elements, which is a powerful way of managing visibility. But to take advantage of this power, you must make sure the content in your project has the appropriate view scale-to-detail level correspondence.

Let's look at another common example. Create a default stair run, as shown in Figure 7.5. Then look at the stair in the South elevation at a couple of different scales (Figure 7.6).

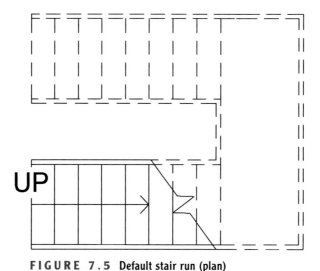

FIGURE 7.5 Default stair run (plan)

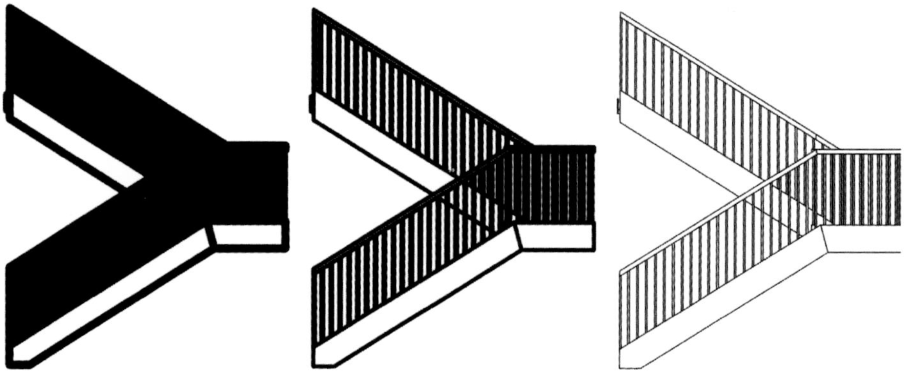

FIGURE 7.6 Default stair run (elevation)

Figure 7.6 illustrates three scales (1′=100′ [1:100], 1′=50′[1:50], and 1′=10′[1:10]). As you can see, the balusters are showing up at every level of detail—even to the point that they're displaying as a solid black line! This isn't the right kind of graphic communication that you want from your Revit project.

Level of Detail

Let's modify the view display and level of detail for both the stair and the desk:

1. Select the desk and choose Edit Family from the Modify menu, or right-click and choose Edit Family from the context menu.

2. Select the hardware (the drawer pulls) and then click the Visibility Settings button on the Modify ribbon to open the Family Element Visibility Settings dialog box.

This dialog box allows you to determine the visibility for both the orientation and level of detail for the hardware. As you can see, the hardware is already set to not show up in plan.

3. The hardware is showing up at all levels of detail (Coarse, Medium, and Fine). Change the settings so that it *only* shows up at a Fine level of detail. Do the same for the hardware on the other side of the desk (Figure 7.7).

FIGURE 7.7 Editing levels of detail for hardware

4. Let's modify the detail level for the faces of the drawers. Change the visibility settings so they show up at the Medium *and* Fine levels of detail (but not Coarse).

5. Reload the desk family into the project. The results are shown at the same detail levels as before (Figure 7.8), but legibility has been increased.

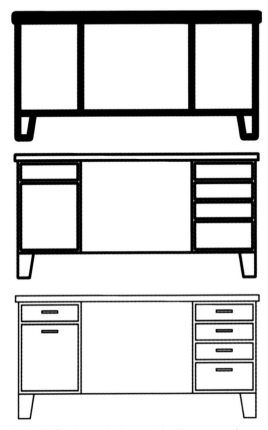

FIGURE 7.8 The level of detail corresponds to scale.

6. Next we'll do the same for the stairs. The trick is that the balusters are not available by selecting the stairs. The stairs are a system family, so you'll have to select the nested family from the Project Browser. In the Project Browser, expand the Families tree, then Railings. Right-click on Baluster-Square and choose Edit to open the element in the Family Editor.

7. Once you have opened the baluster family, select the element on the screen and, using the Properties palette, open the Visibility/Graphic Overrides dialog box. Uncheck the Coarse detail level. Note that the Plan/RCP views are already unchecked, meaning the baluster will not display by default in those views.

8. Reload the family into the project and the balusters will display only at the Medium and Fine levels of detail. You will now see results in a much cleaner graphic display.

Changing the Family Category

Family components schedule according to their category, which is determined when you start to model a new family component. When you're creating a new family component, Revit first prompts you to select the appropriate template.

Certification Objective

But in many cases, you'll realize afterward that you need to change this category to another. You may have to do this for a family component that you created as well as ones you've downloaded. Changing categories is easy to do.

Editing the Family

For this exercise, select the face-based box that we provided from the previous chapter. It's been placed on the top of the desk.

1. Right-click the face-based box and choose Edit Family from the context menu.

2. When the family opens, you'll notice the box is resting on a large platform. Don't worry about this—it's the context for the "face" of the face-based family (Figure 7.9). Face-based and hosted families already have geometric context (along with critical parameters and reference planes) in their templates so you can model in context and test parametric behavior.

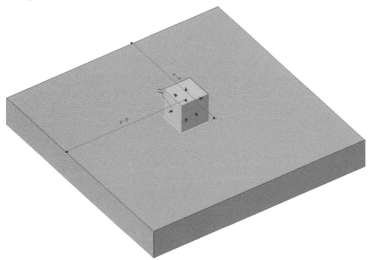

FIGURE 7.9 Editing the face-based family

Family Category and Parameters

When you modeled this component, you didn't know what the category would be, so you just left it as a Generic Model. But now the design has progressed and the component needs to schedule as Specialty Equipment. Not a problem!

 1. Select Family Category And Parameters from the Properties palette on the Home tab.

2. The dialog box shown in Figure 7.10 opens. The current category is selected. Select Specialty Equipment and click OK.

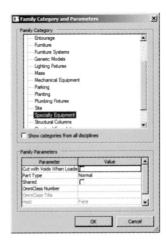

FIGURE 7.10 Changing the family category

3. Reload the family into the project environment; select the option to override the existing version. If you were in CAD, this step would be just like reloading a block—you're simply updating the element with the new information. The family will not appear to have changed, but it will now schedule according to its new category.

Editing the Insertion Point

The other thing that often occurs is the insertion point of a family will need to change. This issue arises for one of two reasons. First, a family will flex about its insertion point. So when the family expands or contracts, the insertion point is maintained. The second reason is that when you replace one family for

another of the same category, they will swap at the same insertion point. So if
you have a family with an insertion point that is at a corner but upon reflection
needs to flex or swap out at another location, you'll have to edit the insertion
point.

1. For this example, go to the Level 1 plan view. Load a chair into your
   project by choosing Place A Component from the Home tab.

2. From the Place Component context menu, click the Load Family button
   and under the Furniture folder, choose the Chair-Executive.rfa family. Place it as shown in the left image in Figure 7.11. Then place the
   chair underneath the desk, as shown in the middle and right images.
   Note that the chair is centered under the desk's opening.

FIGURE 7.11 Loading and placing the chair in the project

3. Now select the desk and change the size from 60"×30" [150cm×75cm]
   to 72"×36" [180cm×90cm]. The desk has grown from the upper-right
   corner; the chair is no longer centered and will have to be moved. If
   there were many chairs and desks in this situation (like an office layout), this task would be very tedious! Let's change the insertion point
   of the desk to avoid this situation in future design iterations.

4. Select the desk and open it in the Family Editor. Open the Ground
   Floor, Floor Plan View. Designate the two reference planes indicated
   with arrows as the insertion point for the family. Select both reference planes and then check the Defines Origin box in the Properties
   menu (Figure 7.12).

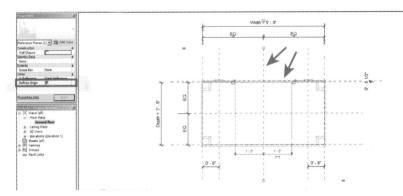

FIGURE 7.12 Editing the origin of a family

5. Reload the family into the project, and select Overwrite The Existing Version. The family will initially move to align the old insertion point with the new insertion point effectively relocating the desk. Select the desk and move it back relative to the chair. Now you can test different desk sizes, and you'll notice that the family will flex with respect to the location of the chair (Figure 7.13).

FIGURE 7.13 Different-sized desks

Modifying Family Geometry

Now comes the tricky part. Even though you're just starting out with Revit and you won't be expected to create new content from scratch, it's likely that you'll be expected to modify existing content that's become part of your project (think of this as completing red lines in Revit).

As the design progresses, generic elements that have been used as meaningful placeholders will in many cases need to be modified to include more detail. In other cases, existing context will be exchanged for components that are already detailed. So let's start editing components of different categories.

Editing the Family

Let's start by modifying a 2D element from the previous chapter. Suppose that according to your firm's graphic standards, the Furniture tag should have rounded sides. Go to the South elevation to see the Furniture tag. The chair has been temporarily hidden for clarity (Figure 7.14).

Certification
Objective

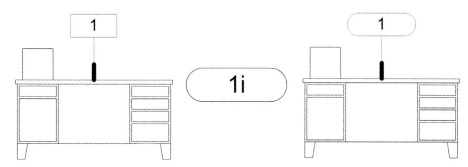

F I G U R E 7 . 1 4 Editing the Furniture tag

Rather than create another Furniture tag for the project, let's modify this one. You'll start by changing the name to reflect its eventual shape.

1. Highlight the name in the Project Browser and rename Boxed to **Rounded**. Now open the tag from the Project Browser or by selecting the tag and selecting Edit Family.

2. Add arc lines to either side of the tag and delete the vertical lines, as shown in the middle image in Figure 7.14. Then reload the tag into the project and overwrite the existing tag. It's really that easy. Every tag throughout the entire Revit project will have updated (see the right image in Figure 7.14).

You've just seen one reason you don't need to have figured out all your standards and settings in order to begin your first Revit project. It's that easy to update your entire project as it develops!

Editing Profiles

Now let's revisit the default handrail profile that was created with our stair. The profiles are located in the Project Browser.

1. Find the Rectangular Handrail family and right-click it. Choose Edit from the context menu and Rectangular Handrail will open in the Family Editor. Since you want to keep your existing handrail profile intact, choose Save As and name the new profile **L Shaped Handrail**.

2. There are some parameters that you'll want to maintain in this family. To make them visible, go to the Visibility/Graphic Overrides dialog box (type **VG** on your keyboard) and select the Annotation Categories tab. Then check all the options, as shown in Figure 7.15. The profile view will then resemble the image in Figure 7.16.

3. Add new profile lines to resemble Figure 7.17. Note that the parameters for Width and EQ have been retained. Now load the profile into your Revit project. The L Shaped Handrail profile family will now be listed in your Project Browser along with the various types.

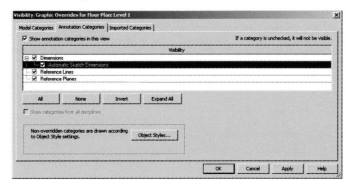

FIGURE 7.15 Adjusting Visibility/Graphic Overrides of the profile

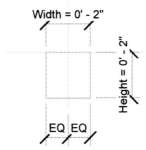

FIGURE 7.16 The modified baluster

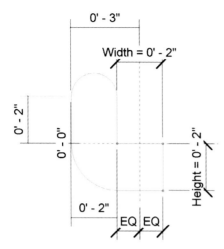

FIGURE 7.17 New handrail profile

4. Now let's create a new railing and then associate the railing to the existing stair. Start by duplicating the railing that is already in use by the stair in the project and then rename the duplicate as **L Shaped Handrail**.

5. You need to modify the properties of the railing to include the new handrail profile. To do so, right-click on the Railing type in the Project Browser and select Type Properties.

6. In the Type Properties dialog box, select Edit from the Rail Structure option. Doing so opens the Edit Rails dialog box (Figure 7.18). Pull down the profile menu and select the handrail, as shown in Figure 7.18.

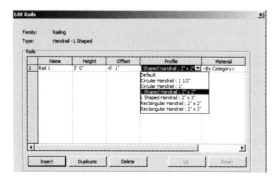

FIGURE 7.18 Editing the type properties of the railing

7. The new profile has been associated to the duplicate railing. All you need to do is swap out the present stair railing for the new one! Select the handrails and then select the new railing from the Properties Pallet (Figure 7.19).

FIGURE 7.19
Selecting the new railing

Now let's edit some detail components!

Detail Components

Here's the scenario: You're working to integrate your office standards into your Revit template and the break line in this project doesn't match the graphic standards of your office. You need to get this consistent, so begin by opening the break line family in the family editor and we'll step through how to make the changes.

1. Browse to the callout of Section 1 or select it in the Project Browser under Detail Items. Then, select Edit Boundary from the Mode palette.
   This element is not a line (see Figure 7.20). It's actually a masking region (kind of like a white solid hatch) that is used to obscure geometry in your project. Some of the boundary line styles are Medium and some are Invisible.

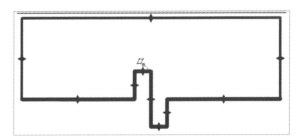

FIGURE 7.20 Editing the detail component break line

2. Select the edge of the masking region and click Edit Boundary
again. Edit or delete the inner lines and add new ones, as shown in
Figure 7.21. Be sure to use the Medium line style.

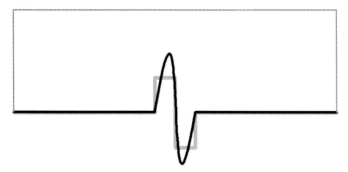

FIGURE 7.21 Editing and reloading the break line

3. Finish the sketch and reload the break line into your project. It will
update in all views, as shown here:

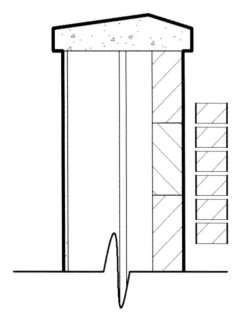

Repeating Details

As mentioned in the previous chapter, repeating details are based on component
families that are given rules to repeat with, based on a defined interval. As an

example, elements like brick or CMU in a wall section or fence posts are elements that repeat typically on a regular interval. Rather than have you create an array to draw these elements in 2D and have to redefine the array if you make changes, Revit allows you to create rules for these components. They will automatically repeat based on the rule structure. It's quite a handy feature. If we place the brick repeating detail on the vertically compound wall, it looks nearly correct (Figure 7.22). What's missing is a mortar joint between courses. This joint will also help obscure the hatch pattern of the wall.

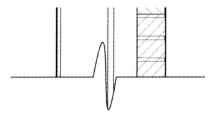

FIGURE 7.22 You'll edit the brick repeating detail.

Because the brick repeating detail is based on a single component that is being nested, you need to go to the original family. You can also find the original component family in the Detail Items drop-down in the Project Browser. Open the family by right-clicking on the component name, Brick Standard, in the Project Browser and selecting Edit from the context menu.

Figure 7.23 shows the default component. Let's add a filled region between the brick and the upper line:

FIGURE 7.23 The default component

1. Choose Transfer Project Standards in the Settings panel on the Manage tab.

2. You will transfer in the fill patterns from our open Revit project into the brick family (which has only a few patterns available). Deselect all the options in the Select Items To Copy dialog box except for Fill Patterns and click OK.

3. A dialog box asks if you want to overwrite all the existing patterns in the family. Select New Only.

4. The fill pattern that you need to indicate a mortar joint is now loaded in this family. Select the Filled Region command from the Detail panel on the Home tab to begin sketching the new boundary that will represent the mortar joint.

5. Draw the boundary as shown using detail lines (Figure 7.24). Before you finish the family, you should assign a new filled pattern to this sketch. Select Edit Type from the Properties palette.

FIGURE 7.24 Sketching the filled region

6. Choose Duplicate and name the new filled region **Mortar Joint**. Next, select the area labeled Diagonal Crosshatch [Drafting] and in the Fill Patterns dialog box select Sand - Dense as the new fill pattern associated with your sketched area (Figure 7.25). Click OK until you close all the dialogs and then finish the sketch.

7. Load the modified family into your project by clicking the Load Family button on the ribbon. Overwrite the existing version in your project when prompted.

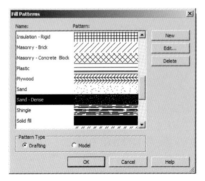

FIGURE 7.25 Creating a new filled region

Now that the family has been modified, the repeating detail that is associated with the same family has been modified as well (Figure 7.26). You can complete the section by adding individual detail components or add additional repeating details.

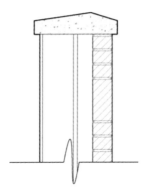

FIGURE 7.26 The repeating detail associated with the same family has been modified.

Now let's investigate editing other 2D annotations by modifying the default title block family.

Title Blocks

Title blocks are also 2D elements. For pilot projects, it's fine to start with the default title block (just select the correct overall size) and then modify it later. Grids are helpful when you're organizing views on title blocks, but as you've noticed by now, the default title block doesn't have a grid. So let's add one.

You'll find title blocks under Sheets in the Project Browser (above the Families node). Double-click the sheet A101 in the Project Browser to open the view. Then follow these steps:

1. Select the sheet, and then choose Edit Family from the context ribbon.

2. Before going any further, let's create a new line type to associate to the grid. It will have a slight color or tint in order to easily distinguish it from the rest of the graphics on the title block as well as any project views. From the Manage tab, select Object Styles on the Settings panel.

3. When the Object Styles dialog box opens, click New under Modify Subcategories. Use the New Subcategory dialog box to create a new line called **Grid Lines**, as shown in Figure 7.27. From the Subcategory Of drop-down, select Title Blocks. Then click OK.

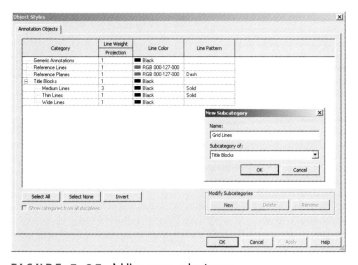

F I G U R E 7 . 2 7 Adding a new subcategory

4. Select the Line Color option (Figure 7.27) and then modify the color to a light blue.

5. Now you're ready to draw the grid lines. Select the Line tool from the Detail panel of the Home tab to open the Modify | Place Lines tab. Select the subcategory Grid Lines.

6. Now draw five vertical lines and four horizontal lines (Figure 7.28). Dimension them as well with a continuous dimension (the dimensions

will not show up in the project environment). Select the EQ option, and all the lines will become equally spaced.

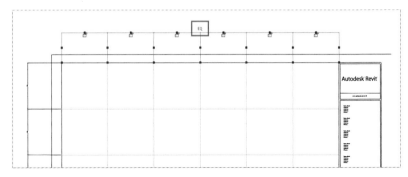

FIGURE 7.28 Adding and dimensioning grid lines

If you were to reload this sheet in the project, you'd be able to control the visibility of the grid like any other object: via Visibility/Graphic Overrides. But it's useful to be able to turn the visibility of the grid on and off throughout the project. You can do this by associating a type parameter to the grid lines that you've just created. Then when you're done using the grid line to set up your project views, you can turn it off with one click!

7. Select all the grid lines that you just created. In the Properties palette, select the small button to the right of the Visible check box.

8. Now you can add a new parameter to associate with these lines. Click Add Parameter to open the Parameter Properties dialog box. In the Name field, type **Grid Visibility**. Click the Type radio button and set Group Parameter Under to Graphics, as shown in Figure 7.29.

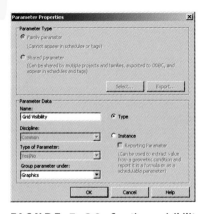

FIGURE 7.29 Creating a visibility parameter

9. When you're finished, click OK. Reload the title block into your project, overwriting the parameters of the existing title block.

10. Select the title block in the project and click Edit Type in the Properties palette to open the Type Properties dialog box (Figure 7.30). If you uncheck the Grid Visibility parameter, it will turn off the grid throughout your project (rather than just one view at a time).

FIGURE 7.30 The Grid Visibility parameter in the Properties palette

11. Deselect the parameter. When you click OK, the grid will no longer be visible in the title block.

Now that you've modified 2D family components, let's experiment with editing 3D elements. You've already modified the geometry of a nonhosted element (the desk in an earlier exercise). So let's modify a hosted component next.

Hosted Components

As mentioned in the previous chapter, a hosted family has a specific relationship to a specific host category, such as a Floor, Wall, Roof, or Ceiling. Without the host, the hosted family can't be placed. A wall-hosted family will only allow itself to be placed in a wall, and so on.

For this exercise, we're going to modify the generic fixed window that is part of the default Revit template. Select the window from the Project Browser and click Edit Family to open the family in the Family Editor (Figure 7.31). You want to keep the existing type, so begin by renaming the family via Save As.

FIGURE 7.31 Window opened in the Family Editor

At the moment, the host part of the family is not visible. Let's turn this on via Visibility/Graphic Overrides (the left image in Figure 7.32). Make sure that all the boxes are checked as shown. The 3D view will now resemble the image on the right of Figure 7.32.

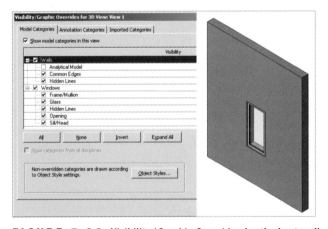

FIGURE 7.32 Visibility/Graphic Overrides for the host wall

You need to be able to see the existing reference planes in the family. Select the Exterior Elevation view (the left image in Figure 7.33). Reference planes serve as guides that allow the geometry to flex. As you can see, the window geometry has not been given parameters. The parameters are associated to the reference planes. The geometry is also associated to the planes.

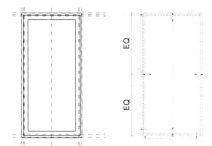

F I G U R E 7 . 3 3 Reference planes and parameters

For this example, you'll start by adding another horizontal reference plane. To keep this reference plane equally spaced with regard to the overall window height, you'll also dimension the reference plane and then set the value to EQ (the right image in Figure 7.33). No matter what the window height, the new reference plane will remain centered.

This process is an important part of modifying existing content! This window family is full of dimension parameters that control different types. These parameters are extremely useful—you don't want to delete them!

You don't need to create new geometry from scratch; you can modify what is already in the family. This approach may seem like "cheating," but in fact this is usually how content is modified in Revit: by editing what is already there. In addition to this process being efficient, the geometry that you modify is likely going to continue to "remember" existing relationships to reference planes and parameters.

1. Start by selecting the Frame/Mullion Extrusion. Once the frame is selected (Figure 7.34), you can choose the Edit Extrusion tool from the Mode palette. Now sketch new internal lines as shown to split the window into three panels. Delete any segments between the new lines before you finish the sketch.

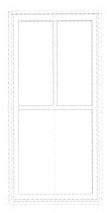

FIGURE 7.34
Editing the existing
window frame

2. After the sketch is finished, it's important to "flex" the family to make sure that the different sizes will behave before you load the family into the project. Select the Family Types command to open a dialog box of all the various family types. Select a few different types, and click Apply after each type is specified (Figure 7.35).

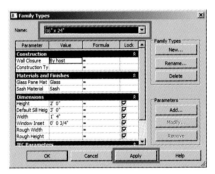

FIGURE 7.35 **Flexing the modified window family**

3. Close the dialog box and look at the window in 3D. Everything is working. But the window pane is still one piece of glazing. Let's modify that now. Select the glazing, and then choose the Edit Extrusion option. Return to the exterior elevation and add sketch lines with regard to your previously modified window trim (see Figure 7.36).

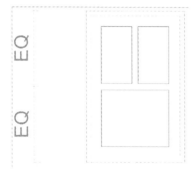

FIGURE 7.36 Modifying the window glazing

Finish the sketch and then repeat the previous process of testing a few different family type parameters in order to make sure that the window glazing is going to flex with the different sizes (Figure 7.37).

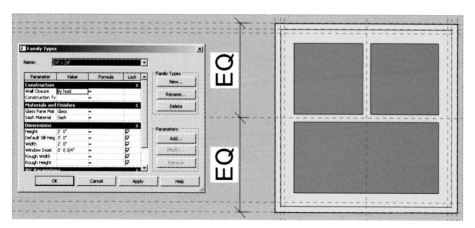

FIGURE 7.37 Flexing the window types

Now that the window has been modified, load it into your project. Select one of the existing windows and then use the Properties palette to swap out the existing window with the component that you've just created. Because the insertion points are the same, the window location will remain consistent.

THE ESSENTIALS AND BEYOND

Rather than starting from scratch, it's often faster to find a family or element close to what you need and modify it. You learned how to edit view display and detail level, as well as change the family category and modify family geometry.

ADDITIONAL EXERCISES

▶ Select another family and modify its level of detail so the appropriate geometry is displayed at the right scale and detail level in the project environment.

▶ Explain how you would modify a family from face-based or hosted to one that is not.

▶ Explain how you would modify a family that is not face-based or hosted to one that is.

▶ Nest a family into another family and select the Shared option. Verify this nested family schedules when placed in the project.

▶ Add a new subcategory to a family and assign geometry to the category. From the project environment, compare the visibility options under the main category (Doors, Furniture, Specialty Equipment, and so forth) of this family before and after the family is loaded into a project.

CHAPTER 8

Groups and Phasing

Overall project management is a large part of the design development process. Much of the time, managing design is a process of managing change. Projects often develop as moving targets; communicating the program results in needing to answer questions that no one anticipated.

So the more the program develops, the more change management is required—sometimes in an exponential fashion. And although managing this kind of change becomes practically untenable in CAD, Revit allows you to manage multiple, simultaneous relationships faster than in any other application.

Groups and phasing is all about quickly and easily managing change in your project. Modifying one family component will update throughout a project. But groups can contain multiple host and family components. Phasing applies to views (filtered to show only a slice of a project's timeline) as well as geometry.

Will design get any easier in the process? It depends on your perspective. You'll be able to make design decisions faster and from nearly anywhere in the project. You'll also be able to find conflicts and poor design decisions far earlier in the process. And in many cases Revit will compel you to resolve them well before you're accustomed to doing in a 2D, CAD-centric world.

In this chapter, you learn the following skills:

▶ **Using groups**

▶ **Using phasing**

Using Groups

There are many different kinds of elements in a Revit project. With regard to geometry, there are *host families* (which are created directly within the project environment) and *component families* (which are created in the Family Editor).

 HOST VS FAMILY

We like to describe a building as fundamentally assembled from "repetitive relationships." Things are connected. Pieces become parts, and parts become assemblages, and assemblages become architectural constructs. The ability to edit the properties of either type of component (host or family) is incredibly elegant, as doing so will in turn have an immediate effect on your entire project.

This is where groups come into play. Groups are created in the project environment and contain collections of component families, host families, or perhaps a combination of both. As a matter of fact, collections of groups can become other groups.

We can't cover every possible bit of obscure functionality in groups. But we do want to make sure that you gain the confidence to use groups in the way that they're most often used.

Creating Groups

We'll start by opening the file c08_Groups_and_Phasing_Start.rvt. It's available for download at this book's web page, **www.sybex.com/go/revit2012essentials**. It's been preloaded with content and context for this typical scenario. As you can see, we've gone ahead and loaded all the furniture you'll use for these exercises in the project (Figure 8.1).

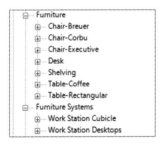

FIGURE 8.1 Groups
and phasing file

Let's start by adding a collection of furniture to one of the offices. First, go to the Level 1 Floor Plan view. Then add the components shown in Figure 8.2. We've added the following components:

▶ Executive Chair (1)

▶ Breuer Chair (2)

▶ Shelf (1)

▶ Desk (1)

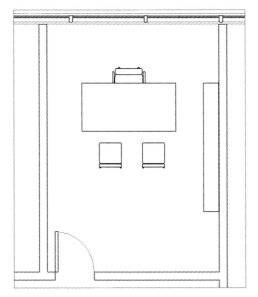

FIGURE 8.2 Adding furniture to the office

Now imagine that you need to copy this configuration through a few offices. You can accomplish this copying easily, but what if one of the elements had to change? That could not be so easily managed; you'd have to manually locate all the components that had to be modified and then change them one by one.

So let's create a group of all these elements. To do this, select all the furniture that you've just added and then select the Create Group tool, as shown in Figure 8.3.

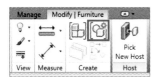

FIGURE 8.3 Creating the group

Revit will prompt you to name the group. To avoid a project full of confusing default names, name the group **Office Furniture 1** (see Figure 8.4). Leave the check box Open In Group Editor deselected and click OK.

FIGURE 8.4 Naming the group

When the group is finished, you'll see all its elements surrounded by a dashed line as well as an insertion point for the group (Figure 8.5). The insertion point is the location that the group will maintain when you exchange one group for another.

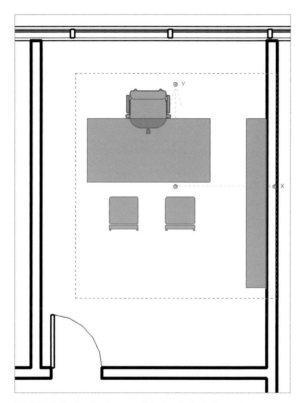

FIGURE 8.5 Group with the default insertion point

Move the insertion point by dragging the center of the insertion to a new location (Figure 8.6). Then rotate the insertion point by dragging either end node, as shown in Figure 8.6.

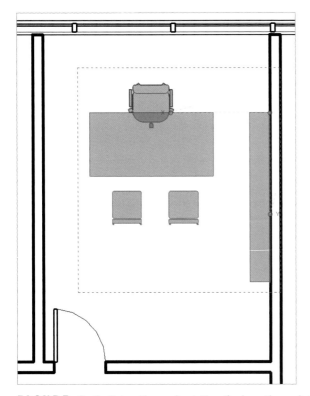

FIGURE 8.6 Relocating and rotating the insertion point

Copying Groups

Now let's copy this group to a few new locations. You have a couple of good options. If there's already an instance of the group in the view that you're working in, select the group and then click Copy (highlighted on the left in Figure 8.7) or Create Similar (highlighted on the right).

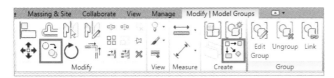

FIGURE 8.7 The Copy and Create Similar tools

The other option you have is to drag an instance from the Project Browser just like any other element. The group that we've just created is shown in Figure 8.8.

FIGURE 8.8 Our new group appears in the Project Browser.

Choose whichever option you like and copy the group around the floor plan as shown in Figure 8.9. You'll also need to rotate the copies in order to orient them properly.

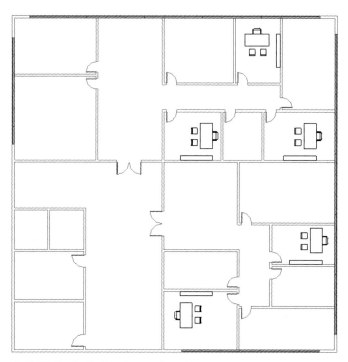

FIGURE 8.9 Creating copies of groups

Duplicating Groups

In many cases you'll start with one group and then create permutations of that group as the design progresses. You can accomplish this easily by duplicating one of the groups in the Project Browser. Another useful option is to select one of the groups that you want to edit and then duplicate it via the Edit Types dialog (Figure 8.10).

FIGURE 8.10 Duplicating the group

First, select the Office Furniture 1 group; then click Edit Type. Now you'll be able to duplicate the group. Name the new group **Office Furniture 2**. The new group will show up in the Project Browser (Figure 8.11).

FIGURE 8.11 The new group in the Project Browser, ready to be edited

Now let's edit this new group.

Editing Groups

Select the group shown in Figure 8.12. On the Group panel of the contextual Modify | Model Groups tab is the Edit Group option. Select this tool and you'll enter Edit Group mode.

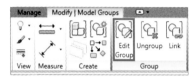

FIGURE 8.12 Selecting Edit Group mode

Everything in the group that you're editing is now shown as usual, while everything not in the group is given a temporary sepia tone (see Figure 8.13).

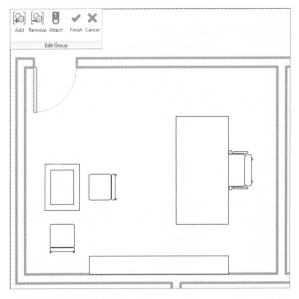

FIGURE 8.13 In Edit Group mode, everything not in the group is given a temporary sepia tone.

Reconfigure the seating and add a coffee table as shown in Figure 8.14. Then finish the group by selecting Finish.

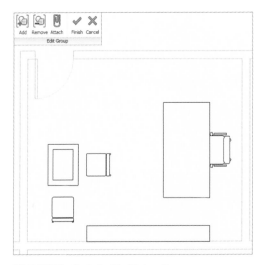

FIGURE 8.14 Modifying the group

Now copy another instance of the group in your project, as shown in Figure 8.15. Keep in mind that with every copy of a group, all your other project views and schedules will be updating in real time!

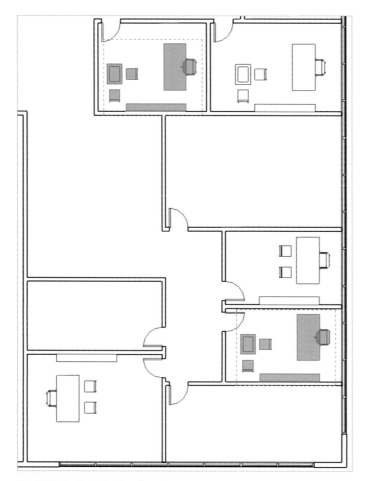

FIGURE 8.15 Copying the group

Exchanging Groups

Any group can be exchanged for any other group. Before you exchange one group for another, you may want to check that the insertion points of the two groups are properly located in order to keep the replaced group from shifting its location.

To replace a group, select it and then click the pull-down menu in the Properties window. You'll see all the other groups in the same category. Model groups may contain geometry and datums, whereas Detail groups will only contain 2D elements like detail items. Exchange the group as shown in Figure 8.16.

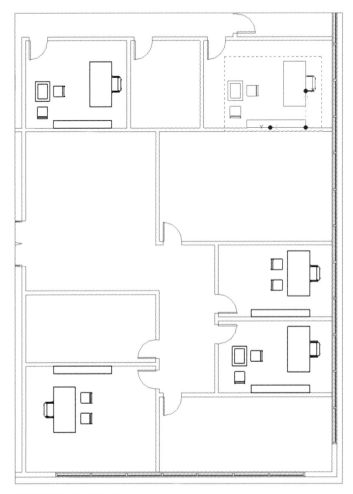

FIGURE 8.16 Exchanging groups

Saving Groups

With very large or complex groups, it may be helpful to work on them outside the project environment and then reload them into your project. To save a group, select the group name from the Project Browser, right-click, and select Save Group, as shown in Figure 8.17.

FIGURE 8.17
Saving the group

By default, you'll then be prompted to save the group with the same name (Figure 8.18). The file is saved as a Revit project (*.rvt) and you can open the file and modify it as required.

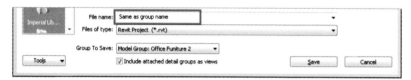

FIGURE 8.18 Group saved with .rvt extension

Loading Groups

When you're finished editing the group, you can easily reload it by selecting the group name, right-clicking, and choosing Reload from the context menu (Figure 8.19).

FIGURE 8.19
Reloading the group

In other cases you'll want to load groups without replacing anything. Such groups are resolved assemblages that can speed the design process. Bathroom and utility cores, office furniture, and meeting rooms (even unit types, like in hotels) can be saved from other successful projects and reused.

To load a group, select Load As Group from the Load From Library panel on the Insert tab (Figure 8.20).

FIGURE 8.20 Loading the group

There's another option still. You can link a Revit file to your project and then bind it. When the file is bound, it will behave as a group (a very helpful function) until you decide to ungroup it. Ungrouping a group breaks it up into all its separate parts. But doing so doesn't delete the group from the project.

Some Best Practices

There are a few good best practices when working with groups that you should know about. It's easy to get carried away with groups because they're effective for maintaining lots of relationships in your projects. On the other hand, you can quickly confuse new team members with an overabundance of groups that bring only diminishing returns.

Don't put datums (levels and grids) into groups.   You don't want to copy datums around your project every time you place a new instance of the group. To avoid this, either create your groups from views that don't have datums shown (like a plan or 3D view) or use the Filter function to make sure there are no levels or grids in your selection.

Avoid nesting groups within groups.   Nesting may seem like a good idea, but you'll probably want to avoid it. It'll lead to an overabundance of groups, which in turn will lead to a lot of confusion as your project develops.

Keep the host and hosted together.   When you're creating groups that contain hosted families, it's a good idea to keep the host and hosted together. Otherwise, you have to remember to create the host on which one of the grouped elements depends. Deleting the host (outside the group) that has a relationship to elements within the group can lead to project errors

Avoid attached relationships with walls. For example, if a wall is attached to a top level and then added to a group, everything will be fine as long as all the levels are equally spaced. But if one of the levels moves, all the other walls in the group will try to update accordingly. Because the levels they're associated to have not moved, you'll get errors and strange wall overlaps.

Create left and right options when necessary. While mirroring CAD files (or even 3D components) seems fine in principle, a lot of content doesn't get manufactured in left and right options. Unfortunately, content in Revit doesn't have an option to "disallow mirroring," so if someone mirrors a component, it may look fine in the plan. But in reality, they're indicating to another team member (like an engineer) that a piece of equipment is going to be serviced on a side that doesn't exist. For example, mirroring can put the hot water on the right and the cold on the left. So, we suggest you create left and right options. Yes, updating two options will take a bit more time—but doing so will help you avoid expensive field changes that result from someone unknowingly mirroring fixtures, furniture, and equipment.

CREATE
LEFT / RT
SEPARATELY

Using Phasing

Phasing allows your project to express the component of time. All project geometry has a phase component (when created and demolished). And all views have a component in order to allow you to filter within a specific range of time. Let's take the previous exercise and continue to create a phasing exercise. But if you haven't finished the previous exercise, you can start with the file 08_Groups_ and_Phasing_Middle.rvt from the book's web page.

Certification
Objective

Geometry Phases

First of all, let's look at the phasing properties for some of the walls in the project. Select the wall, as shown Figure 8.21. Note that there are properties for Phase Created and Phase Demolished. As a matter of fact, all the elements in this file present when we first started this chapter (all the walls, doors, curtain walls, and so forth) were created on the *Existing phase*. All the furniture and groups were placed on the *Proposed phase*. Imagine a scenario where you have an existing tenant space that is empty and needs to be configured for a new use, and you'll get the idea of where this exercise is headed.

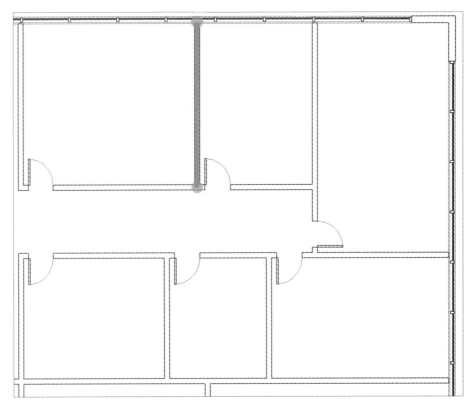

FIGURE 8.21 Geometry phases

At the moment, there are only two phases in the project (Existing and Proposed), and these properties can be assigned to any geometry. Don't worry about having a distinct Demolition phase, as demolition occurs during either Existing or Proposed.

View Phases

Views have phases as well. These phases allow you to filter views so that you can isolate geometry based on when it's created, demolished, or proposed. Figure 8.22 shows the present view phase of the Phase filter.

First of all, it's important to note that the phase of the view is the same phase that will be assigned to the geometry that you create in that view. So if View Phase is set to Existing, the geometry will be considered existing; if View Phase is set to Proposed, the geometry will be given the Proposed phase. But don't worry if you get this wrong or need to change a phase property later—this property is easily modified.

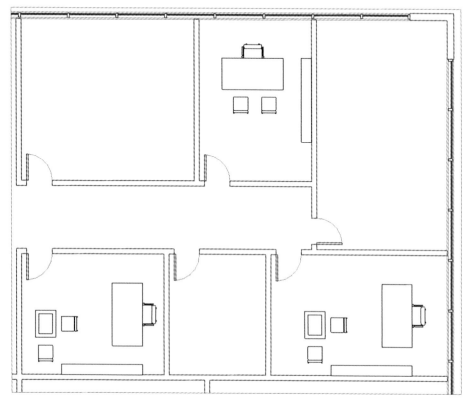

FIGURE 8.22 View phases

Second, there are a number of Phase filters defined in a Revit template (Figure 8.23), and we won't need to cover them all now. But we do want to point out what the various phases do.

FIGURE 8.23 Phase filters

At the moment, Phase is set to Proposed and Phase Filter is set to Show All, so both existing and proposed elements are being shown. Let's see how you can easily isolate the geometry from either phase.

Figure 8.24 shows what is visible if you set Phase Filter to Show Previous Phase. Since the phase of the current view is Proposed, the previous phase shows existing elements.

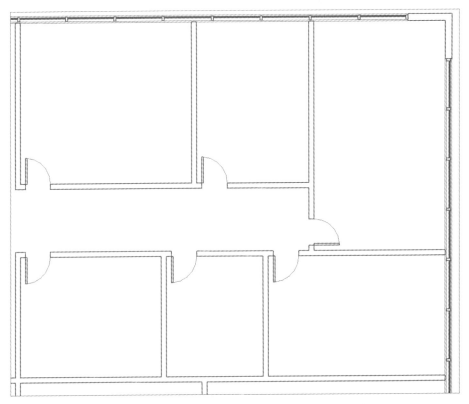

FIGURE 8.24 You'll see this if Phase Filter is set to Show Previous Phase.

Now select Show New. Now only the new, or proposed, elements are shown, as you can see in Figure 8.25.

If you choose Previous + New, the existing and proposed elements will be shown (Figure 8.26).

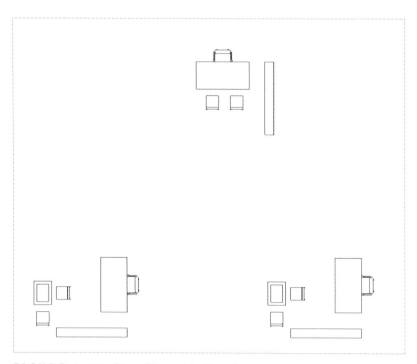

FIGURE 8.25   Phase Filter set to Show New

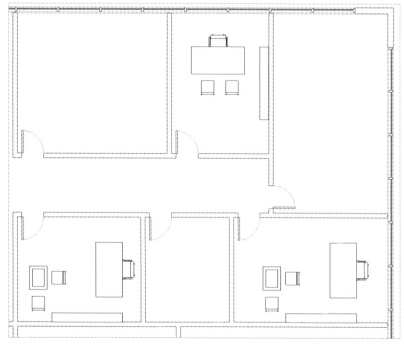

FIGURE 8.26   Geometry phases

Now set the view back to Show All for the remaining exercises.

Demolition and Proposed Elements

As part of this scenario, we're going to turn these two separate tenant spaces into a single space. We'll do so by demolishing a few elements and adding proposed elements.

Start by selecting the Manage tab and clicking the Demolish tool in the Phasing panel (Figure 8.27). Now you can demolish a few elements.

FIGURE 8.27 Demolition tool

Next, select the two doors and walls shown in Figure 8.28. Notice as you select the elements for demolition they're given a dashed representation in plan (a common graphic convention to indicate demolition).

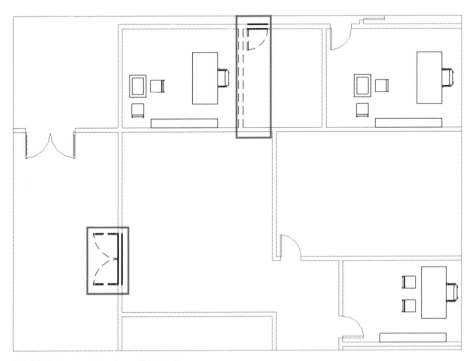

FIGURE 8.28 Demolished elements

If you look at the view in 3D, the demolished walls are indicated by a red color. And if you look closely, you'll notice that Revit has replaced the demolished door with a new wall (Figure 8.29).

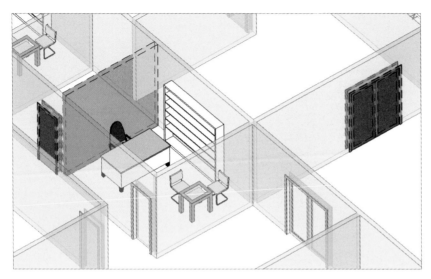

FIGURE 8.29   Demolished view in 3D

Now you need to reconfigure this office to accommodate passage to the other space. Start by moving the furniture group to the right and add a new wall and door to complete the revised office space (Figure 8.30). Be sure that the new walls have a height of 10' to match the existing walls.

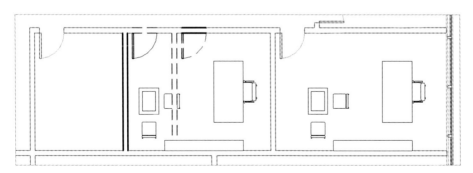

FIGURE 8.30   Proposed elements in 2D

You'll notice that Revit has automatically demolished the portion of the existing wall that needs to accommodate the proposed door (Figure 8.31).

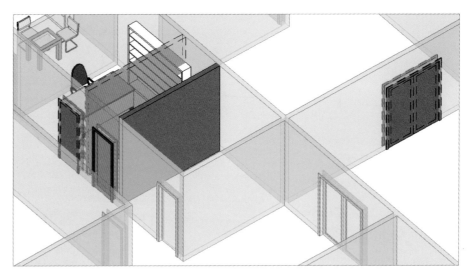

FIGURE 8.31 Proposed elements in 3D

৬✓

Finally, you need to use the Split Element tool to split the upper wall at the intersection of the new wall so you can demolish only a portion of the existing wall (Figure 8.32).

FIGURE 8.32 Split Element tool

Split the wall at the location shown in Figure 8.33.

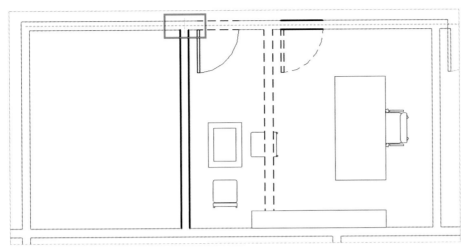

FIGURE 8.33 Splitting the wall

Now demolish the two left walls as shown in Figure 8.34. Note that the door (a hosted element) has been automatically demolished as well. This makes sense as the door would not be able to exist without the wall.

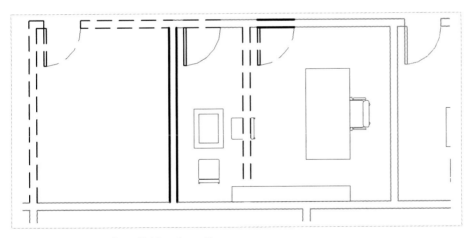

FIGURE 8.34 Demolishing the walls

Now split the lower wall as shown in Figure 8.35.

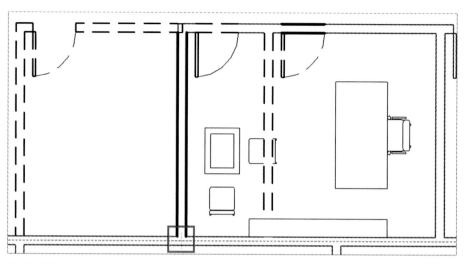

FIGURE 8.35 Splitting the lower wall

CLEANUP WALL ✳ When using the phasing tools, you'll often have to clean up wall conditions between the intersection of existing walls that remain and their demolished walls. First, select the demolished wall. You'll notice that blue nodes indicate each endpoint of the wall. By default, the wall attempts to automatically join the other walls.

To modify this condition, right-click on the blue node and select Disallow Join from the context menu (Figure 8.36). Now you can drag the wall away from the undesirable joined condition. Once you do this the remaining walls will join properly.

Repeat the process for all the intersections marked in Figure 8.37.

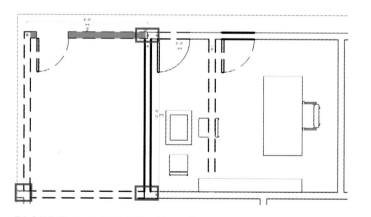

FIGURE 8.36 Splitting the wall

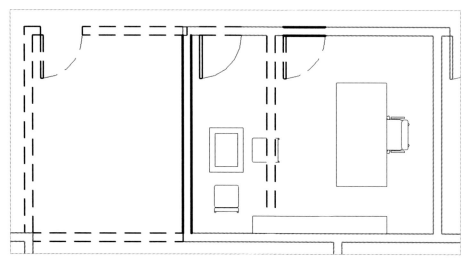

FIGURE 8.37 Cleaning wall joins

We think it's a good idea to resolve wall joins periodically as you work, rather than put them off to do at the last minute.

Completed Views

Now go back to your 3D view and let's see what the different stages of existing we need to complete look like. First, set Phase to Existing and Phase Filter to Show New. That way, you will see only the existing elements (before any demolition or proposed furniture), as shown in Figure 8.38.

FIGURE 8.38 Existing phase

Now set Phase to Proposed and Phase Filter to Show Previous + Demo. None of the proposed elements are shown, but the existing elements are displayed along with the elements that will be demolished (Figure 8.39).

Now set Phase Filter to Show Complete. The existing walls remain along with the newly proposed elements (Figure 8.40).

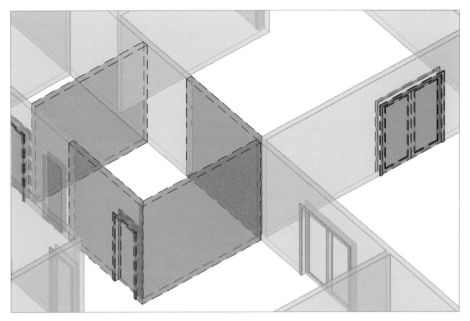

FIGURE 8.39 Existing and demolition shown

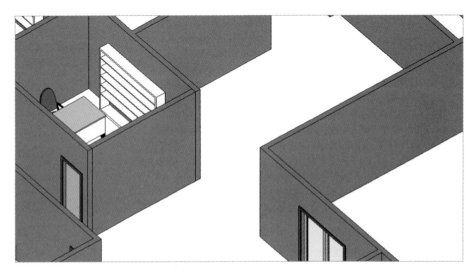

FIGURE 8.40 Show Complete filter

Figure 8.41 shows the same view in 2D.

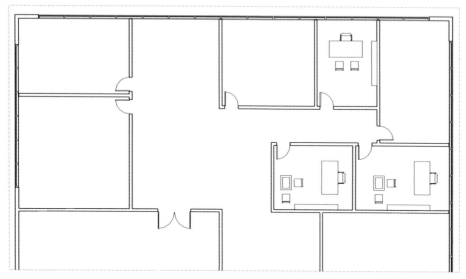

FIGURE 8.41 Show Complete filter in 2D

THE ESSENTIALS AND BEYOND

If this were a real project, you'd simply duplicate your project views and give them different Phase and Phase Filter settings. Then you'd take the multiple views (2D, 3D, and even schedules) and assemble them on multiple sheets for documentation. The great thing about Revit is that, as a phased project evolves and you need to demolish, propose, and even "undemolish" project elements, all of the project views and documentation remain fully coordinated.

If you'd like to review the completed file, go to **www.sybex.com/go/ revit2012essentials** and download c08_Groups_and_Phasing_Finish.rvt.

ADDITIONAL EXERCISES

▶ Revit files may also be linked and later bound. The bound link becomes a group in the project. Link and bind another RVT file into your project. What are the advantages? Disadvantages?

▶ Create a group and copy a few instances. Exclude elements from one of the groups. What are some of the advantages to doing this in a real project?

▶ How might you indicate a "Future" phase to show a present condition in context with the finished version?

▶ Create groups of frequently used assemblages and put them in a central location (like family components) so other design teams have access to them.

CHAPTER 9

Rooms and Color Fill Plans

The ability to add spaces to rooms has terrific implications. Keeping room names and areas coordinated frees hours of manual effort for more productive and meaningful design-related tasks. Once rooms are tagged, you'll be able to create coordinated color fill plans that automatically reflect the data in the room's space. Any changes to the space are immediately reflected throughout the entire Revit project.

In this chapter, you learn the following skills:

▶ **Tagging spaces with room tags**

▶ **Creating room keys**

▶ **Generating color fill room plans**

Tagging Spaces with Room Tags

Start by opening the Revit file that you completed at the end of Chapter 8, "Groups and Phasing." If you haven't yet completed the chapter, you can go to the book's web page and download the Revit file cO9_Rooms_and_Color_Fills_Start.rvt. Figure 9.1 shows a view of the Level 1 floor plan when you open the file. Set the scale to ¼″ = 1′-0″ [1:50].

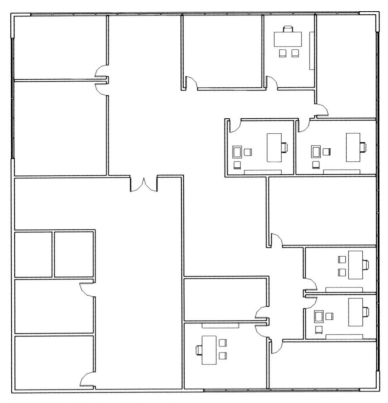

FIGURE 9.1 Level 1 floor plan

When you've finished the exercises in this chapter, you can inspect the file in its finished state on the book's web page at **www.sybex.com/go/ revit2012essentials**. Download the file titled cO9_Rooms_and_Color_ Fills_Finish.rvt.

Room Tags

Rooms and room tags are two different things and the distinction is important. The room is the spatial object that contains all the metadata about the space. The tag merely reports those values. In many cases you can edit the tag and the room values will update (and vice versa). But whereas deleting the room will delete the tag, the opposite is not true. You can delete a tag, and the room will remain. This makes sense, as the room will not be tagged in all views.

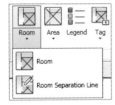

To add a room to your project, select Room tool on the Room & Area palette of the Home tab. Two options are available: Room and Room Separation Line. Select the Room option.

Now the context menu that lets you modify and place rooms becomes available. As you hover over enclosed spaces, the room boundary will highlight, indicating the space you're about to tag (Figure 9.2). You don't have to tag rooms as you place them, but by default this option is selected.

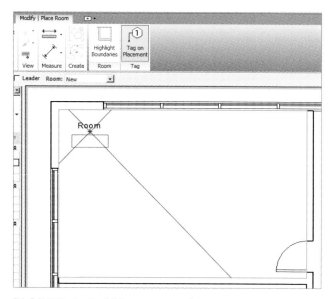

FIGURE 9.2 Adding a room and room tag

The tag that has been selected only indicates the room name and number (Figure 9.3), but more options are available. If you select the room tag and pull down the Properties menu for the tag, you'll see that the same tag contains several parameters.

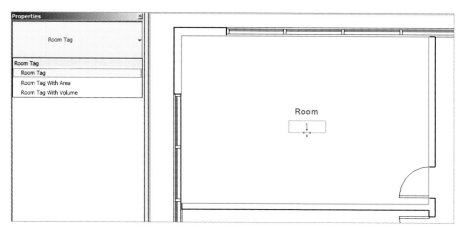

FIGURE 9.3 Room tag

Select the Room Tag With Area option. Once the option is selected, the room tag will show the area based on your project units (Figure 9.4). In this case, the room is 274 square feet. This feature is incredibly helpful if you want to create rooms as your design develops that allow you to constantly confirm that your design program parameters are being maintained.

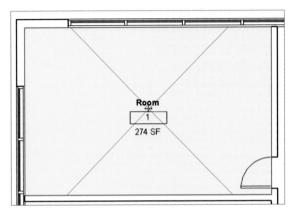

FIGURE 9.4 Room Tag With Area

Select the room and the properties for the space will display in the Properties Pallet. You can quickly and easily modify both the room number and name here (Figure 9.5).

FIGURE 9.5 Changing the room number and name

Room Boundaries

Now let's see what happens if you move a wall that defines this space. Select the wall at the right as shown in Figure 9.6 and move it 2′ [600 mm]. The moment that you release the wall, the space updates with the new information, which is immediately reported by the room tag (Figure 9.7).

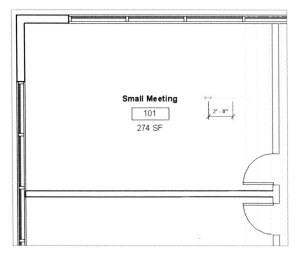

FIGURE 9.6 Moving the wall

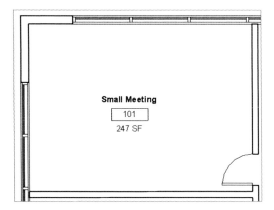

FIGURE 9.7 Updated room space and tag

Let's continue to add spaces and tags as shown in Figure 9.8.

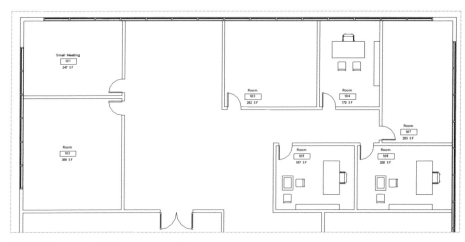

FIGURE 9.8 Adding rooms and tags

Room Separation Lines

As you start to add a tag to the large, central open space, it's obvious that it will be tagged as a single room (Figure 9.9). But in many cases, open spaces need to be tagged in smaller areas. You don't want to add walls to help you carve the large space into smaller areas, and fortunately there's a better option.

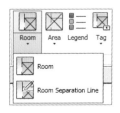

To break the large space into smaller areas, return to the Room tool and select Room Separation Line. These are model lines, and they'll show up in 3D views. The great thing about them is they'll allow you to create spaces without using geometry.

By default, these lines are thin and black, which is fine. But we want to give you a hint on how to distinguish these lines from other elements. As great as Revit is as a WYSIWYG environment, sometimes it can be confusing to see all black lines and geometry. We'll help clarify this now.

Select Line Styles from the Additional Settings panel of the Manage tab. The dialog in Figure 9.10 will open. You want to edit the default values for the <Room Separation> lines. In this case, you're making them wider, blue, and with a very fine dotted pattern.

After you complete the changes, sketch the lines as shown in Figure 9.11. Then add rooms and room tags to the spaces as shown in the figure.

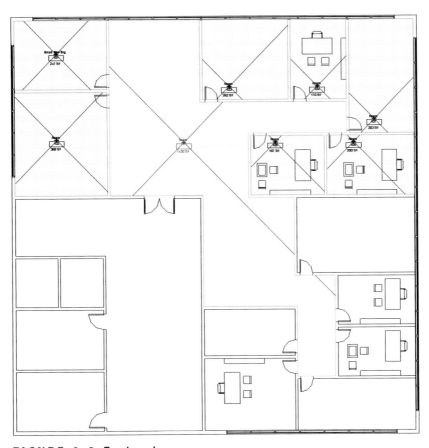

FIGURE 9.9 Tagging a large space

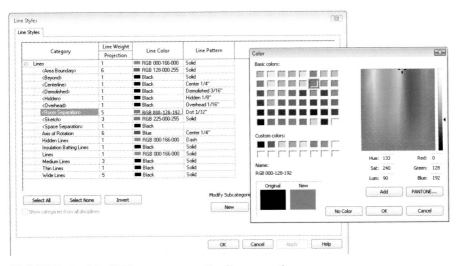

FIGURE 9.10 Editing room separation line properties

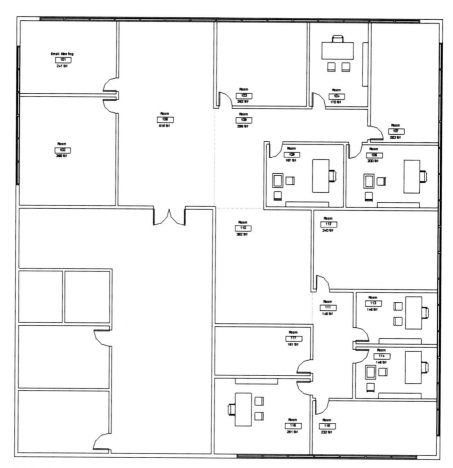

FIGURE 9.11 Adding room separation lines

Creating Room Keys

You could certainly continue editing all the room names manually (and this is regularly done during early design). But in many cases—and particularly on larger projects—the program is very specific about room names and other values given to spaces. Another factor is that rooms are often identically and repeatedly named. If multiple room names need to be edited, this can be a time-consuming and tedious process.

A better option is to quickly create a room key. This key will contain all the values for the rooms in your room program. The key value is then associated to one or many rooms. And in the event of a change, you only need to edit the value in the key, and all the rooms update instantly.

To create a room key, start by creating a schedule. The Schedules menu is accessed from the Create panel of the View tab.

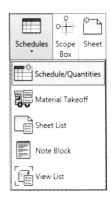

The next step is particularly important. From the New Schedule menu, select Schedule Keys as the option (not Schedule Building Components). Then name the schedule as shown in Figure 9.12.

FIGURE 9.12 Creating a schedule key

The Key Name field is already selected by default. The only other field you want to add is Name, which will contain the name of the room in the key (Figure 9.13). When you finish the dialog by clicking OK, nothing will schedule and you'll have no line items. This is because you didn't create a schedule; you created a schedule key. You'll add the key fields in the next step.

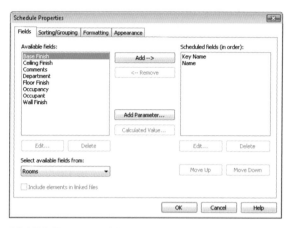

FIGURE 9.13 Adding fields to the room key

Creating Key Fields

From the Rows panel on the context menu, select the New option. Now you can add rows to your schedule key. Add a total of six rows.

At this point, you can edit the fields in the schedule key as shown in Figure 9.14. The key description will not show up in your room tag. (Hint: Use a real-world description that helps the design team understand the context of the tag beyond a one-word name.) Finally, add numbers to the prefix of the key descriptions as an ordering device.

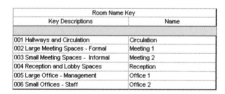

Room Name Key	
Key Descriptions	Name
001 Hallways and Circulation	Circulation
002 Large Meeting Spaces - Formal	Meeting 1
003 Small Meeting Spaces - Informal	Meeting 2
004 Reception and Lobby Spaces	Reception
005 Large Office - Management	Office 1
006 Small Offices - Staff	Office 2

FIGURE 9.14 Room name key

Now go back to the Floor plan view of Level 1, select the room, and assign a key value from the Room Style drop-down. You'll see something like Figure 9.15.

FIGURE 9.15 Assigning a key value to the room

Modifying Key Fields

When you pull down a menu on the Schedule tab, all of the key values become available (Figure 9.16). This helps remove doubts that come with naming all rooms manually (where spelling and syntax errors can lead to unexpected problems).

FIGURE 9.16 Key values from the Room Style drop-down menu

The great thing about this is that if the room names need to change, you only need change them in one location—the room key. In Figure 9.17, we've changed the Name fields for Office 1 and Office 2. This change is immediately reflected throughout the project.

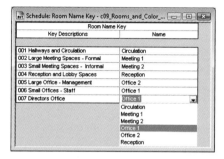

FIGURE 9.17 Updating the room key

Generating Color Fill Room Plans

Creating color fill plans in Revit is easy to do and once again, color fill plans constantly update as existing information is modified or new information is added. This allows you to focus on communicating rather than coordinating your design information—as if resolving your design isn't already hard enough!

Adding a Color Legend

To create a color fill plan, select the Room And Area panel of the Home tab, and then select the Legend tool. Place the start location for the legend as shown in Figure 9.18. You'll then be shown a dialog that allows you to select the space type and color scheme. In this case you're creating a Room type with a color scheme based on the name of the space.

FIGURE 9.18 Defining the space type and color

Keep in mind that these values don't have to exactly correspond. For example, you could show room names in the tag, while the color fill illustrated the department or other value of the space in the fill plan.

Once these values are defined, the color fill is automatically generated. And by default, only the values in the view are indicated. For example, if you had many more room styles in the project but not in the view, this could get confusing. The default parameter is to only create colors for values that are shown (Figure 9.19).

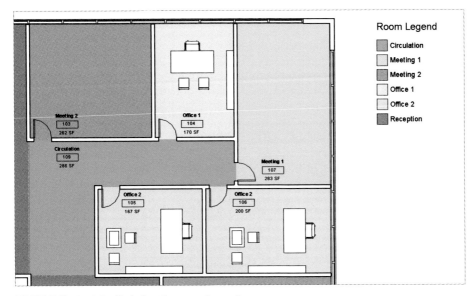

FIGURE 9.19 **Updating the room Legend**

To edit the default color assignments, select the color fill legend in the plan view. You'll then be able to select the Edit Scheme tool from the Scheme panel in the context menu.

Selecting the Edit Scheme tool opens the Edit Color Scheme dialog. All the values are available for editing (Figure 9.20). You can edit the color as well as the fill pattern. Doing so is helpful if you want to create an analytic fill pattern for a black and white or grayscale print.

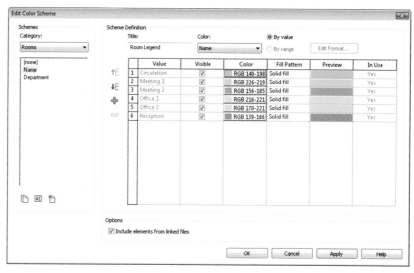

FIGURE 9.20   Edit Color Scheme dialog

Modifying Color Legends

Let's edit the color of the Circulation fill. Select the Color field and another dialog will open. Modify the values to R 255, G 128, and B 128. When you complete the changes, Revit automatically updates the fill color to reflect your changes (Figure 9.21).

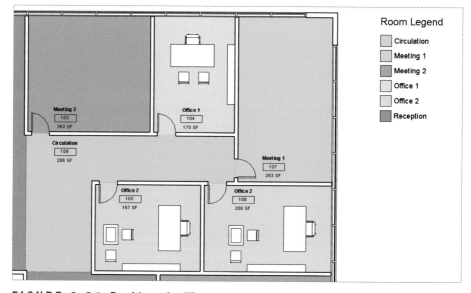

FIGURE 9.21   Resulting color fill

As you can tell, Revit created a color fill in the project view based on all the room names that were assigned to that view. So what would happen if you created a new room? Well, let's find out.

Start by modifying the room key as shown in Figure 9.22. In this scenario, you're adding a new style to accommodate a director's office. Just add another field to the key and then edit as shown.

Room Name Key	
Key Descriptions	Name
001 Hallways and Circulation	Circulation
002 Large Meeting Spaces - Formal	Meeting 1
003 Small Meeting Spaces - Informal	Meeting 2
004 Reception and Lobby Spaces	Reception
005 Large Office - Management	Office 2
006 Small Offices - Staff	Office 1
007 Directors Office	Office 3

FIGURE 9.22 Adding a new key value

Now that the room key has been added to the project, let's associate it to one of the rooms. Do so by selecting the room for Meeting 2 and reassigning this space to the newly created Office 3 key. Immediately the color fill modified on the floor plan and the new value are added to the existing color fill legend (Figure 9.23).

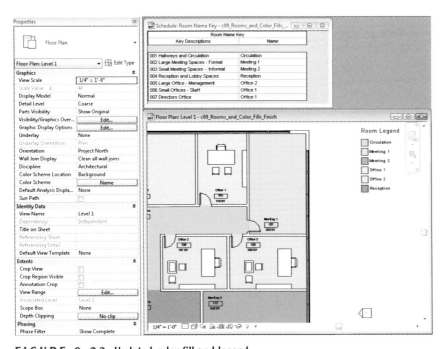

FIGURE 9.23 Updated color fill and legend

Now let's experiment by moving a wall on the floor plan. At the moment this hallway is 6'-6" [2m] wide (wall center to wall center), as shown in Figure 9.24. Let's change this value to 5'-0"[1.5m]. You can do so easily by selecting the highlighted, temporary dimension and changing the value to 5, which equals 5'-0" [1.5m].

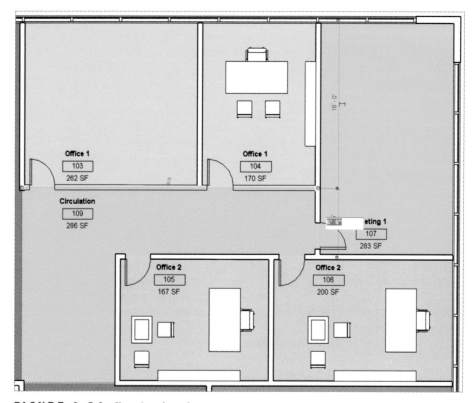

FIGURE 9.24 Changing the value

The room tags immediately update to reflect their new area and the color fills update to reflect their new boundary condition (Figure 9.25).

Let's take this exercise one step further. Room information in section is incredibly helpful for communicating your design intent.

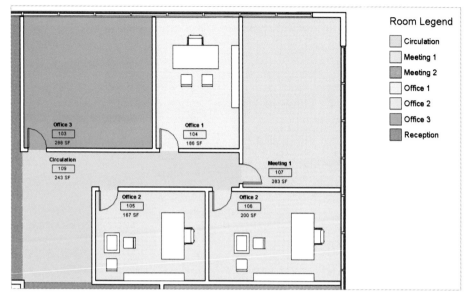

FIGURE 9.25 Updated color fill

Adding Tags and Fill Colors in Section

We'll start by creating a section across the project plan view (Figure 9.26). Then double-click the section head to open the new view.

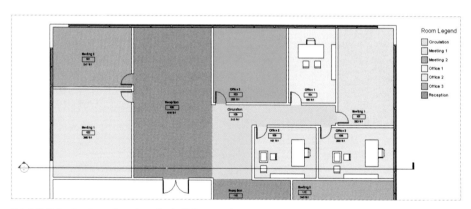

FIGURE 9.26 Creating the building section

Figure 9.27 illustrates the new building section. While all the geometry is shown correctly, it would certainly help to tag the spaces with their room names.

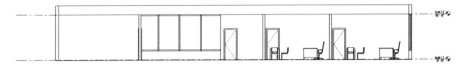

FIGURE 9.27 Resulting building section

You have two options to tag the room spaces. If you select Room Tag, you'll be able to place each tag manually. This approach is fine for a small project, but on a larger project it would take a considerable amount of time.

For this exercise, let's select Tag All Not Tagged. Selecting this option will open allow you to tag numerous element categories in a view all at once. But you only need to tag rooms. Select the Room Tags category as shown in Figure 9.28. Then click OK.

Immediately the view is populated with room tags (Figure 9.29). Keep in mind that Revit will center the tags in the room, so you will need to move their location slightly if the tag is overlapping geometry and unclear.

So what about color fills? Well, let's find out. Select the Legend tool and place the legend in the section view. The rooms are immediately filled with the same pattern and color in section as the color fill in plan (although this doesn't have to be the case), as shown in Figure 9.30. Again, there's no reason the fill in section couldn't describe Department or other values, while the room tags displayed the room name.

FIGURE 9.28 Adding room tags to the section view

FIGURE 9.29   Room tags shown in section

FIGURE 9.30   Room colors fill in section to match plan colors

THE ESSENTIALS AND BEYOND

User-defined parameters can be used to manage room and program data in a way not practical before Revit. Even the desired program areas can be added to the room key, allowing you to compare proposed and actual areas. There's a lot of wonderful functionality with regard to rooms, room tags, and color fills that we haven't been able to cover in this brief chapter. Instead, we focused on the typical uses to get you up to speed so that you're confident and productive as quickly as possible.

ADDITIONAL EXERCISES

▶ Create a single room and add a room and room tag. Now add a wall across the middle of the room. Which side of the room contains the space of the room? What denotes the origin of the room?

▶ Create a room color fill that uses black and white patterns rather than color. Why might this be useful?

▶ Create a room tag that displays information not visible in the default tag (such as Department).

▶ Create a room key with desired room areas and compare them to actual room areas.

▶ Create a color fill in your office's project template.

CHAPTER 10

Worksharing

Understanding multiuser workflow is essential to completing your pilot project in Revit. There's plenty of work to go around between the design, development, and eventual documentation of a building project.

If you've never used Revit before, what you're probably used to is CAD. Multiuser workflow in CAD is a very different animal, so you may need to suspend your expectations of what it'll be like in Revit.

Whereas CAD projects are typically divided along the lines about what needs to be drawn (plan, section, elevation at various levels of detail), Revit envelops you in the entire process. 2D, 3D, schedules, and so on are in a single database waiting for the input and direction of your team.

The great thing is that this is a far more elegant and efficient process than manually managing 2D files (which only one person can work on at a time). If anything, expect a large CAD-based project that would require 5–6 staff working in CAD to require about half that number working in Revit.

In this chapter, you learn the following skills:

▶ **Enabling worksharing**

▶ **Creating central and local files**

▶ **Adding worksets**

▶ **Assigning elements to worksets**

▶ **Saving to the central file**

▶ **Creating new elements**

▶ **Using workset display filters**

▶ **Using worksharing to work with consultants**

▶ **Using guidelines for worksharing**

Enabling Worksharing

**Certification
Objective**
The first thing that you'll need to do is open the file from the end of Chapter 9, "Rooms and Color Fill Plans." If you don't have the file, go to the book's web page at **www.sybex.com/go/revit2012essentials** and download c10_Worksharing_ Start.rvt.

Saving the File

We'd strongly suggest that before you enable worksharing, you create a new copy of the file in order to back up your old work. For example, you may have been doing some schematic design planning in Revit and now it's time to add more people to the project in order to meet a deadline. Creating a copy of your old file (before enabling worksharing) is just good practice in case you need to return to your previous work.

In this case, we're preparing for this file to be the central file by naming it c10_Worksharing_Central.rvt (Figure 10.1).

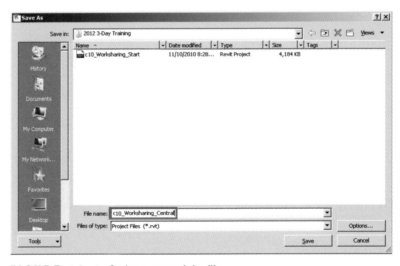

FIGURE 10.1 Saving a copy of the file

Once the file is open, go to the Collaborate tab. The tool to enable and access worksets is on the Worksets palette of the Collaborate tab.

When you select the Worksets tool, the following dialog box appears telling you three important things:

▶ Worksharing can't be undone (aren't you glad you saved a copy?).

▶ Datum is moving to a workset called Shared Levels and Grids.

▶ Project content that is not view specific (geometry and rooms) is all being assigned to Workset1.

All of this is fine and will allow you to enable worksharing. Click OK to continue (Figure 10.2).

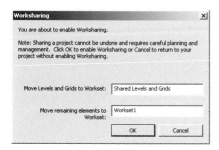

FIGURE 10.2 The initial worksharing dialog box

Next the dialog box shown in Figure 10.3 will display. Your workset username will appear in the Owner field. At present, you own everything in the project. No one else can work on the project without your permission.

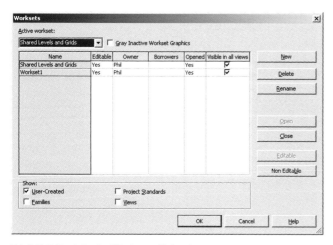

FIGURE 10.3 Worksets dialog box

Creating Central and Local Files

If this were a real project, you would likely want to save the central file on a local server so that your other team members can have access to the file. They're not going to work directly in the central file, but they'll need to have access to it in order to make their own local copies, and so that those local copies can communicate to the central file from a central location.

Creating the Central File

It's a good idea to save the project, which will establish it as the central file (Figure 10.4). Select the desired location for the central file. Be aware that you can't just move it after the fact. It's a bit more complicated, because moving a central file will create a local copy. We don't want to get into all the details now—just know that you want to save the file in the desired location.

Now close the central file and let's create our local copy.

Save File as Central File   ×

This is the first time that the project has been saved since
Worksharing was enabled. This project will therefore
become the central file. Do you want to save this project as
the central file?

If you want to save the file as the central file with a different name
and/or different file location, click No and use the Save As command.

[Yes]   No

FIGURE 10.4 Saving the central file

Creating the Local File

When you work in Revit with worksharing enabled, it's unlikely that you'll be working in the central file. Rather, you will work on your own local copy of the central file, as will everyone else. These local copies are constantly communicating and syncing to the central file in order to avoid conflicts.

Click Open in Revit and browse to your central file. Select it once but don't double-click. As you can see in Figure 10.5, ensure that the Create New Local option is selected. Selecting this option will not open the central file but rather create a copy of the central file.

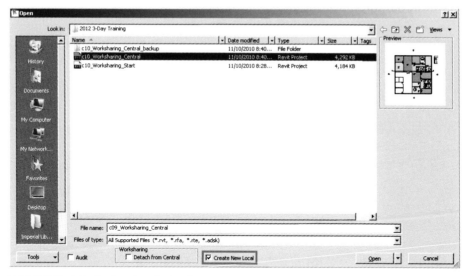

FIGURE 10.5 Creating the local copy

By default, your local copy is placed in your Documents folder with a suffix based on your username in Revit. In this author's case, the username is Phil. So the local file has been saved in the Documents folder as c10_Worksharing_Central_Phil.rvt (Figure 10.6).

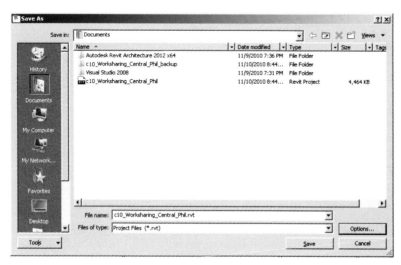

FIGURE 10.6 Saving the local copy

Now that the local file has been created, we're ready to create some user-defined worksets and then assign geometry to those worksets. Theoretically, other users could also start to access the central file and make their own local copies. But in practice, they'll probably wait until the user-defined worksets are created and the geometry has been properly assigned.

Adding Worksets

Open the Worksets dialog box by using the same Workset tool we used to activate worksharing previously. Click New and then create three additional worksets, as shown in Figure 10.7. Keep in mind that worksets are not "layers" and a lot of granularity isn't required. Basically worksets are for broad collections of objects based on their relationship to the project.

The project that we're using for this exercise is fairly modest. Interior, exterior, and core worksets are sufficient. If this were a multistory project, you would likely create interior worksets for each building level, as well as another workset for the roof and roof-related elements (such as equipment and skylights). Once you've created the worksets, click OK.

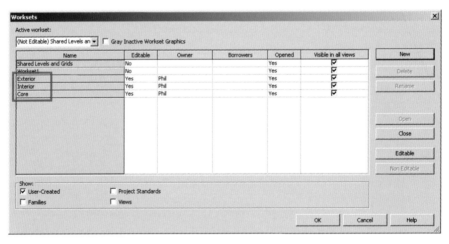

FIGURE 10.7 Creating additional worksets

Now let's open the Visibility/Graphic Overrides dialog box for the view (press VG on the keyboard). As you can see in Figure 10.8, there's an additional tab for worksets. This tab didn't exist before worksharing was enabled. This tab allows you to turn off elements based on their workset assignment.

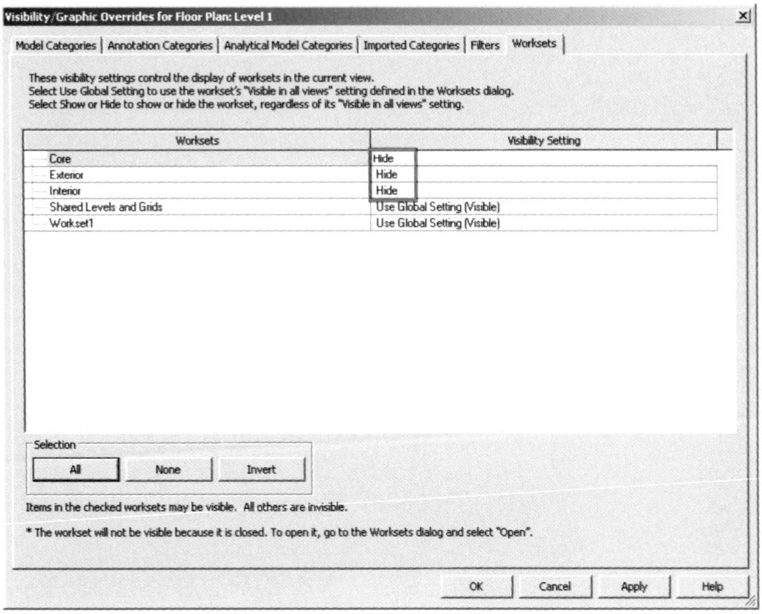

FIGURE 10.8 The Worksets tab

Workset Visibility

You're about to begin assigning portions of the project to your user-defined worksets. As you do this, you want to be able to clear the view of elements that have already been assigned to one of your newly created worksets. Basically, you want to work "subtractively" by removing elements.

To do this, set the Visibility Setting column for the active view to Hide, as shown in Figure 10.8. As geometry is assigned to each of those worksets, it will disappear from view and keep you from accidentally selecting it again.

By the way, don't delete Workset1 from your project. It's a great place to put content when you're not sure which workset something is supposed to belong to. Also, we've encountered many projects that midstream were introduced to staff who had minimal Revit experience. Rather than have them obsess over which workset should be active as they work, we told them to put all their work in Workset1 and that we'd move things around later. This also helped us isolate and review their work.

Now you can begin assigning elements to your user-defined worksets.

Assigning Elements to Worksets

Assigning elements to worksets is easily done. Just be sure of what you're selecting. You will often use the Filter tool and may work in more than one view. Except for rooms, it's often easier to select elements in 3D views. But for this exercise, we'll keep it simple by working from the 2D Level 1 floor plan view.

Start by selecting the elements shown in Figure 10.9—the walls in the lower-left corner of the plan.

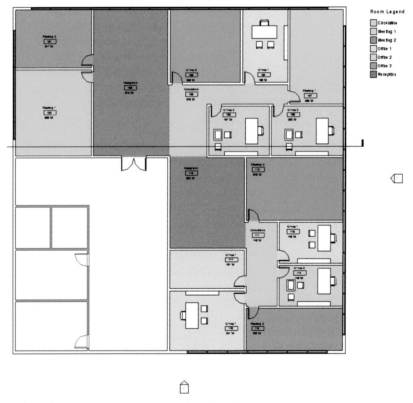

FIGURE 10.9 Assigning user-defined worksets

On the Properties palette you'll now see a field that indicates the workset assignment. Change this value from Workset1 to Core. Once you do so, the elements assigned to the core workset will no longer be visible in this view. Don't be alarmed! If you'll recall from the previous step, we turned off the visibility for this (and other) worksets, so this should be expected.

Now let's select all the interior elements and move them all to a new workset rather than selecting one element at a time. To select all the elements described, draw a selection window starting at the lower right to the upper left inside the exterior walls. Windowing from this direction will include every element you've crossed or included within the window you drew. Should you have windowed left to right, it would have selected *only* the elements that were fully contained within the selection box.

All of the selected elements can't be assigned to user-defined worksets, so you'll need to use the Filter tool to deselect some of the elements you've selected. Click the Filter tool from the Modify menu. In the Filter dialog box, deselect Room Tags and Views, as shown in Figure 10.10.

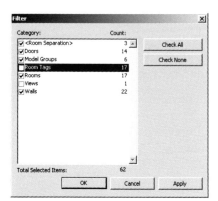

FIGURE 10.10 Deselecting elements with the Filter tool

Now assign these elements to the interior workset. Once again, don't be alarmed when those elements seem to disappear.

For the final selection, select all the remaining walls that are visible in the view and then select the Filter tool again. This time, only select Walls in the Category list (Figure 10.11). Elements like curtain panels, grids, and mullions automatically belong to their parent workset of walls.

Now all the geometry and rooms will not be visible in your project. So open the Visibility/Graphic Overrides dialog box for the view and reset the visibility settings as shown in Figure 10.12. All the elements will once again be visible in your view. At this point, you can save your project and synchronize it with the central file.

FIGURE 10.11 Isolating walls with the Filter tool

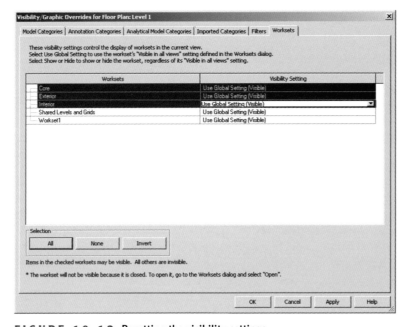

FIGURE 10.12 Resetting the visibility settings

Saving to the Central File

When you want to save your work to the central file, there are a number of options to fit your workflow. On the Synchronize panel of the Collaborate tab, you can click Synchronize With Central to see the first two ways to save: Synchronize And Modify Settings and Synchronize Now.

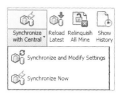

Synchronize And Modify Settings is a more explicit process by way of the dialog box shown in Figure 10.13, which gives you options to relinquish worksets, compact the central file, and save your local file after the sync with the central file is complete.

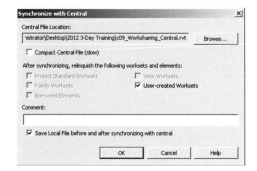

FIGURE 10.13 Synchronize And Modify Settings

The Synchronize Now option is probably the more frequently used option. Consider creating a keyboard shortcut so you don't have to return to this tab as you work and want to save to Central. This option will save your local copy and sync with the central file as well as update your file with any changes from the central file. Any borrowed elements are also relinquished. But if you have any workset checked out or editable, it's not checked back in. It will still be editable by you.

The Reload Latest option allows you to reload the latest version of the central file in your local project. However, it doesn't publish any of your work in the central file.

Finally, the Relinquish All Mine option allows you to check back in elements that you may have borrowed but not changed. If you've made changes, you either have to sync them with the central file or discard the changes without saving. You cannot relinquish elements in a file that has been modified.

So what do you do if you've made changes that you want to get rid of? The only way to do this is to close the file and select the Do Not Save The Project option (Figure 10.14). This will close the project without saving your work or syncing with the central file.

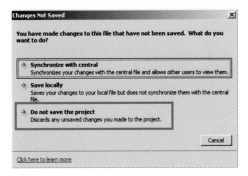

FIGURE 10.14 Closing the file without saving changes

If you select this option, Revit will ask you what to do with the elements that you've borrowed or worksets that you have enabled (Figure 10.15). If you relinquish the elements and worksets, other people will be able to modify them in their local files. If you keep ownership, the changes you've made will be lost, but you'll still have the elements and worksets enabled.

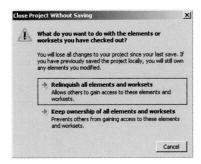

FIGURE 10.15 Relinquishing elements and worksets

When you have no elements or worksets enabled in a project, you can confirm this by opening the Worksets dialog box in Figure 10.16.

Let's continue by adding new elements to our local file.

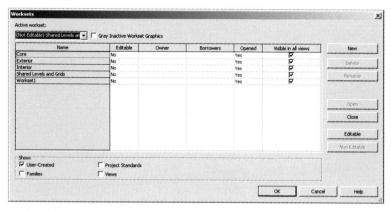

FIGURE 10.16 Relinquished elements and worksets

Creating New Elements

When worksharing is enabled, you'll want to make sure that any new geometry or rooms you're adding are being assigned to the right workset. You're going to add some new furniture to the project, so you'll want to make the interior workset active.

First let's copy a group of furniture from room 105 to room 103, as shown in Figure 10.17. Since the active workset is interior, the elements in the group are assigned to this workset.

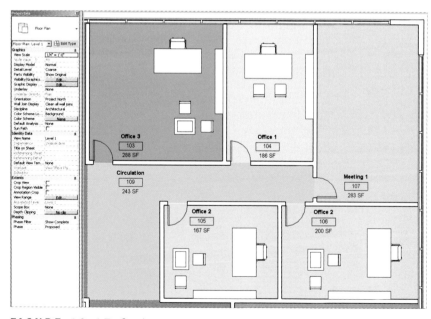

FIGURE 10.17 Copying a group

It's not possible to have elements in a workset assigned to a different workset as the group. Revit automatically assigns the elements within a workset to the same workset as the group.

Now let's duplicate an existing component and create a new type, and then use this new type in our project. Start by duplicating the table. In the Project Browser, right-click 72″×30″ [180cm×75cm] and choose Duplicate from the context menu (Figure 10.18).

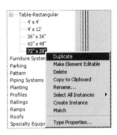

FIGURE 10.18
Duplicating an existing type

Next, modify the duplicated table. Select the table again in the Project Browser, right-click, and choose Type Properties.

Rename the type to **144″ x 48″ [350cm x 120cm]** using the Rename button. Next, modify the dimensional parameters as shown in Figure 10.19, changing the Height, Length, and Width values. This will create a significantly larger table for use in our conference rooms. Click OK to finish editing the family.

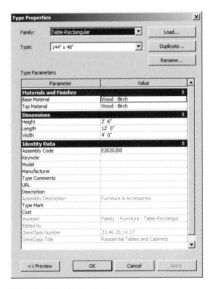

FIGURE 10.19
Modifying the type parameters

Now you can place a new instance of the table in our project (Figure 10.20). Again, since interior is the active workset, the table has been assigned accordingly. Place chairs around the table, as shown in Figure 10.21.

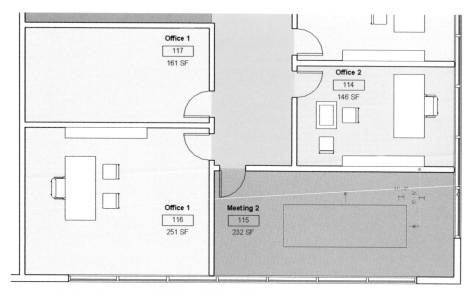

FIGURE 10.20 Adding the table to the project

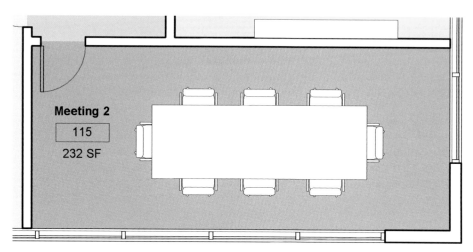

FIGURE 10.21 Adding chairs to the table

This grouping of furniture will be a useful addition to other meeting spaces in our project. But rather than copy them around as separate elements, it'll be more helpful to create a group and then copy this group in the project.

Select all the elements and then select the Group tool. Name the model group **Large Table and Chairs.** Click OK. Note that the group has also been assigned to the active workset (Figure 10.22).

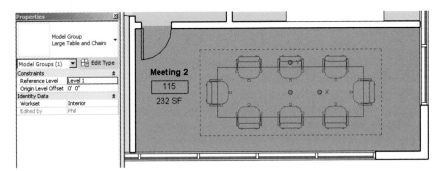

FIGURE 10.22 Workset assignment for the new group

Opening and Closing Worksets

As you work on larger and larger projects (of even very dense small projects), worksets are a great way to help you isolate and focus on what you're trying to accomplish. And while each view has its own visibility settings, when you want to isolate (or hide) elements throughout your project, worksets offer helpful options.

Open your Worksets dialog box and you'll notice that at the moment all the user-created worksets are set to Opened. This is fine if you need to see everything at once. But for larger projects or in cases where you want to limit what you're seeing across all project views, you can selectively open and close worksets. Do so now and click OK to close the dialog box.

The results are immediate (Figure 10.23). Only the interior workset is shown in all your project views (3D, perspective, plan, elevation, section, etc.).

Now that you have a good understanding of how to place elements on an active workset as well as open and close worksets selectively, let's explore workset display filters.

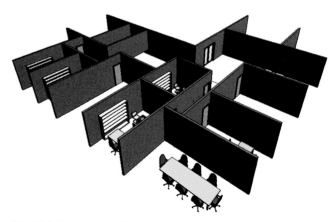

FIGURE 10.23 Interior workset isolated

Using Workset Display Filters

Workset filters are new to Revit 2012 and are a great way for visually understanding many things about your project. To create this scenario, all three authors are accessing this file at the same time. There's a central file on the server and we're all working from our local copies.

Furthermore, all of us have borrowed elements in the central file. In the past, who had ownership of certain elements was difficult to see, and this issue often created workflow problems when borrowed elements were modified.

In Figure 10.24, you can see in the Worksets dialog box that no worksets are editable but that other users have borrowed elements.

Editable	Owner	Borrowers	Opened	Visible in all views
No			Yes	☑
Yes	eddy		Yes	☑
No			Yes	☑
No			Yes	☐
No		eddy	Yes	☑

FIGURE 10.24 Borrowed elements in the Worksets dialog box

Now let's look at the worksharing display options settings, which are available from the lower portion of the Revit project window 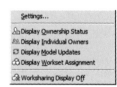. Select the Settings option.

Figure 10.25 illustrates the four sets of settings available for worksharing display in our project: Ownership Status, Individual Owners, Updates, and Worksets. Notice that the settings are based on the particular parameters in our project (number of worksets, active users, and so forth). Let's make some of these options active one at a time and view the results. Start with the

Ownership Status tab. Ownership status helps you distinguish between elements that are owned by you, others, or no one.

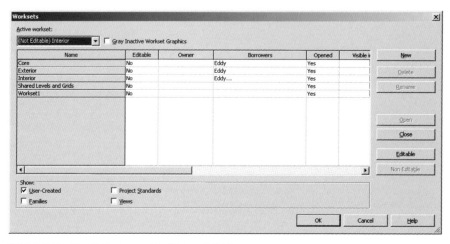

FIGURE 10.25 Ownership Status visibility

To activate any of these settings, click the icon and choose one of the menu items from the list. Doing so will toggle your visibility settings and apply an orange border to the view you're in, alerting you that you've engaged the settings. To turn them back off, choose the Worksharing Display Off option. Individual owners will help you visualize exactly which elements belong to which users (Figure 10.26).

Finally, the Workset Assignments tab helps you visualize elements based on the workset to which they're associated (Figure 10.27).

We're really glad these worksharing improvements have made it into Revit!

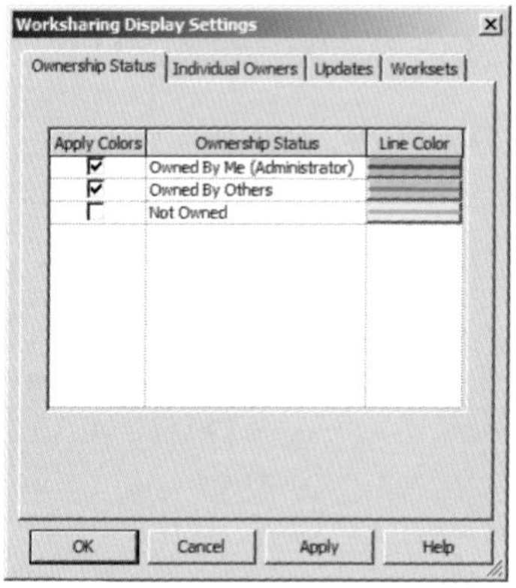

FIGURE 10.26 Individual Owners

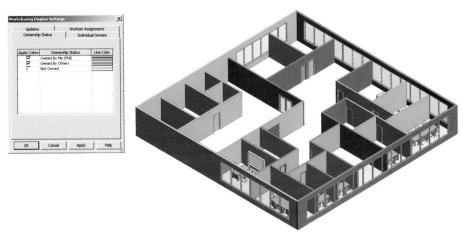

FIGURE 10.27 Workset visibility

Using Worksharing to Work with Consultants

One of the great benefits of worksharing is sharing your work with others. So far, we've discussed how to do this within your team, but what happens when you want to share with a larger team—like structural or MEP consultants?

Revit allows you to link in other Revit files which we covered earlier in this book. But once those files are loaded into your model, there are some key tools that allow you some additional leverage over the information you just linked so you can work more seamlessly with your expanded team. This is called the Copy/Monitor tool.

rtification bjective

The Copy/Monitor command allows you to create local copies of linked elements for better graphic control of the elements, while maintaining an intelligent bond to the linked elements.

With the project file saved from the previous exercise, switch to the Collaborate tab and select Copy/Monitor ➢ Select Link. Pick the linked architectural model and the ribbon will change to Copy/Monitor mode. Click the Options icon to open the dialog box shown in Figure 10.28; note that the options seen in the Copy/Monitor tool in Revit Architecture are slightly different from those in the Structure and MEP products. For the purpose of this book, we will focus only on the options available in Revit Architecture.

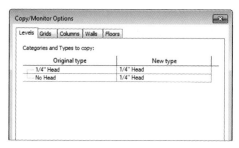

FIGURE 10.28 Element tabs
available for Copy/Monitor in Revit Architecture

As shown in Figure 10.28, the Copy/Monitor Options dialog box in Revit Architecture is divided into five tabs representing the elements available to be copied and/or monitored. For each element tab, there is a list called Categories And Types To Copy. As shown in Figure 10.29, the Floors tab lists the available floor types in the linked model in the left column and host model floor types in the right column. Notice that any of the linked types can be specified with the option Don't Copy This Type. This feature can be used for quality control if your project's BIM execution plan states that certain elements are not to be copied. For example, if walls are not to be copied, switch to the Walls tab and set all linked wall types to Don't Copy This Type.

Original type	New type
6" Foundation Slab	Don't copy this Type
Generic - 12"	Generic - 12"
Generic - 12" - Filled	Generic - 12"
LW Concrete on Metal Deck	LW Concrete on Metal Deck
Steel Bar Joist 14" - VCT on Concrete	Steel Bar Joist 14" - VCT on Concrete
Wood Joist 10" - Ceramic Tile	Wood Joist 10" - Ceramic Tile
Wood Joist 10" - Wood Finish	Wood Joist 10" - Wood Finish
Wood Truss Joist 12" - Carpet Finish	Wood Truss Joist 12" - Carpet Finish

FIGURE 10.29 Some of the elements you
can choose to monitor in the Copy/Monitor dialog box

At the bottom of the Copy/Monitor Options dialog box, you will find a section called Additional Copy Parameters for each element tab (Figure 10.30). Note that the additional parameters are different for each element category. For example, when levels are copied and monitored, an offset and naming prefix can be applied to accommodate the difference between the finish floor level in a linked architectural model and the top of steel level in the host structural model.

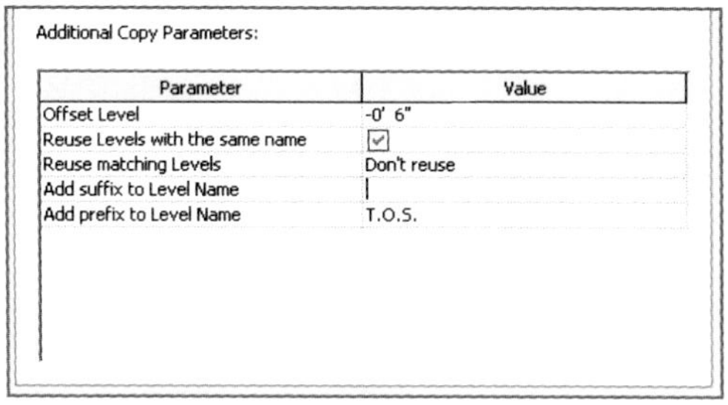

Additional Copy Parameters:	
Parameter	Value
Offset Level	-0' 6"
Reuse Levels with the same name	☑
Reuse matching Levels	Don't reuse
Add suffix to Level Name	|
Add prefix to Level Name	T.O.S.

FIGURE 10.30 Additional copy parameters can be applied to each element category.

Let's take a closer look at each of the element category options available for the Copy/Monitor tool:

Levels In most cases, the difference between the location of a structural level and an architectural level may lead to the presumption that you would not want to copy levels between files; however, this is a good case where you can apply additional copy parameters to build in an offset distance. Keep in mind the offset will apply to all Copy/Monitor selections. Thus, if a structural level needs to be offset by a different value, create the level in the host model and use the Monitor command to create the intelligent bond to the linked model's level. The difference will be maintained through any modifications in the linked model.

Grids Copying in the grids is usually a strong workflow. You can use the options on these tabs to convert the grid bubbles used by the architect into those used by the structural engineer. It is also possible to add a prefix to the grid names. For instance, you could add the value "S-" in the prefix field and then grid "A" from the architectural model will come into the structural model as "S-A."

Columns The structural engineer can choose to replace any column— architectural or structural—in the architectural model with an appropriate structural column; however, this implies that the architect will maintain an understanding of where differentiating column types would exist. Realistically, the structural elements should only exist in the structural engineer's model and then link into the architectural model. The architect may then choose to either Copy/Monitor the linked structural columns with architectural columns (which act as finish wrappers) or place architectural columns along the monitored grid lines. In the

latter option, architectural columns will move along with changes in grid line locations, but would not update if structural columns are removed in the linked model.

Walls and Floors   Similar to columns, structural walls that are important to the
coordination process may be better managed in the structural model and linked
into the architectural model. If you decide to use a Copy/Monitor relationship for
these types of elements, it is best to create uniquely named wall types for structural coordination. Name such wall types in a manner that makes them display at
the top of the list in the Copy/Monitor Options dialog box. You can do so by adding
a hyphen (-) or underscore (_) at the beginning of the wall type name.

Finally, make sure that you select the check box Copy Windows/Doors/
Openings for walls or Copy Openings/Inserts for floors so that you also get the
appropriate openings for those components in the monitored elements.

Use the Copy/Monitor tools in Monitor mode to establish the relationships of
the grids between host and linked models. Doing so will ensure that changes to
grids in either model will be coordinated.

DOWNLOADING THE COMPLETED FILE

If you want to download this completed file, go to the book's web page
at **www.sybex.com/go/revit2012essentials** and download the file
c10_Worksharing_Central.rvt. Keep in mind that although this is a
central file, the copying will automatically create a local copy. To resolve
this, open Revit and browse to the downloaded file. Select the file and then
choose the Detach From Central option. Selecting this option will create a
central file rather than an orphaned local copy.

Using Guidelines for Worksharing

Now that you have a general understanding of how worksharing and worksets
operate, let's take a moment to consider a few best practices.

Think of worksets as containers.   Worksets aren't "layers" like in CAD. Think
of them as containers for majors systems in your building (interior, exterior,

roof, core, etc.). You only need to manage or be mindful of stuff that belongs to user-created worksets:

- ▶ Datum (Levels and Grids)

- ▶ Geometry (Building elements that show up in multiple views)

- ▶ Rooms (the spaces that can be tagged)

Be mindful of the active workset.   If you're creating one of those three things, be mindful of the active workset. And keep in mind that Revit manages the worksets for everything else (views, families, and project standards).

Borrow elements on the fly.   Don't enable entire worksets by making the entire workset editable. Instead, just borrow elements on the fly. This approach lets you avoid many conflicts that occur when one person needs to modify something you own (but don't really need) in the model. With the interconnected nature of buildings, you don't even need to deliberately make an element editable. The simple act of modifying something that exists (or placing a new element) will borrow it for you.

Associate linked files to their own workset.   Associate any linked files to their own workset. Then you can open and close the worksets associated to those links. This strategy is much more predictable than loading and unloading links (which will have an effect on everyone working on the project). Opening or closing a workset only affects your project.

Stay out of the central file.   Stay out of the central file—don't move it and don't rename it (unless you know what you're doing). Opening the central file restricts access by the files that are trying to connect to it. And if you "break" something in the central file, you'll break the connections that others have from their local copy. Which means they may end up losing their work. Which means your team will not like you.

Open and close worksets selectively.   Selectively opening and closing worksets is a lot faster than opting to modify multiple view visibility settings or use hide/isolate on a view-by-view basis. If you're only supposed to be working on the core and internal areas of a multistory building, only opening the worksets associated to those areas will save a lot of computing power.

THE ESSENTIALS AND BEYOND

Worksets are straightforward once you get down the basics. Larger projects will require more granular workset assignments, but the principles are the same.

ADDITIONAL EXERCISES

▶ Use the previous exercise with a friend or coworker to access the same project at the same time.

▶ Link a Revit project into a file that has worksharing enabled. Assign the linked file to a workset and then practice "opening" and "closing" the workset. What happens to the linked file?

▶ Create a workset named Entourage and make it not visible by default. Use this workset for elements that are useful for visualization but not documentation.

▶ Practice "locking" the datum (levels and grids) by making the workset editable to you and not relinquishing it. Others will be able to graphically adjust the endpoints, but they won't be able to move or delete the datum.

CHAPTER 11

Details and Annotations

As you've seen so far, you can use Revit to create walls, doors, roofs, and floors; to define space; and to bring your architectural ideas into three-dimensional form. In each of these cases, the geometry is typically modeled based on a design intent, meaning that your goal isn't to model everything but enough to demonstrate what the building is going to look like. To this end, it becomes necessary to embellish parts of the model or specific views with detailed information to help clarify what you've drawn. This embellishment takes the shape of 2D detail elements in Revit that you will use to augment views and add extra information.

In this chapter, you learn the following skills:

▶ **Creating details**

▶ **Annotating your details**

▶ **Legends**

Creating Details

Even when you're creating details, Revit provides a variety of parametric tools that allow you to leverage working in a BIM model. You can use these tools to create strictly 2D geometry or to augment details you're trying to create from 3D plans, sections, or callouts. To become truly efficient at using Revit to create the drawings necessary to both design and document your project, you must become acquainted with these tools—you'll find yourself using them over and over again throughout your project.

All of these view-based tools are located on the Detail panel of the Annotate tab (Figure 11.1). This small but very potent toolbox is what you will need to familiarize yourself with in order to create a majority of the 2D linework and components that will become the details in your project. To better understand how these tools are used, let's quickly step through each of them.

FIGURE 11.1 The Detail panel
of the Annotate tab

Detail Line

The Detail Line tool is the first tool located on the Detail panel of the Annotate tab. This tool is the closest thing you'll find to CAD drafting. It allows you to create view-specific linework using different lineweights, tools for drawing different line shapes, and many of the same manipulation commands you would find in a CAD program.

Detail lines are view specific—they will only appear in the view in which they're drawn. They also have an arrangement to their placement, meaning that you can layer them underneath or on top of other objects. This feature is especially important when you begin using regions, detail lines, and model content to create your details.

Using the Detail Line tool is fairly easy. Selecting the tool will change your ribbon tab to look like Figure 11.2. This new tab will have several panels that allow you to add and manipulate linework.

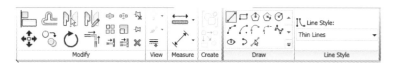

FIGURE 11.2 The Detail Line toolset

This new tab contains three panels: Modify, Draw, and Line Style. The Modify panel has the host of tools you've used so far for your walls, doors, and other elements. Here you can copy, offset, move, and perform other tasks. The Draw panel allows you to create new content and define shapes, and the Line Style drop-down allows you to choose the line style you'd like to draw with.

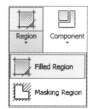

Regions

The next tool on the Detail panel of the Annotate tab is the Region tool. *Regions* are areas of any shape or size that you can fill with a pattern. This pattern (much like a hatch in AutoCAD) will dynamically resize with the region boundary. Regions layer just like detail lines do and can be placed on top of, or behind, linework and model objects. Regions also have an opacity and can be completely opaque (covering what they are placed on) or transparent (letting the elements show through).

There are two types of regions: filled regions and masking regions. *Filled regions* allow you to choose from a variety of hatch patterns to fill the region. They are commonly used in details to show things like rigid insulation, concrete, plywood, and other material types. *Masking regions*, on the other hand, come in only one flavor. They are white boxes that can have (or not have) discernable borders to them. Masking regions are typically used to "hide" or *mask* certain content from a view that you don't want shown or printed.

**Certification
Objective**

Components

The Component drop-down menu allows you to insert a wide array of component types into your model. These are 2D detail components, or collections of detail components in the case of a repeating detail. Detail components are schedulable, taggable, keynotable 2D families that allow an additional level of standardization within your model. Some examples of when you'd use detail components are blocking in section, steel shapes, and metal studs in plan or section—just about any replicated 2D element that comes in a standardized shape.

Detail Components

Detail components are 2D families that can be made into parametric content. In other words, a full range of shapes can be available in a single detail component. Because they are families, they can also be stored in your office library and shared easily across projects.

To add a detail component to your drawing, select Detail Component from the Component drop-down list located on the Annotate tab and use the Type Selector to choose from ones that are already inserted into the model. If you don't see a detail component you want to insert in the Type Selector, click the Load Families button on the Modify | Place Detail Component tab and insert one from the default library or your office library.

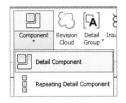

Creating a Detail

Making a detail component is much like creating a 2D family. Let's step through making a simple 2D detail component.

From the book's web page (**www.sybex.com/go/revit2012essentials**), download the Detail-Start.rvt file and open the view Exterior Detl, Typ. You'll create some detail components and regions to get started with a typical window detail. The first thing you'll want to do is use the Callout tool to create a new detail of the window sill. Create a new callout and name it **Exterior Window Sill, Typ.** The starting view will look like Figure 11.3.

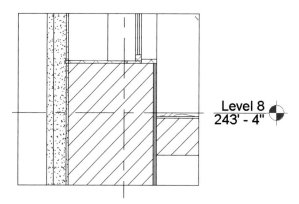

FIGURE 11.3 The window sill detail before embellishment

 Certification Objective

Now, let's make the detail:

1. You'll notice that you have some detail elements that can't exist in real-life construction. For example, you'd never run the sheetrock back behind the floor slab, and there's no room for flashing or blocking below the window. You'll need to modify this view to rectify these conditions. Let's start with the floor slab and fix the sheetrock. To do this, you'll cover a portion of this area with a filled region. So to begin, select the Filled Region button from the Annotate tab.

2. Set the line style to invisible and create a box bounding the floor slab (Figure 11.4). You'll notice three of the bound lines are on cut planes: the top and bottom edges of the box. Select these edges and use the Line Style drop-down to change the lineweight to Medium.

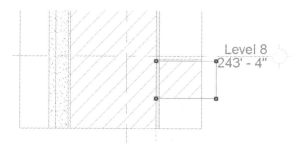

FIGURE 11.4 Modifying the boundary of the filled region

3. Click the Edit Type button in the Properties palette to open the Type Properties dialog box. Since there is no defined region type that is identical to existing materials, you'll need to make one. Click Duplicate, name the new region type **00 Existing**, and click OK.

4. Now you need to modify the settings:

   Fill Pattern: Set this field to Drafting and choose ANSI31.

   Background: Opaque

   Line Weight: 1

   Color: Black

   Click OK when you're done.

5. Now that the region is defined, click the green check mark ✔ to complete the sketch. Your finished filled region will look like Figure 11.5.

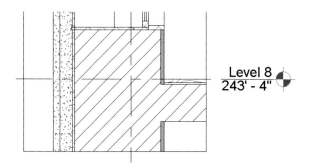

FIGURE 11.5 Adding the filled region

6. As part of the window sill condition, say you know you have a 1″ [25 mm] gap between the bottom of the window sill and the existing masonry opening. This gap isn't reflected in the window detail currently because the window family was created to cut a square opening just big enough for the window. For this detail, you need to create a masking region under the window sill so you can add some other components like blocking. Choose the Masking Region tool from the Region flyout on the Annotate tab.

7. With Line Style set to Thin Lines, create a box 1″ [25 mm] deep under the window sill (Figure 11.6).

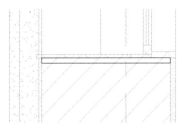

FIGURE 11.6 Adding a masking region

8. With the box created, click the green check to complete the sketch. The finished sill will look like Figure 11.7.

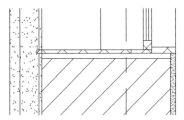

FIGURE 11.7 The completed sketch

The next step is to add some detail components for blocking and trim. Click the Application menu, choose File ➢ New ➢ Family, and choose `Detail Component.rft`. When creating detail components, as with any other family, you'll start with two reference planes crossing in the center of the family. This crossing point is the default insertion point of the family. The first family, blocking, is straightforward:

1. Start by selecting the Masking Region tool on the Home tab and drawing a box with the lower-left corner at the origin. The box should be 1″ [25 mm] high and 3″ [75 mm] wide. You're using the Masking Region instead of the Lines tool so you can have a clean, white box that you will be able to use to layer over other elements you might not want to see.

2. On the Home tab, click the Lines tool and draw a line across the box denoting blocking. The family should look like Figure 11.8.

FIGURE 11.8 Creating a blocking detail component

3. With the drawing finished, click the Application menu, select Save As ➤ Family, and name the family **06 Blocking**. Place it in a folder with the Jenkins model.

4. With the family named, click the Load Into Project button to add the family to the Jenkins model.

5. On the Annotate tab, click the Detail Component button. The component you insert will be the one that will become the default component, and you will be able to see the name 06 Blocking in the Type Selector. Insert a piece of blocking at the left, right, and center of the sill (Figure 11.9).

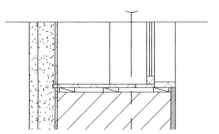

FIGURE 11.9 Inserting and placing the blocking

6. With the blocking inserted, you want to make one more detail component for the baseboard. Create a detail component using the same steps as earlier measuring 1″ [25 mm] wide by 6″ [150 mm] high and called **06 Baseboard**. The reason you want to create these elements as families and not just as filled regions is so that later in the detailing process you can annotate them using the Revit Keynote tool. Families will have a lot more functionality and versatility later down the line for faster documentation. With the baseboard added, the detail looks like Figure 11.10.

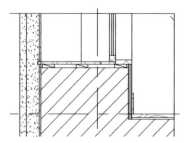

FIGURE 11.10 The sill detail with base

7. Not all of the detailing will be able to be completed using components. Sometimes, it is easier and more effective to simply use linework to create the necessary features in a detail. For these purposes, you want to create some flashing at the window sill. To do so, you'll use the Detail Line tool. Choose the tool and select Medium Lines from the Line Style drop-down menu.

8. Using the Detail Line tool, draw in some flashing for the window sill (Figure 11.11).

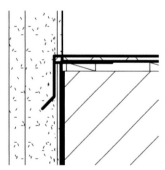

FIGURE 11.11 Adding flashing using detail lines

Arranging Elements in the View

So far you have created all of the content in order and have not had to change the arrangement of any of the elements. However, knowing how to change arrangement is an important part of detailing so you don't have to draw it all in exact sequence. Arrangement allows you to change the position of an element, such as a line or a detail component relative to another element. Much like layers in Photoshop or arrangement in PowerPoint, Revit allows you to place some elements visually in front of or behind others. Once an element or group of elements is selected and the Modify menu appears, on the far right you'll see the Arrange panel.

From here, you can choose among four options of arrangement: Bring To Front, Bring Forward, Send To Back, and Send Backward. Using these tools will help you get your layers in the proper order.

Repeating Detail Component

Certification
Objective

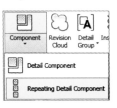

Repeating elements are common in architectural projects. Masonry, metal decking, and wall studs are some common elements that repeat on a regular interval in architectural projects. Revit's tool to help create and manage these types of elements is called the Repeating Detail Component and is located in the Component flyout on the Annotate tab.

This tool allows you to place a detail component in a linear configuration where the detail component repeats on a set interval. This allows you to draw a "line" that then becomes your repeating component. The default Revit repeating detail is common brick repeating in section. Creating elements like this not only lets you later tag and keynote the materials, but also allows you some easy flexibility over arraying these elements manually. Choose the Repeating Detail Component tool and draw a section of brick (the default tool).

Before you create a repeating detail component, we'll cover the properties behind one so you can get a better idea of how they work. Selecting the Brick component and choosing Properties gives you the Type Properties dialog box shown in Figure 11.12.

FIGURE 11.12 Type Properties
dialog box for a repeating detail

Here's a brief description of what each of these settings does:

Detail   This setting allows you to select the detail component to be repeated.

Layout   This option offers four modes:

>   **Fixed Distance**   This represents the path drawn between the start and end point when the repeating detail is the length at which your component repeats at a distance of the value set for spacing.
>
>   **Fixed Number**   This mode sets the number of times a component repeats itself in the space between the start and end point (the length of the path).
>
>   **Fill Available Space**   Regardless of the value you choose for Spacing, the detail component is repeated on the path using its actual width as the Spacing value.
>
>   **Maximum Spacing**   The detail component is repeated using the set spacing, and the number of repeated components is set so that only complete components are drawn. Revit creates as many copies of the component as will fit on the path.

Inside   This option adjusts the start point and end point of the detail components that make up the repeating detail.

Spacing   This option is active only when Fixed Distance or Maximum Spacing is selected as the method of repetition. It represents the distance at which you want the repeating detail component to repeat. It doesn't have to be the actual width of the detail component.

Detail Rotation   This option allows you to rotate the detail component in the repeating detail.

With these settings in mind, you need to create a custom repeating detail for the sill detail you've been working on. The exterior of the building is terracotta brick and will have visible joint work every 8″ [200 mm].

1. Begin by selecting a new Detail Component family. Click the Application menu, select New ➤ Family, and choose Detail Component.rft from the list.

2. Create a masonry joint 6″ long and ⅜″ [10 mm] high with a strike on one of the short ends (Figure 11.13) using a filled region. Save the family as **04 Grout** and load it into the project.

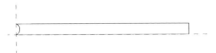

FIGURE 11.13 The grout detail component

3. Now, back in the project, choose the Repeating Detail Component tool. Choose Edit Type from the Properties palette and Duplicate from the Type Properties menu. Name the new type 04 **Terracotta Grout** and click OK.

4. You need to change the properties of this new type to reflect the detail component you just created and its spacing. Change the following fields:

Detail: Set this field to 04 **Grout**, the family you just created.

Spacing: Set this value to 8″ [200 mm].

You can leave the rest of the fields alone. Click OK when you're finished. The Type Properties dialog box will look like Figure 11.14.

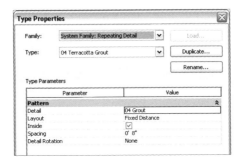

FIGURE 11.14 The repeating detail's type properties

5. Since you're still in the Repeating Detail command, you can simply begin drawing a "line" with the repeating detail. Starting at the base of the view, draw a line all the way up the left edge, placing the new joint over the terracotta exterior.

6. You can further finesse the appearance by placing one of the joints directly below the window sill. This will appear placed on top of the flashing you drew earlier, so select the flashing detail line and choose Bring To Front. The completed detail will look like Figure 11.15.

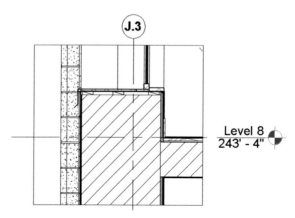

FIGURE 11.15 The finished window sill detail

Although this detail still needs annotations before you could think about placing it onto a sheet, you can begin to see how you have used the 3D geometry of the model and were able to quickly add some embellishment to it in order to create a working project detail. For now, save this detail. You'll return to it later in the chapter.

Insulation

The best way to think of the Insulation tool is like a premade repeating detail. You'll find this tool on the Detail panel of the Annotate tab.

Selecting this tool allows you to draw a line of batt insulation, much like a repeating detail. When selecting the insulation tool, you can modify the width of the inserted insulation from the Options Bar (Figure 11.16). The insulation is inserted using the centerline of the line of batt, and you can shorten, lengthen, or modify the width either before or after inserting it into your view.

FIGURE 11.16 Modifying the Insulation width in the Options Bar

Detail Groups

Detail groups are similar to blocks in AutoCAD and are a quick alternative to creating detail component families. These are collections of 2D graphics and can contain detail lines, detail components, or any collection of 2D elements. While you will probably want to use a detail component to create something like blocking, if you plan to have the same blocking and flashing conditions in multiple locations, you can then group those conditions and be able to quickly replicate them in other details. Like blocks in AutoCAD, manipulating one of the detail groups will change all of them consistently.

There are two ways to make a detail group. Probably the most common is to create the detail elements you'd like to group and then select all of them. In the Modify context tab that shows up, click the Create Group button. When you're prompted for a group name, name the group something clear rather than accepting the default name Revit wants to give it (Group 1, Group 2, and so on).

The other way to create a detail group is by clicking the Create Group button in the Detail Group flyout on the Annotate tab. You will then be prompted for the type of group (Model or Detail) and a group name before you can select any elements for the group.

When selecting the elements, you'll be taken into Edit Group mode. Your view will have a yellow transparency overlaid on top of it, and elements within the view will appear gray. To add elements to the group, select Edit Group and then click the Add button (Figure 11.17). Here you can also remove unwanted elements from your group. When you're finished, simply click the Finish check.

FIGURE 11.17
The Edit Group panel

You can place any group you've already made using the Place Detail Group button from the Detail panel of the Annotate tab. Groups insert like families, and you can choose the group you'd like to insert from the Type Selector on the Properties palette.

Linework

Although not part of the Annotate tab, the Linework tool is an important feature in creating good lineweights for your details. Revit does a lot to help manage your views and lineweights automatically, but it doesn't cover all the requirements all the time. Sometimes the default Revit lines are heavier or thinner than you'd desire for your details. This is where the Linework tool comes in handy; it allows you to modify existing lines in a view-specific context.

To use the Linework tool, choose the Linework button from the View panel on the Modify tab. Doing so will add the familiar Line Styles Type Selector panel on the right of the tab and allow you to select a line style from the list. Simply choose the style you want a particular line to look like and select that line in the view. The lines you pick can be almost anything; cut lines of model elements, families, components, whatever. Selecting the line or boundary of an element will change the line style from whatever it was to whatever you have chosen from the Type Selector. Figure 11.18 shows a before and after of your sill detail with the linework touched up.

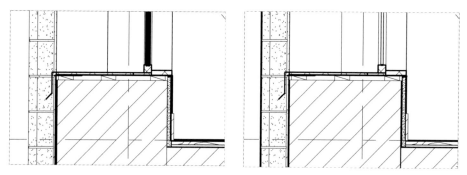

FIGURE 11.18 Before and after the Linework tool

You can also choose to remove lines using this tool. By selecting the <Invisible> line type, you can make some linework disappear. This is a good alternative to having to cover unwanted linework with a masking region.

Annotating Your Details

Certification Objective

Notes are a critical part of communicating design and construction intent to owners and builders. No drawing set is complete without descriptions of materials and the work. Now that you've created a detail, you need to add the final touches of annotations to communicate size, location, and materiality. The tools you will use for annotation are found on the same Annotate tab that you used to create your details. These are the Dimension, Text, and Tag panels shown in Figure 11.19.

FIGURE 11.19 Revit's annotation tools

Dimensions

In our detail, we have made some modifications that you might notice. We've added some detail to the window family to reflect some of the details needed for construction. Using this revised detail, let's begin by adding dimensions to the detail you just created. The dimension tool you will use the most often is the Aligned dimension tool located on the left side of the Dimension panel and highlighted in Figure 11.19. It can also be found on the QAT bar ✐ .

1. To begin, select either of the Aligned dimension tools and place a dimension string from the grid line to the centerline of the wall, as shown in Figure 11.20.

Certification
Objective

FIGURE 11.20 Adding a dimension string

2. Now that you've placed the dimension, you realize it's in the wrong location and you want the left side at the exterior wall. Dimensions are dynamic in Revit and easy to relocate. By highlighting the dimension string, you will see two sets of blue dots on either side. One set controls the length of the witness line, and the other one (the one that overlaps the tick mark) controls that witness line's location. Select this blue dot and drag it to the exterior of the wall. You'll notice the dimension automatically updates.

3. Add another dimension string from the grid line to the back of the window jamb.

4. Once you've added this dimension, you'll notice it doesn't read very well since it's located over the window sill. You need the dimension located there, but you can relocate the text. Grab the blue dot under the text and drag the text string to the right. You'll notice once the dimension text is outside of the dimension string, Revit will add an arc associating the text to the dimension (Figure 11.21).

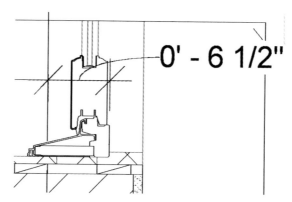

FIGURE 11.21 Modifying the text location

5. Now, add another dimension locating the gypsum board relative to the grid line (Figure 11.22).

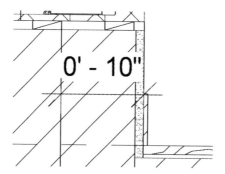

FIGURE 11.22 Dimensioning the wall location

6. In this dimension, notice that the dimension text has a white box similar to a masking region that lies behind the text and covers some of the detail of the sill condition. As a preference, you want to eliminate this box and have the dimension string read clear. To do this, highlight the dimension by left-clicking it and select Edit Type from the Properties palette. You'll get the Type Properties dialog box shown in Figure 11.23 for dimensions.

7. This dialog box allows you to change all of the settings in the dimension: text, color, length of each dimension element, and so forth. Scrolling to the bottom you'll notice the Opaque/Transparent setting. This controls that white box behind the dimension. Select this and set it

to Transparent. Click OK. Notice the dimension now reads with a transparent background.

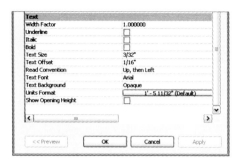

FIGURE 11.23 Dimension type properties

8. Let's add one final dimension string. Add a dimension locating the window sill relative to the floor, as shown in Figure 11.24.

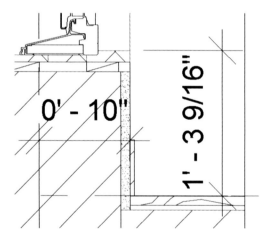

FIGURE 11.24 Dimensioning the window sill

9. Notice that this dimension is an awkward number and probably not something we want to include in the CD set. Remember that in Revit, dimensions simply report the relative location of objects—they cannot be forced with values. So to change the dimension string, you'll need to change the location of one of the two objects you've dimensioned. Since the floor is probably not going to move, you can reposition the window slightly. By selecting the window, notice that the dimension string turns blue and the numbers get very small (Figure 11.25).

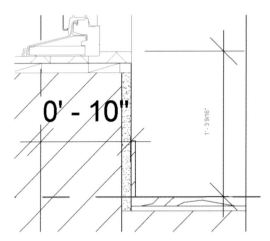

FIGURE 11.25 To change the dimension string value, change the location of the objects dimensioned by selecting the window.

10. Here you can key in a more reasonable value. Select the blue text and type **1 4 [400 mm]** in the text box (Figure 11.26). Press Enter and the window will push up just a bit and reset the dimension string.

11. With all the dimensions on the detail, it should look like Figure 11.27.

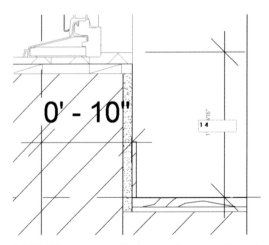

FIGURE 11.26 Keying a value into a dimension string

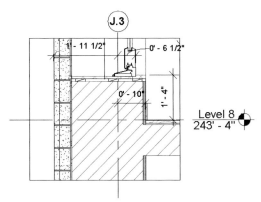

FIGURE 11.27 The dimensioned detail

Tags

Now that you have dimensions on the detail, it's time to add some tags. In this detail, you're going to tag the window as well as some of the materials in the detail to help identify them to the contractor. Material tags can be added in two ways: through the Material Tag button located in the Tag panel of the Annotate tab or through text.

1. To begin, start by tagging the window. Choose the Tag By Category button from the Tag panel and select the window.

2. When the window is selected, Revit will give you the warning shown in Figure 11.28. This warning tells you that Revit has added a tag but it has fallen outside of your view. By default, Revit places tags in the center of the element being tagged. In our case, the tag resides in the middle of the window cut in section, which is above our crop box.

FIGURE 11.28 The tag fell outside of the crop window.

3. To remedy this, select the box that defines the crop region for the detail. Doing so will highlight the crop box, but also an invisible, dashed box called the annotation crop box. This crop window can be turned on and off through the Properties palette.

4. By dragging the upper limit of this box higher, you will eventually see the Window tag you placed on the window (Figure 11.29).

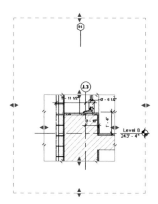

FIGURE 11.29 Extending the annotation crop window

5. Notice that the tag has a leader line associated with it. You'll want to move the tag, but also remove the leader line. To do so, highlight the tag, and in the Options Bar, deselect the Leader check box (Figure 11.30). Doing so will allow you to drag the tag down—leader free—and place it within the crop region.

FIGURE 11.30 Removing the leader from the Window tag

6. With the Window tag in place, now let's add a Material tag. Choose the Material Tag button from the Tag panel. You'll be prompted to load the family, so navigate to Annotations ➤ Architectural again and choose `Material Tag.rfa`. Material tags allow you to tag materials consistently through out the model. This means if you tag something like Concrete once in the model, the material will remember the tag you used and will show that same tag every time you tag it in any other view. Once the tag is selected, mouse over the vertical panel shown in Figure 11.31. The material there has been prepopulated with 5/8″ GYPSUM BD as a tag. Select the material and place the tag.

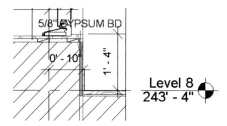

FIGURE 11.31 Using the Material tag

7. With the tag placed, you'll notice that by default there is no arrow-head. Select the tag and choose Edit Type from the Properties palette. Here you can give the tag an arrowhead. Choose 30 Degree Arrow and click OK (Figure 11.32).

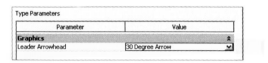

FIGURE 11.32 Adding an arrowhead to the tag

In the same way, you can populate the remainder of the materials in the detail. For materials that aren't already specified, Revit will provide you with a question mark. Simply click on the question mark and you can enter the text describing that material. Once entered, all other materials of that type within the model will automatically show what you just typed. Changes made to this material will also be broadcast through the model.

Text

Not all elements in Revit have materiality to them and there are times when tags are not the best way to convey information. For the rest of the information you want to communicate, use Text. The Text tool is located on the Text palette of the Annotate tab. When you're using text in your model, it's important to remember that text is not linked to any element or material. Labeling something with text or using text to call out notes doesn't dynamically update as elements change within the model.

1. In our example detail, the shims you placed as part of the window family do not have a way to tag a material and need to be called out using text. Choose the Text command from the Annotate tab. Doing so opens the Modify | Text tab and you'll see the tools on the Format panel. These tools control the leaders, leader location, justification, and font formats, respectively.

   For now, leave the selections at the defaults, choose a location on the screen, and click the left mouse button. This begins a text box. Type 1/2″ SHIMS (Figure 11.33).

FIGURE 11.33
Adding text to the detail

2. Once you've added text to the box, you'll notice that the Modify menu has changed. You now have the option to add and remove leaders. To add a leader, click the Add Leader button at the upper left of the Format panel ⊞A .

With the leader added, you can move the text and leader into position with the other notes. In this way, you can complete the annotations on the detail (Figure 11.34) and begin the next one.

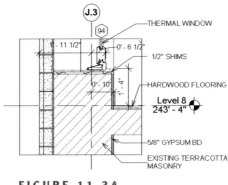

FIGURE 11.34
Finishing the detail

Legends

Legends are unique views in Revit as they are the only view type you can place on more than one sheet. These can become great tools for things like general notes, key plans, or any other view type that you will want to have consistent across several sheets. It's also important to note that anything you place inside a legend view—doors, walls, windows, and so on—will not appear or be counted in any schedules. Legend elements live outside of any quantities present in the model.

The Legend tool is located on the View tab. There are two types of legends you can create from this menu: a legend, which is a graphic display, or a keynote legend, which is a text-based schedule. Both legend types can be placed on multiple sheets, but for this exercise, you'll focus on the legend.

As part of the sample workflow, you may want to present some of the wall types as part of your presentation package to demonstrate the Sound Transmission

Class (STC) of the walls and the overall wall assembly. Since these wall types will be appearing on all the sheets where we are using them in the plan, you'll make them using a legend.

To make a legend, start with the `c11-Sample-Building.rvt` file found on the book's website. Open the file and choose the Legend button from the View tab under the Legends flyout. Creating a new legend is much like creating a new drafting view. You'll be presented with a New Legend View dialog box (Figure 11.35) where you can name the legend and set the scale. For this legend, name it WALL LEGEND and choose 1″ = 1′-0″ [1:10] for the scale.

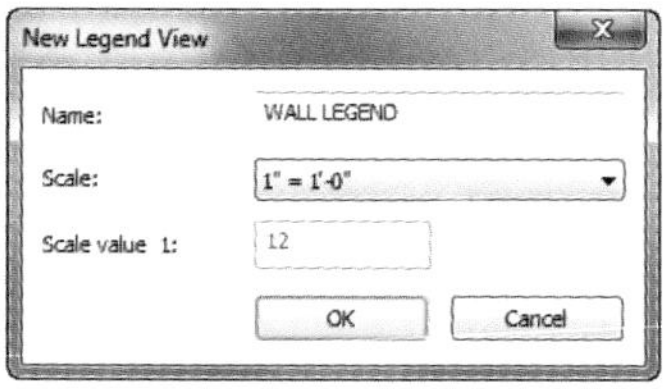

FIGURE 11.35 Creating a legend

The legend you've created will look like a blank view. At this point, it's up to you to add content. The simplest type of legend would be adding notes such as plan or demolition notes that would appear in each of your floor plans. You could do this simply by using the Text tool and adding text within this legend view; however, in this example you want to add more than just text.

To add wall types or any other family to the legend view, expand the Families tree in the Project Browser and navigate to the Wall family. Expand this node and then expand the Basic Wall Node. Select the `Interior - 4 7/8″ Partition (1-Hr)` wall type and drag it into the view.

With the family inserted into the view, it will appear as a 3′ [1000 mm] long plan wall. Change your view's detail level from Coarse to Medium or Fine so you can see the detail within the wall. With that done, highlight the inserted wall and look at the Modify | Legend Components settings in the Options Bar (Figure 11.36).

FIGURE 11.36 Select a legend component to access its properties in the Options Bar.

This menu will be consistent for any of the family types you insert. The menu consists of three sections:

Family   This drop-down menu allows you to select different family types and operates just like the Type Selector does for other elements within the model.

View   The View option lets you change the type of view from Plan to Section.

Host Length   This option changes the overall length (or in the case of sections, height) of the element selected.

Let's make some minor adjustments to the wall. Let's change View to Section and change Host Length to 1'-6" [500 mm].

The wall now looks like a sectional element. By adding some simple text we can embellish the wall type to better explain the elements you're viewing (Figure 11.37).

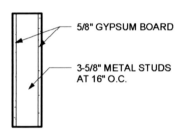

FIGURE 11.37 Add other annotation to embellish the wall type section.

Continue the exercise by adding the Exterior - EIFS on Metal Stud wall type to the legend along with some additional text notes.

THE ESSENTIALS AND BEYOND

The process of embellishing the model to reflect the design intent and detailing gets easier with practice. Remember that you won't have all the detail you need in the model to show the details you'll need in your documents. By embellishing the callouts and sections with additional information, you can quickly add the detailed information you will need to show.

THE ESSENTIALS AND BEYOND *(Continued)*

ADDITIONAL EXERCISES:

▶ You need to detail the window head condition for a full set of documents. Using the section you've already created, create a detail view of the window head, and using the same tools and workflow demonstrated in this chapter, add a similar level of detail to the condition. Some of the elements—like keynotes or some of the filled regions—can be reused from the previous detail, making this effort a bit quicker. Don't be afraid to copy and paste filled regions or other elements from one detail to another.

▶ In this chapter, you added a level of detail to the window family by adding some CAD details. Replicate the same level of detail in the head condition. You can reuse the information in the sill to expedite the process.

CHAPTER 12

Creating Drawing Sets

While the industry continues to move toward a 3D BIM model as a construction deliverable, today we still need to produce 2D documents for a construction set. Fortunately because of Revit, we can create these sets with more accuracy and dependability than in the past. In this chapter, you will work on taking the elements and creating documentation.

In this chapter, we're going to introduce a scenario that will mimic what might happen on a real project in preliminary design. You'll be using the Residence.rvt model from the book's web page (**www.sybex.com/go/ revit2012essentials**) in the Chapter 12 folder.

Here's the story: You have recently completed some design work in advance of your upcoming pricing package for a residential design project. You will need to lay the plans, elevations, and perspectives out on some sheets for the package. But you want to help the contractor with some quantities, so you also want to include some schedules. With this scenario in mind, you need to lay out the views already created onto sheets, create some schedules, and then get the drawing set printed.

In this chapter, you learn the following skills:

▶ **Creating schedules**

▶ **Placing views on sheets**

▶ **Printing documents**

Creating Schedules

Schedules are lists and quantities of elements and element properties within the model. They itemize objects, including building families such as walls, doors, and windows; calculate quantities, areas, and volumes; and quantify elements such as the number of sheets, keynotes, and so on. They are another way to view a Revit model. Once created, they are dynamically kept up-to-date with any changes that occur to the model itself.

Understanding Schedules

Certification
Objective

In a project workflow, creating schedules of objects, areas, or quantities is usually one of the most laborious tasks for architects. When this process is performed manually, it can take a very long time and typically results in errors requiring much checking and rechecking of the information. In Revit, all the elements have information about their properties defined within the model. You also have the option to add information or categories to any existing element. For example, in Revit, doors have properties such as size, material, fire rating, and cost. All of this information can be scheduled and quantified. As those doors are changed within Revit, the properties update in the schedule.

Revit lets you schedule elements based on the element's properties. This means that almost anything placed in a Revit model can be scheduled and quantified. Because the schedule is simply viewing the elements within the model in a non-graphical way, making change to the elements in a schedule view makes changes to the element in the model, and vice versa.

WINDOW SCHEDULE				
WINDOW TYPE	Type Mark	WIDTH	HEIGHT	COUNT
Double Hung: 32" x 82"	A	2' - 8"	6' - 10"	5
Double Hung: 34" x 82"	B	2' - 10"	6' - 10"	2
Double Hung: 28" x 63.5"	C	2' - 4"	5' - 3 1/2"	1
Casement: 18" x 54"	D	1' - 6"	4' - 8"	1
Double Hung: 29" x 60"	E	2' - 5"	5' - 0"	6
Fixed: 29" X 48"	F	2' - 5"	4' - 0"	1
Double Hung: 29" x 64 3/4"	G	2' - 5"	5' - 4 3/4"	1
Casement: 18" x 64.75"	H	1' - 6"	5' - 4 3/4"	1
Fixed: 36" X 12"	J	3' - 0"	1' - 0"	2

Revit has several types of schedules. They can all be accessed from the Create panel of the View tab. The Schedule flyout is shown in the margin. There are five primary types of schedules you can create using Revit. Let's look at each:

Schedule/Quantity   This is the most commonly used schedule type in Revit. This schedule allows you to list and quantify all the element category types in Revit. You would use this type to make door schedules, wall schedules, window schedules, and so on. These schedule types are limited to scheduling properties within the same category.

Material Takeoff   This type of schedule lists all the materials and subcomponents of any Revit family category. You can use a material takeoff to schedule any material that is placed in a component or assembly. For example, you might want to know the cubic yardage of concrete within the model. Regardless of whether the concrete is in a wall or floor or column, you can tell the schedule to report the total amount of that material in the project. Material takeoffs will report material properties across multiple categories.

Sheet List   This schedule allows you to create a list of all the sheets in the project.

Note Block   This schedule lists the notes that are applied to elements and assemblies in your project. You can also use a note block to list the annotation symbols (centerlines, north arrows) used in a project.

View List   This schedule shows a list of all the views in the Project Browser and their properties.

Each of these schedule types has a host of categories that you can mix and match to make schedules and track elements within the model. All of these schedules are broken down into some common elements that allow you to build and customize your schedules. Let's step through these elements and see how they can be used.

To begin a schedule, select Schedule/Quantity since it is the most widely used of schedule types. Selecting any of these schedule types will give you the New Schedule dialog box (Figure 12.1).

FIGURE 12.1 Creating a new schedule

This dialog box allows you to choose the category you would like to schedule. As you move through the list on the left, you can see a host of different schedule categories, as listed here:

Areas (Gross and Rentable)	Gutters	Rooms
Casework	Lighting Fixtures	Site
Ceilings	Mass	Slab Edges
Curtain Panels	Mass Floors	Specialty Equipment
Curtain Systems	Mechanical Equip.	Stairs
Curtain Wall Mullions	Parking	Structural Columns
Doors	Planting	Structural Foundations
Electrical Equipment	Plumbing Fixtures	Structural Framing
Electrical Fixtures	Property Line Seg.	Topography
Fascias	Property Lines	Wall Sweeps
Floors	Railings	Walls
Furniture	Ramps	Windows
Furniture Systems	Roofs	

If there aren't enough categories for you to choose from to create customized schedules, Revit provides a venue to add additional options. At the bottom-left corner of the New Schedule dialog box is the Show Categories From All Disciplines check box. Selecting this check box gives you the ability to schedule elements from MEP and Structural categories. This option can be useful when you have those disciplines supplying Revit files to you and you are linking them into your architectural model.

Revit also gives you the opportunity to create schedules that span categories. The first option in the dialog box in Figure 12.1 is the Multi-Category schedule. You might want to schedule all the casework and furnishings in a project simultaneously. Or perhaps you want to schedule all the windows and doors if they are being ordered from the same manufacturer. A Multi-Category schedule allows you to combine a number of categories into one schedule. One of the limits of this schedule type is that you cannot schedule host elements (walls, floors, ceilings, and so on) but only their materials and family components.

With this description in mind, let's look at the other options when creating a schedule. Choose Walls and click OK. Doing so opens a new dialog box called Schedule Properties. Here, you can set the various properties of a schedule that define not only how it looks, but what information it reports.

There are five tabs across the top: Fields, Filter, Sorting/Grouping, Formatting, and Appearance. Each of these controls different aspects of the schedule. Let's step through each of these tabs and see how they affect the look and reporting of the schedule:

Fields   The Fields tab (Figure 12.2) lets you select the data that will appear in your schedule. For the wall schedule, it shows all the properties available in the wall family (we chose Family And Type, Type Mark, and Volume). The list of available fields on the left will vary based on the family you chose to schedule. If you've added any project-based parameters to those family categories, they will be available here as well. Also notice at the lower-left corner is the option Include Elements In Linked Files. Enabling this option allows you to schedule across multiple files and can be a great tool on larger projects.

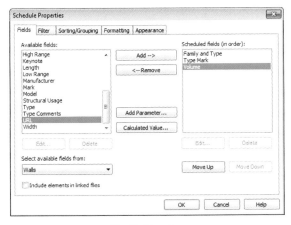

FIGURE 12.2 The Fields tab

Filter   On the Filter tab (Figure 12.3), you can filter out the data you don't wish to show in your schedule. Filters work like common database functions. For example, you can filter out all the sheets in a set that don't begin with the letter A. Or you can filter a material list so that it shows only items containing Concrete.

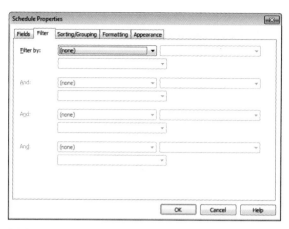

FIGURE 12.3 The Filter tab

Sorting/Grouping   The Sorting/Grouping tab (Figure 12.4) lets you control the order in which information is displayed and which elements control that order. For instance, if you are creating a sheet index you can choose to sort by Sheet Number or Sheet Name, depending on how you'd like the information displayed. You can also decide whether you want to show every instance of an item or only the categories for a family by using the Itemize Every Instance check box at the bottom.

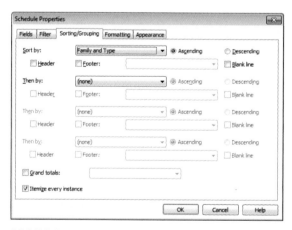

FIGURE 12.4 The Sorting/Grouping tab

Formatting   The Formatting tab (Figure 12.5) controls the display heading for each field and whether the field is visible on the schedule. It also controls other elements of the field, such as justification, display name, and orientation of the header. This tab also allows you to use the Calculate Totals check box. Not all Revit fields will calculate their total values at the bottom of the schedule. By highlighting the field on the left, you can check the Calculate Totals box and show a sum at the bottom for any numerical column.

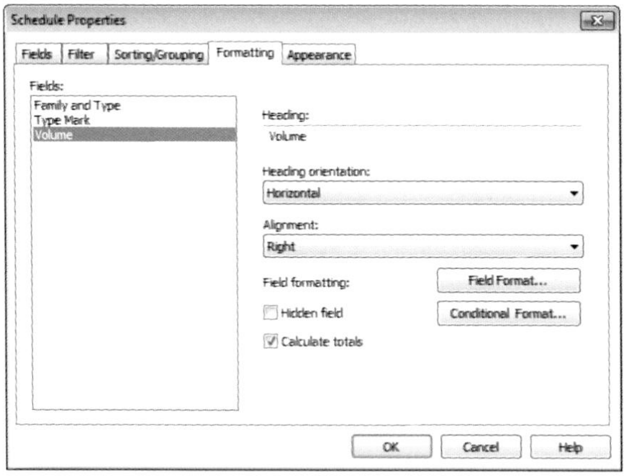

FIGURE 12.5 The Formatting tab

Appearance   The Appearance tab (Figure 12.6) controls the graphical aspects of the schedule, such as font size and style of text for each of the columns and headers in the schedule. It also allows you to turn the schedule grid lines on and off, as well as modify the line thickness for the grid and boundary lines.

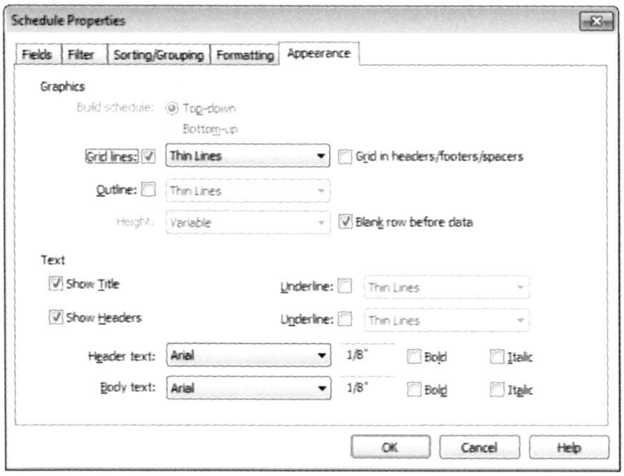

FIGURE 12.6 The Appearance tab

Once you've established the fields and look of your schedule, clicking OK gives you a preliminary layout. This layout can be modified at any time during the project, but it gives you a basis from which to begin. To modify the schedule at any time, simply click the Element Properties button or right-click and choose Element Properties from the context menu.

Schedules have their own special tab on the ribbon that is active when you are viewing the schedule outside of a sheet. The tab (Figure 12.7) allows you to select the properties, add and delete rows, and show or hide columns within the schedule.

FIGURE 12.7 The Schedule tab buttons

Another key feature of this menu bar is Highlight In Model. This button allows you to select any element in the schedule from any cell and locate that element in the model. Let's say you want to locate a particular door from your door schedule. Highlight the door in the schedule and click the Highlight In Model button, and Revit will take you to a different view with that door highlighted. This feature can be a useful way to locate elements in the model, especially for larger models.

Now that you have an idea of the elements that compose a schedule, let's return to our demonstration workflow and create a Rentable Area schedule based on the areas we've defined earlier in this chapter.

Making Schedules

Now that we've discussed some of the features of the Schedule tool, let's open the Residence.rvt model and make a couple of schedules. When you first open the model, you'll notice that there are several views and sheets already created. This model is a work in progress—it's a private residence of 1,230 square feet. The project is a renovation of a 1890s two-story brick. In the design, all the interior walls have been eliminated and put on a "demo" phase, which keeps the 19′ clear span as open as possible. All new interior walls have been added and the entire interior refreshed within the historic shell. Since the renovation is so substantial, the designer chose to replace all the existing original windows with new insulated, wood windows. To assist the window manufacturer with the custom sizes, you need to create a window schedule. To begin, choose the Schedule/Quantity button from the Schedule drop-down menu on the View tab.

The New Schedule dialog box (shown earlier in Figure 12.1) opens. Here you'll make a series of selections to create the schedule. Follow these steps:

1. From the Categories list, select Window at the bottom. Since this project has multiple phases, you want to make sure the phase is set to New Construction—you don't need to schedule the windows you're removing. Click OK when you've finished.

2. We're now going to step through the five tabs in the Schedule Properties dialog box. This will help you format the schedule and choose what you'd like to see. Starting with the Fields tab, choose the following fields:

   Type   This represents the family type or, in our case, the window name.

   Type Mark   This is the letter that you'll use on the elevations to define the window type in your document.

   Width   Specify the window width.

   Height   Specify the window height.

   Count   Specify the number of times a window type appears in the model.

   Choose these fields from the Fields list on the left and, using the Add button, move them to the right (Figure 12.8). You can use the Move Up or Move Down button to change the order of the fields.

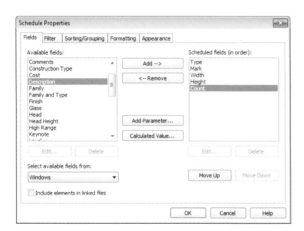

FIGURE 12.8 Adding fields to our Window schedule

3. Choose the Sorting/Grouping tab. From the Sort By drop-down, choose Type.

4. In our schedule, you want to make the window count read as it would in a spreadsheet: right-justified. Choose the Formatting tab and select Count from the list on the left. Change the Alignment setting to Right (Figure 12.9). In the same way, you can choose the Type Mark field and choose to center-justify it so all the letters will align nicely.

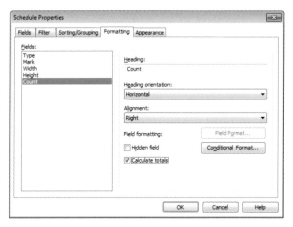

FIGURE 12.9 Formatting the schedule

5. We're going to leave the rest of the schedule at the defaults, so click OK. Revit will follow the directions you have given it to display the schedule that appears in Figure 12.10. Note that you can also change any of the heading names by simply typing inside the box. Since Type Mark isn't a value that most people relate to, we've simplified it to Type and made the rest of the field names all uppercase.

WINDOW SCHEDULE				
OPENING SIZE	TYPE	WIDTH	HEIGHT	COUNT
18" x 54"	D	1' - 6"	4' - 8"	1
18" x 64.75"	H	1' - 6"	5' - 4 3/4"	1
18" x 82"	FF	1' - 6"	6' - 10"	1
28" x 63.5"	C	2' - 4"	5' - 3 1/2"	1
29" X 48"	F	2' - 5"	4' - 0"	1
29" x 60"	E	2' - 5"	5' - 0"	6
29" x 64 3/4"	G	2' - 5"	5' - 4 3/4"	1
32" x 82"	A	2' - 8"	6' - 10"	5
34" x 82"	B	2' - 10"	6' - 10"	2
36" X 12"	J	3' - 0"	1' - 0"	2

FIGURE 12.10 The Window schedule

Following these simple guidelines, you can create all kinds of schedules in your project.

Creating a Room Schedule

Creating other schedule types is fairly simple if you follow the guidelines we just went over and step through the tabs in the Schedule Properties dialog box. Since you have one schedule under your belt, let's try another one—this time, you'll create a room schedule. To do this, begin by choosing the Schedule/Quantity button from the Schedule drop-down on the View tab, and then follow these steps:

1. Choose Rooms from the New Schedule dialog box and click OK.

2. Choose the following fields from the Schedule Properties dialog box:

   ▶ Number

   ▶ Name

   ▶ Floor Finish

   ▶ North Wall

   ▶ East Wall

   ▶ South Wall

   ▶ West Wall

   ▶ Area

   ▶ Comments

   When you're done, click OK.

3. On the Sorting tab, choose Number.

4. On the Formatting tab, choose Area and justify to the right. Click OK to get the schedule you see in Figure 12.11.

ROOM SCHEDULE								
NUMBER	NAME	FLOOR	NORTH WAL	EAST WALL	SOUTH WAL	WEST WALL	AREA	REMARKS
100	LIVING ROOM	WOOD					307 SF	a.
101	DINING ROOM	WOOD					99 SF	a.
102	OFFICE	WOOD					71 SF	a.
104	KITCHEN						134 SF	
103	1/2 BATH	WOOD					25 SF	a.
200	BEDROOM 1	WOOD					161 SF	a.
201	BATH 1						39 SF	
205	HALL	WOOD					95 SF	a.
202	BEDROOM 3	WOOD					121 SF	a.
203	BATH 2						41 SF	
206	Room						7 SF	
207	Room						15 SF	
208	Room						7 SF	
209	Room						22 SF	
210	Room						12 SF	

FIGURE 12.11 Our Room schedule

Now, let's do something slightly different with this schedule. Since four of our columns are dealing with wall finishes, let's add a header to those columns so you can group them under one header, Wall Finishes. To do so, start by selecting the four headers as shown in Figure 12.12. Grab one with your mouse and holding down the left mouse button, drag across to select all four.

FIGURE 12.12
Selecting the wall finishes

With the four columns selected, choose the Group button from the Headers panel. This will give you a new row above your existing headers. Now you can type **Wall Finishes** to complete your schedule (Figure 12.13).

| ROOM SCHEDULE | | | | | | | | |
| | | | WALL FINISHES | | | | | |
NUMBER	NAME	FLOOR	NORTH WALL	EAST WALL	SOUTH WALL	WEST WALL	AREA	REMARKS
100	LIVING ROOM	WOOD					307 SF	a.
101	DINING ROOM	WOOD					99 SF	a.
102	OFFICE	WOOD					71 SF	a.
104	KITCHEN						134 SF	
103	1/2 BATH	WOOD					25 SF	a.
200	BEDROOM 1	WOOD					161 SF	a.
201	BATH 1						39 SF	
205	HALL	WOOD					95 SF	a.
202	BEDROOM 3	WOOD					121 SF	a.
203	BATH 2						41 SF	
206	Room						7 SF	
207	Room						15 SF	
208	Room						7 SF	
209	Room						22 SF	
210	Room						12 SF	

FIGURE 12.13   **The Room schedule**

Once this schedule is complete, you'll notice that some of the fields already have data in them. This is due to the fact that some of this information is generated automatically by Revit (like room areas) and some of it was added earlier in this process by adding room numbers to the plans or room names. Remember, schedules are just a nongraphical way of viewing the model—changes to the schedule will alter what you see in the model.

Creating a Sheet List

Sheet List is a different schedule type that you can create in Revit. The Sheet List schedule allows you to create a list of sheets in your project that are found within the Project Browser. This can be handy, especially on larger projects where the sheet list can tend to get long. This tool is also located in the Schedules flyout on the View tab.

This schedule has a feature that allows you to create placeholders for sheets that are not yet created or will not be a part of your discipline's drawings. You can use this feature to create full sheet schedules including all consultant drawings. It also allows you to create placeholder entries in the sheet schedule before you've created the sheets.

In our sample workflow, you have created several drawings and sheets, and you want to schedule them so you can add a sheet list to your drawings. To do so, begin by selecting the Sheet List tool from the Schedules flyout.

1. You'll see the now familiar Revit schedule dialog box starting with the Fields tab. From this tab, you need to select two fields from the categories on the left and move them to the column on the right. Select the Sheet Number and Sheet Name categories (Figure 12.14).

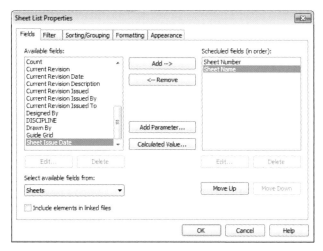

FIGURE 12.14 Creating the sheet list

2. On the Sorting/Grouping tab, choose to sort by Sheet Number and make sure the Itemize Every Instance check box is checked (Figure 12.15).

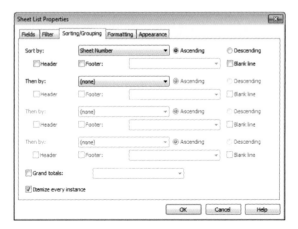

FIGURE 12.15 Sorting by Sheet Number

3. Now, choose the Filter tab. You'll be creating a sheet index for your presentation sheets, so you don't want to include all the sheets in the set. You already have some of the construction documentation sheets in the file (the A series sheets), and you don't want those reported in your schedule. You want to filter out all the sheets that don't begin with the letter K (for the Kitchen sheets in this set).

4. On the Filter tab, choose to filter by Sheet Number.

5. From the next drop-down, choose Begins With.

6. In the third field, enter the letter **A**. The filter should look like Figure 12.16.

7. Be sure to use an uppercase A, as the Boolean queries in Revit are case sensitive. When you're done, click OK.

   What you should have is a schedule with nothing in it but sheet numbers that begin with the letter A. Now you need to populate the rest of the sheet list.

Certification Objective

8. To begin adding sheets to the sheet list, select the New Sheet button from the Create panel. This will give you a row with a blank for both of your headings, Sheet Number and Sheet Name.

9. To your sheet list, you'll add one of the two sheets you need for this set. You need a Plan sheet – A100. Clicking the New Sheet button will give you the New Sheet dialog box so you can add a sheet to the set (Figure 12.17).

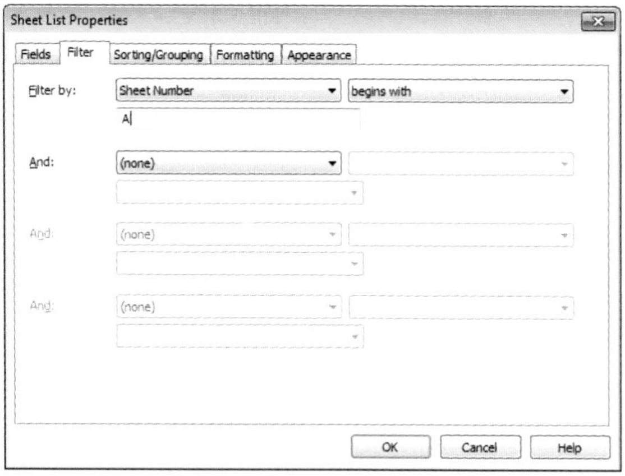

FIGURE 12.16 Filtering out sheets

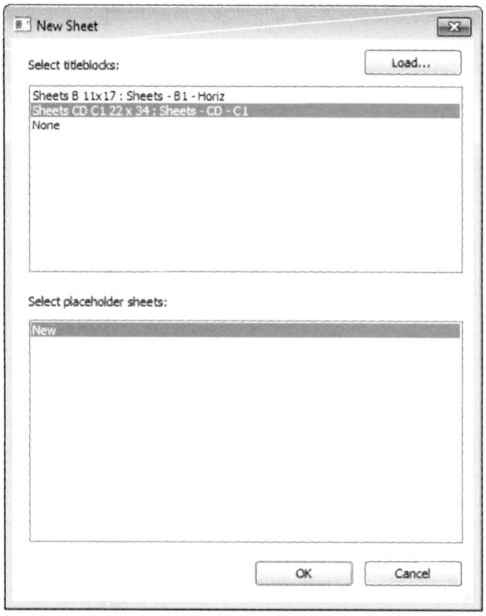

FIGURE 12.17 Adding sheets to the list

10. Choose the 22×34 Sheet CD – C1 sheet and click OK. This will add a sheet to your project browser. By default, the sheets are added in sequential order, so whichever sheet was added the most recently will be the next sheet in the list. In this example, it will appear as A051, right after the A050 sheet. Right-click the sheet and choose Rename from the context menu. Rename the sheet to **A100 – Floor Plans.**

You'll see a blank sheet in your view window. Closing this view will take you back to the schedule view with your new sheet in the list (Figure 12.18).

SHEET LIST	
SHEET NO	Sheet Name
A050	SITE PLAN
A100	FLOOR PLANS
A150	REFLECTED CEILING PLANS
A500	INTERIOR ELEVATIONS

FIGURE 12.18
Adding sheets to the set

Placing Views on Sheets

Throughout this book, you have created several different kinds of views, from plans to elevations to perspectives. Eventually, you will need to lay out those views onto sheets so they can be printed or converted to PDF format and sent to clients or team members for review.

Creating sheets in Revit is very easy. As you've already seen, they can be created through a Sheet List schedule. You can also create sheets by right-clicking the Sheet node in the Project Browser and selecting New Sheet from the context menu. Regardless of which method you use to create them, let's walk through laying these views out on sheets and see how each view can be further manipulated once it's placed on a sheet.

Adding Floor Plans to the Sheet

Certification
Objective

Since you have already created a series of views, let's use the sheet you've just made for this purpose. Open the A100 – Floor Plans sheet in the view window by double-clicking it in the Project Browser. Now, let's add our first view: the Basement floor plan. To begin, drag and drop the plan from the Project Browser and onto the sheet. The view will show at the proper scale and with a View Title already established. You can then drag the view across the sheet to place it where you'd like to have it (place it on the left side—you'll add more). Figure 12.19 shows the view placed on the sheet.

Now, since we have a bit more space left on the sheet, let's add a couple of other views. Add Level 1 and Level 2 by dragging and dropping them from the Project Browser and on to the sheet. You should notice when you're placing your second and third views on the sheet that you will be presented with an outline of the plan view with a dashed line in the center of the view. This is an alignment tool; Revit is assuming that you want the plans to align on the sheet and it is intelligent enough to aid you in this process. You can casually drag the views around on the sheets enough to find the alignment lines and to ensure that all your plans will line up (Figure 12.20). Your sheet full of views should look like Figure 12.21.

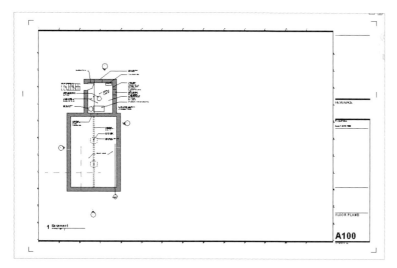

FIGURE 12.19 Placing the view on a sheet

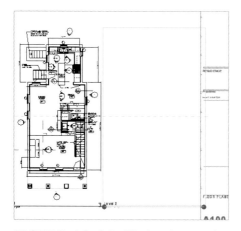

FIGURE 12.20 Aligning views on sheets

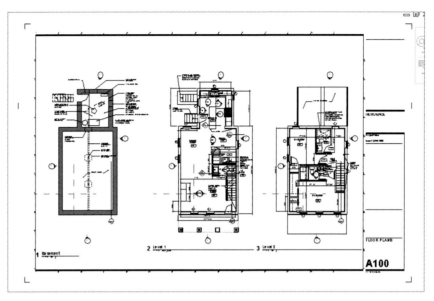

FIGURE 12.21 All the views placed on the sheet

Once the views are placed on a sheet, there will inevitably be a bit of cleanup you'll want to do to the drawings to get everything placed properly and looking good. First of all, by default, Revit will place the View tag in roughly the same place for each view, and that might not be the location you ultimately want it to be in. Revit will also number the views sequentially (1, 2, 3,…) in order of placement.

Let's adjust the view tags a bit on the sheets. To adjust the text in the tags, start by selecting the view itself—*not the tag*. To adjust the tag location, you'll want to select the tag itself.

1. Start by selecting the view for the Basement. The tag will highlight in blue. You want to change two things on the tag: the number and the length of the line.

2. Select the number 1 and change it to A1 to reference the ConDoc drawing system—letters vertically along the side of the sheet and numbers across the bottom of the sheet. Move the detail to the location on the lower-left corner of the detail on the drawing sheet.

3. Next, using the blue grips on the view tag line, drag the right grip closer to the end of the Basement text. Your tag will look like Figure 12.22.

FIGURE 12.22 The edited view tag

4. Now, clearly you can't leave the view tag there as it's falling off the left edge of the sheet—you need to move it to a better position. Click off the tag, anywhere in the view, to deselect the tag. You can also press the Esc key twice or select the Modify arrow at the upper left. Then, select the tag itself. It will highlight blue again, but without the grips on the line. Now, you can click and drag the tag to any location on the sheet (Figure 12.23).

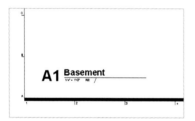

FIGURE 12.23 Moving the view tag

5. Do the same to the other two views. Rename Level 1 to **A6** and Level 2 to **A11** to match their location on the sheet as shown, shortening the view tag lines to a more appropriate length (Figure 12.24).

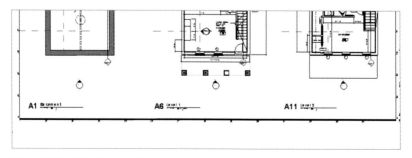

FIGURE 12.24 Laying out the rest of the sheet views

To finish organizing your sheet, you want to add a few lines to divide the different views. You can do so easily by using the Detail Line tool 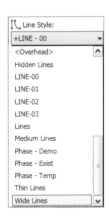, which can be found on the Annotate tab.

1. Choose Detail Line from the Detail Panel.

2. Doing so activates the Modify | Place Detail Lines context menu. From the Line Style panel on the far right, choose Wide Lines from the drop-down.

3. Once the desired line style is selected, you're ready to start drawing lines. By default, the straight line tool is active, and you can select one of the nodes on the sheet between views and draw a vertical line between the Basement and Level 1 and between Level 1 and Level 2 (Figure 12.25).

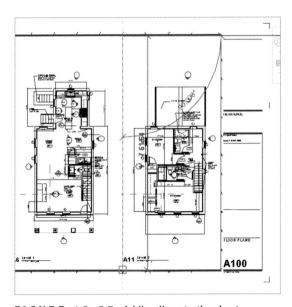

FIGURE 12.25 Adding lines to the sheet

With these dividing lines in place, you notice that one of your annotations in the Basement view is a little too close to the drafting line (Figure 12.26). You want to adjust it.

To do this, you could simply open the view and adjust the text box, but you wouldn't have the sheet as a reference. Instead, you're going to use a command called Activate View.

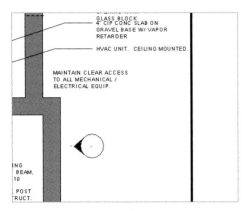

FIGURE 12.26 Adjusting text
in the sheet view

Activating a view is like working in model space through paperspace in CAD. You're working on the actual view but you're doing so while it is placed on the sheet. This approach allows you the benefit of seeing how changes to the view will affect the layout of the view on the sheet.

1. To begin, right-click the view and choose Activate View from the context menu (Figure 12.27).

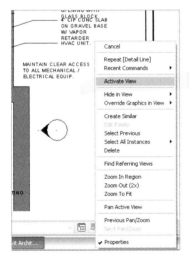

FIGURE 12.27 Activating the view

2. With the view activated, you'll notice that the other views have become grayed out. Revit is showing you only the elements you can currently edit—those within the view. Select the text box that you've identified and, using the grips, drag the right grip inward so the text wraps (Figure 12.28).

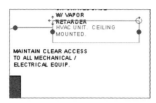

FIGURE 12.28
Modifying the text box

3. To complete your edits, you now need to deactivate the view. Right-click anywhere outside the view and choose Deactivate View from the context menu (Figure 12.29).

FIGURE 12.29
Deactivating the view

Adding the Schedules

With your A100 sheet laid out and ready to print, you can quickly finish your sheet set by adding the Window schedule you created earlier. Adding a schedule is just like adding any other view—you simply drag and drop it from the Project Browser onto the sheet.

1. Open sheet G000 Cover Sheet by double-clicking it in the Project Browser (Figure 12.30).

2. Grab the Window schedule from the Project Browser and drag and drop it into the open area on the sheet.

FIGURE 12.30 G000 Cover Sheet

With the schedule on the sheet, it looks like it needs a bit of adjustment. You can redefine the column spacing so you can make any visual adjustments to the schedule while it is on the sheet to help it read better. Such adjustments do not change the actual schedule but just its appearance on the sheet itself.

To do so, highlight the schedule by selecting it. The schedule will turn blue and you'll have a few new grips to help you make changes (Figure 12.31). The blue inverted triangles at the top of each column allow you to modify the column widths. Grab one and drag it left or right to change the column sizing.

OPENING SIZE	TYPE	WIDTH	HEIGHT	COUNT
\multicolumn{5}{c}{WINDOW SCHEDULE}				
18" x 54"	D	1' - 6"	4' - 8"	1
18" x 64.75"	H	1' - 6"	5' - 4 3/4"	1
18" x 82"	FF	1' - 6"	6' - 10"	1
28" x 63.5"	C	2' - 4"	5' - 3 1/2"	1
29" X 48"	F	2' - 5"	4' - 0"	1
29" x 60"	E	2' - 5"	5' - 0"	6
29" x 64 3/4"	G	2' - 5"	5' - 4 3/4"	1
32" x 82"	A	2' - 8"	6' - 10"	5
34" x 82"	B	2' - 10"	6' - 10"	2
36" X 12"	J	3' - 0"	1' - 0"	2

FIGURE 12.31 Modifying the schedule on the sheet

You'll also notice a blue cut symbol . This cut symbol allows you to break the schedule into parts while on the same sheet. This can be especially handy if you have a long schedule like a room or door schedule and it has too many rows to fit on your sheet vertically. Selecting this tool breaks the schedule in half (and you can break it into half again and again) so that you can take advantage of the horizontal real estate on your sheet. If you choose to separate your schedule in this fashion, it still retains all the necessary information and all the portions continue to automatically fill themselves out dynamically as a single schedule would. You also have the opportunity to change the overall height of the schedule once it is broken up by grabbing the grips at the bottom of the schedule and dragging up and down.

With your schedule on the sheet and the columns properly formatted, you can drag the schedule around on the sheet until it's located where you'd like to have it. To move it around, click and hold the left mouse button down on the schedule. As you move it around on the sheet, you'll notice that like other views in Revit, the schedule will justify with the other schedules on the sheet and give you a light green dashed line to help align the two. Your finished sheet will look like Figure 12.32.

WINDOW SCHEDULE				
OPENING SIZE	TYPE	WIDTH	HEIGHT	COUNT
18" x 54"	D	1' - 6"	4' - 8"	1
18" x 64.75"	H	1' - 6"	5' - 4 3/4"	1
18" x 82"	FF	1' - 6"	6' - 10"	1
28" x 63.5"	C	2' - 4"	5' - 3 1/2"	1
29" X 48"	F	2' - 5"	4' - 0"	1
29" x 60"	E	2' - 5"	5' - 0"	6
29" x 64 3/4"	G	2' - 5"	5' - 4 3/4"	1
32" x 82"	A	2' - 8"	6' - 10"	5
34" x 82"	B	2' - 10"	6' - 10"	2
36" X 12"	J	3' - 0"	1' - 0"	2

FIGURE 12.32 The finished sheet G000

Printing Documents

With all of your documents and sheets laid out, you will eventually need to get the sheets out of Revit and into a printed format. If you've been working in the Windows environment, you'll find that printing from Revit is straightforward, because it's similar to other Windows-based applications.

The Print Dialog Box

To print, you do not need to be in any particular view or sheet. Select the Application menu and choose Print ➢ Print to open the dialog box shown in Figure 12.33. All the features for printing are found here. Let's step through this dialog box and explore each element.

FIGURE 12.33 Print dialog box

The drop-down menu at the top of this dialog box allows you to select the printer or plotter you wish to print to. This can be a physical printer or a virtual one (like Adobe Acrobat Distiller). You add printers to this list using your Windows Printer control panel. Most of the controls you need to use can be found at the bottom of this dialog box in the Settings section on the right and the Print Range on the left.

Print Settings

The printing environment is set up using the Print Setup dialog box (Figure 12.34). Here you set up a printer and settings for printing. You can save these settings with a name so that you can reuse them in later Revit sessions. These settings can also be transferred to other Revit projects if need be, using the Transfer Project Standards tool located on the Manage tab. Let's take a look at some of the printing options available to you.

Hidden Lines Views

Views in Revit can be displayed in four graphic modes: Wireframe, Hidden Line, Shaded, and Shaded With Edges. The most commonly used type is Hidden Line. You'll choose this type for floor plans, sections, and elevations, and sometimes even for 3D.

Revit lets you select whether you wish to print this type of view with vector processing or raster processing of the hidden lines. Vector is faster; however, you need to be aware of some nuances when working with hidden line views. For example, transparent materials (like glass) print transparent with raster processing but opaque with vector processing.

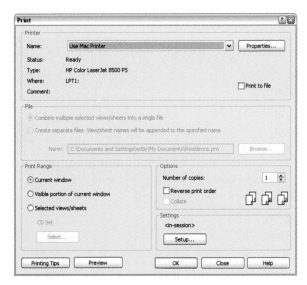

FIGURE 12.34 The Print Setup dialog box

Options

The Options pane is at the lower left in the Print Setup dialog box. The pane includes these options:

View Links In Blue   View links are hyperlinked tags that lead you from one view to another or from a sheet to a view. They appear blue in Revit and print black by default, but you can specify to print them in blue, which is how they appear on the screen.

Hide Ref/Work Planes; Hide Scope Boxes; Hide Crop Boundaries   These three check boxes let you decide whether to print various Revit-specific graphics, including reference planes, scope boxes, and crop boundaries.

Hide Unreferenced View Tags   During the course of a project, you may create a lot of elevation tags, section flags, or detail callouts for working purposes that you don't wish to be printed in the final documents or placed on any sheet. These view tags are referred to as *unreferenced*, and Revit gives you the option to not print them.

Once all of your options are set, you have the ability to save the settings so you can quickly reuse them on future prints. Choose the Save As button on the right, name the setting **11×17**, and click OK. Now, click OK to close this dialog box. This will take you back to the Print dialog box.

Print Range

The other important part of the Print dialog box is the Print Range. In this section, you can define exactly what areas, sheets, or views you want to print. It includes these options:

Current Window   This option prints the full extent of the open view, regardless of what extents of that view are visible currently on your screen.

Visible Portion Of Current Window   This option prints only what you see in the frame of the open window framed for the sheet size you've selected.

Selected Views/Sheets   This option allows you to define a reusable list of views, sheets, or any combinations of views and sheets. This way, you can essentially batch-print a job by sending large quantities of sheets to the printer in one shot and save these selections for later print jobs.

This dialog box lets you pick any view or sheet to include in the View/Sheet Set. If you only want to include sheets in a set, use the Show options at the bottom of the dialog box to shorten the visible list. Doing so allows you to select only sheets or only views if you so choose.

This is a great tool to help define print lists. Some examples of what you might want to use these selections for would be a 100 percent construction document package or a specific set of presentation sheets.

1. In our example, you want to print a set of sheets. Deselect the View check box at the bottom of this dialog box and Revit will display a list of the sheets you've created to date.

2. Next, check the A series sheets, the D100 sheet, and the G000 sheet you just added the schedule to (Figure 12.35).

3. Since you will more than likely want to print this set again, choose Save As from the menu on the right and name the set **Set 1**. This will keep your current collection of sheets together, and if you want to reprint this set, grab the set name from the drop-down menu. Remember, if you add more drawings to the set, by default they won't be added to this print set. You'll need to revisit this dialog box, add the sheets, and click the Save button. For now, click OK to close this dialog box.

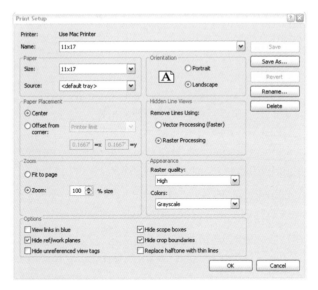

FIGURE 12.35 Checking the desired sheets

4. Our final dialog box looks like Figure 12.36. Clicking OK here will print the six selected drawings to the printer listed at the top. Clicking Close saves your print setup and closes the dialog box.

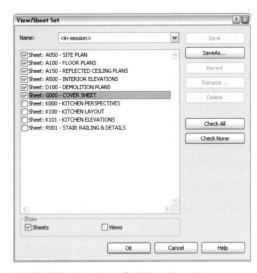

FIGURE 12.36 Finishing the prints

THE ESSENTIALS AND BEYOND

In this chapter, you learned how to quantify the elements in the model by using schedules. We used this same Schedule tool to create a standard door schedule and added a new schedule type for wall quantities. You also learned how to place all the views we've made over the course of the book onto sheets and print them. Finally, you learned how to combine these two techniques and schedule the sheets you created.

ADDITIONAL EXERCISES

▶ Create a door schedule adding the following fields:

Mark

Type

Width

Height

Thickness

Material

Finish

Comments

▶ Lay out this new schedule on sheet G000; be sure to align it with the schedule you already created on that sheet.

CHAPTER 13

Workflow and Other Revit Essentials

Understanding Revit and how to use the software is not a difficult challenge. The real challenge is determining how using Revit and BIM changes your organization's culture and your project's workflow—especially if you're coming from a CAD-based environment. Revit can be more than just a different way to draw a line. In this chapter, we'll focus on what those changes are and provide some tools on how to manage the transition.

In this chapter, you learn the following skills:

▶ **Understanding a BIM workflow**

▶ **Modeling site**

▶ **Detailing in Revit**

▶ **Performing quality control on your Revit model**

Understanding a BIM Workflow

Regardless of the workflow you have established, moving to Revit is going to be a change. You'll still need some tools to help transition from your current workflow to one using Revit. To begin, we'll cover some of the core differences between a CAD-based system and a BIM-based one.

Moving to BIM is a shift in how designers and contractors look at the design and documentation process throughout the entire life cycle of the project, from concept to occupancy. In a traditional CAD-based workflow, represented in Figure 13.1, each view is drawn separately with no inherent relationship between drawings. In this type of production environment, the team creates plans, sections, elevations, schedules, and perspectives and must coordinate any changes between files manually.

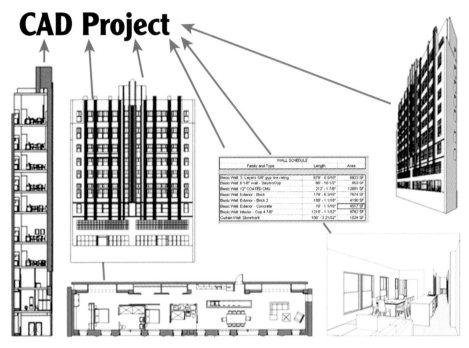

FIGURE 13.1 A CAD-based workflow

In a BIM-based workflow, the team creates a 3D, parametric model and uses this model to automatically generate the drawings necessary for documentation. Plans, sections, elevations, schedules, and perspectives are all by-products of creating an embellished a BIM model, as shown in Figure 13.2. This enhanced documentation methodology not only allows for a highly coordinated drawing set but also provides the basic model geometry necessary for analysis such as daylighting studies, energy, material takeoffs, and so on.

Using Revit becomes more than a change in software; it becomes a change in workflow and methodology. As various design specializations interact and create the building model (Figure 13.3), you can see how structure, mechanical, energy, daylight, and other factors inform design direction. You can also draw relationships between some of these elements that might not have been as obvious in a more traditionally based approach. Although some of these specialties (such as structure and mechanical) are historically separate systems, by integrating them into a single design model, you can see how they interact in relation to other systems with a building. Analysis such as daylighting can inform your building orientation and structure. Depending on your glazing, it can also affect your mechanical requirements (as solar gain). You can see some of these effects through a computational fluid dynamics (CFD) model (used to calculate airflow). Geographic information system (GIS) data will give you your relative location globally and allow you to see how much sunlight you will be receiving or what the local temperature swings will be during the course of a day. As you can see, all of these variables can easily affect building design.

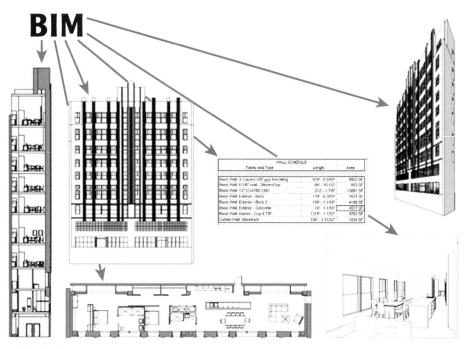

FIGURE 13.2 A BIM workflow

As with any methodological change, you'll have success if you address all the factors. Project success happens on more than a financial or chronological level. It is also determined by a team's ability to replicate successful results. A difficult aspect of transitioning to BIM is predictability. Any system or method, even if it is inherently inefficient, is at some level successful if the system is predictable. If you can say that x effort + y time will yield z result, there is an established comfort level with that system even if it is an inefficient system. When you move to BIM, the system automatically becomes unpredictable because team members need to experience the new system to establish a comfort level with the given results. No longer does x effort + y time yield z; instead, the result is unknown.

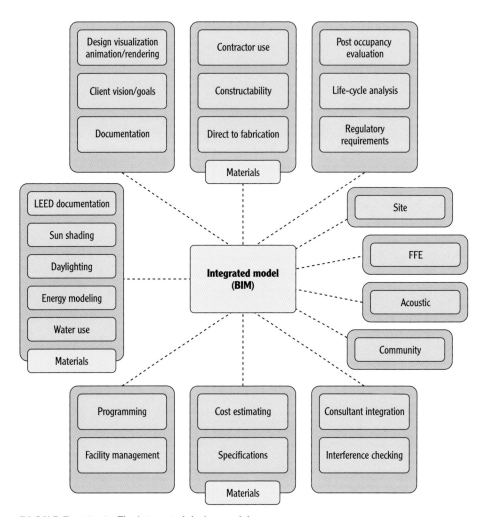

FIGURE 13.3 The integrated design model

Eventually, you reach a point of temporary diminishing returns. The amount of effort you need to put into understanding the new process feels like it has begun to exceed the value you derive from the change, and happiness plateaus. At a point during this plateau, you're put in a position where you need to perform a task in a given amount of time using the new technology. It might be represented by needing to get a schematic-level design sent out to a contractor or create something as simple as a stair. Regardless, the process is a foreign one and by its nature is unpredictable in time. You'll be faced with a decision to forge ahead using an unpredictable method or revert to a more familiar yet inefficient process.

Here your path can split. By regressing to your previous process, you'll enjoy an immediate increase in happiness with the familiarity and predictability of the former method, but this will only level out and never reach any greater heights than it did before you contemplated the initial change. If you stay the course with the new process, happiness will decrease (and frustration consequently increases) as you struggle with the change. However, eventually as the new method becomes more predictable and comfortable, your happiness can achieve greater value.

Although this might be an oversimplification of a process change, the core meaning is critical. Change can be challenging. However, to realize greater goals and adapt to an ever-changing environment both professionally and globally, you will need to rethink your process in order to achieve success. Moving to BIM is acknowledging a change in workflow and process—from abstraction to virtualization (Figure 13.4). As you transition from a traditional workflow to a BIM-based one, keep in mind the change in culture. It will help you to manage expectations, time, and team members' stress levels.

FIGURE 13.4 From abstraction to virtualization

Staffing a BIM project

As you rethink the process of design and documentation, one of the semantic changes you will need to address is staffing. A common misconception of project management when teams are first moving from CAD to BIM is that staffing the project will be the same in both workflows. This couldn't be further from the truth. When the workflow changes, staffing allocations, time to complete tasks, and percentage of work by phase are all affected as a by-product of the change of method.

In a CAD-based project, the level of effort during each of the phases is fairly well known. The industry has been using some metrics over the past several years that should be fairly familiar. There is modest effort and staffing in conceptual design and schematic design phases, and this effort builds until it crescendos during construction documentation. At this phase, a CAD project can greatly increase the number of staff in an effort to expedite the completion of the drawing set. This staff increase can be effective because the CAD drawings are typically separate files and moving lines in one drawing won't dynamically change another.

In a BIM-based framework, there is still a gradual increase of staffing and effort through conceptual design and into the schematic phase, but the effort during schematic design is greater using BIM than in CAD. During schematic design and design development, the project team is still performing all the same tasks that occur in any design process: testing design concepts, visualizations, or design iteration. The increase in effort during the early design phases allows the team to use the parametric nature of the model to significantly reduce the effort later during construction documents, allowing for a decrease in the overall effort over the project cycle.

Project Roles Using Revit

With such a significant change in the effort behind a BIM-based project flow, it's also important to understand how this can change the various roles and responsibilities for the project team. The changes in traditional roles can become a barrier to many projects successfully adopting BIM. Project managers need to be able to predict staffing and time to complete tasks throughout the project phases and have relied on past precedent of staff and project types to do this. Since a BIM-based project can significantly alter the project workflow, many of the historic timetables for task completion are no longer valid. However, a

BIM-based project can be broken down into a few primary roles that will allow you some level of predictability through the various project phases. Although the specific effort and staffing will vary between offices (and even projects), there are some general roles that will need to be accounted for on every project.

There are three primary roles on every BIM project:

Architect   Deals with design issues, code compliances, clear widths, wall types, and so on

Modeler   Creates content in 2D or in 3D

Drafter   Deals with annotations, sheet layout, view creation, and detail creation

These roles represent efforts and general tasks that you need to take into account on any Revit project. On a large project, these roles could also represent individual people, whereas on a smaller project they might be all the same person or one person might carry multiple roles. We'll now cover each of these in a bit more detail and discuss how these roles interact with the project cycle.

Architect

The role of the architect is to deal with the architectural issues revolving around the project. As the model is being created, you will naturally have to solve issues like constructability and wall types, set corridor widths, deal with department areas, and deal with other issues involving either codes or the overall architectural design. This role will be the one applying standards to the project (as in wall types, keynotes, and so on) and organizing the document set. This role will need to be present on the project from the beginning to ensure consistency of the virtual building creation and isn't necessarily limited to only one person. This role also might or might not be a "designer." Although it is possible to do early design in Revit, many project teams prefer to utilize other tools such as Google SketchUp or even pencil and trace paper. The job of the architect is steering the creation of the building within Revit. Tasks for this role include the following:

- ▶ Leading the creation of architectural elements and building from within the model

- ▶ Designing around code requirements and other building logistics

- ▶ Constructability and detailing aspects of the design

Modeler

The role of the modeler is to create all the 2D and especially the 3D content needed in the project. This content includes all the parametric families for elements such as windows, doors, casework, wall types, stairs, railings, and furnishings. Typically, this role is the responsibility of less experienced staff, who might not be able to fulfill the role of architect. These less experienced positions tend to have longer periods of undisturbed time, making them better suited to deal with some of the longer, more involved tasks in modeling content. Finally, they also tend to have some 3D experience coming out of school. They might not have worked with Revit directly but possibly with Autodesk 3ds Max or Google SketchUp, and are thereby familiar with working in a 3D environment. Tasks for this role include:

Drafter

The role of the drafter is to create sheets and views and embellish those views with annotations or other 2D content. This role will be doing the bulk of the work needed to document the project. In earlier stages of the project, this role is typically assumed by either the architect or the modeler, but as documentation gets moving into high gear, it can quickly become the role of multiple people on a larger project. Tasks for this role include the following:

- ▶ Keynoting
- ▶ Dimensioning
- ▶ Setting up sheets and views
- ▶ Creating schedules

From a staffing planning purpose, we are discussing the ideal times to bring in some of these various roles into the project. At the inception of a project design, a modeling role will be of the best use. This person can help create building form, add conceptual content, and get the massing for the building established. If you're using the conceptual modeling tools, the modeler can even do some early sustainable design calculations.

Once the project begins to take a more established form and you complete conceptual design, you'll need an architect role to step into the project. As in a typical project, you'll have to mold the form into a building by applying materials, applying wall types, and validating spatial requirements and the owner's program.

During schematic design, you'll need to include the role of the drafter to begin laying out sheets and creating views. These sheets and views don't have to be for a construction document set yet, but you'll have to establish views for any schematic design submittals. If these views are set up properly, they can be reused later for design development and construction document submittals as the model continues to gain a greater level of detail.

What you'd like to avoid for your project staffing, if possible, is adding staff during the construction document phase. In a BIM/Revit workflow, this can sometimes cause more problems than it solves and slow down the team rather than get work done faster.

Adding Team Members to Fight Fires

In many projects, there comes a time when the schedule gets tight and project management wants to add more staff to a project to meet a specific deadline. When in a 2D CAD environment, new team members would be added to help meet a deadline and would have the burden of trying to learn the architecture of the building, the thoughts behind its design, and how its various systems interact. In a Revit project, they have that same obligation, but they have the additional task of learning how the *model* goes together. The model will have constraints set against various elements (such as locking a corridor width) as well as various digital construction issues (such as how floors and walls might be tied together, what the various family names are, or workset organization). This "ramping-up" period consumes additional time.

Regardless of planning, deadlines escape the best of architects and project managers. It's a good idea to know when and how you can staff to make sure you meet deadlines. Keeping in mind that any team members new to the project have to learn about *both* the design and the model they have been thrown into, follow these suggestions so new staff can help production and don't accidentally break anything along the way:

Create content, content, content. You will find that you will be making model families or detail components until the end of the project. This process will help get the newbie engaged in a specific part of the project and also isolate them enough until they learn more about how the model has gone together.

Put them into a drafting role. Even if this isn't their ultimate role on the project, having staff new to the design help create views and lay out sheets will get them familiar with the architecture while still allowing the team to progress on the document set.

Start them to work on detailing.   Every project can always use someone who knows how to put a building together. If you have someone new to the project and possibly even new to Revit, let them embellish some of the views already created and laid out on sheets. These views can be layered with 2D components, linework, and annotations.

Modeling Site

In the previous sections of this chapter, you learned about the fundamental tools for editing and modifying model elements. Another set of tools you should become familiar with are the site tools. They allow you to create a context within which your building models can be situated. For example, a toposurface will create a hatched area when you view your building in a section, and it will function as a hosting surface for site components such as trees, shrubs, parking spaces, accessories, and vehicles (Figure 13.5).

FIGURE 13.5 A toposurface can host components such as trees, entourage, and vehicles.

The site tools in Revit are only intended to be used for the creation of basic elements, including topography, property lines, and building pads. Although editing utilities are available to manipulate the site elements, these tools are not meant to be used for civil engineering like the functionality found in AutoCAD Civil 3D.

In the following sections you'll learn about the different ways to create and modify a toposurface, how to generate property lines with tags, and how to model a building pad within a toposurface.

Using a Toposurface

As its name suggests, a toposurface is a surface-based representation of the topography context supporting a project. It is not modeled as a solid in Revit; however, a toposurface will appear as if it were a solid in a 3D view with a section box enabled (Figure 13.6).

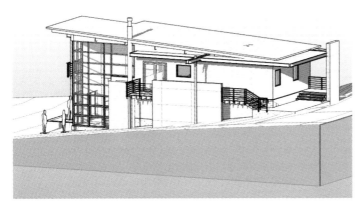

FIGURE 13.6 Toposurfaces will appear as a solid in a 3D view only if a section box is used.

You can create a toposurface in three different ways: by placing points at specific elevations, by using a linked CAD file with lines or points at varying elevations, or by using a points file generated by a civil engineering application. We'll examine these techniques in the following exercises.

Creating a Toposurface from Imported Data

A common workflow you may encounter involves the use of CAD data generated by a civil engineer. In this case, the engineer must create a file with 3D data.

Certification
Objective

Blocks, circles, or contour polylines must exist in the CAD file at the appropriate elevation to be used in the process of generating a toposurface in Revit.

In the following exercise, you will download a sample DWG file with contour polylines. You must link the file into your Revit project before creating the toposurface.

1. Create a new Revit project using the default.rte or DefaultMetric .rte template.

2. Download the file c13-Site-Link.dwg from this book's web page.

3. Activate the Site plan in the Project Browser.

4. Go to the Insert tab in the ribbon and click the Link CAD button. Select the c13-Site-Link.dwg file and set the following options:

   ▶ Current View Only: Unchecked

   ▶ Import Units: Auto-Detect

   ▶ Positioning: Auto - Center To Center

   ▶ Place At: Level 1

5. Click Open to close the dialog box and complete the insertion of the CAD link. Open a default 3D view to examine the results (Figure 13.7).

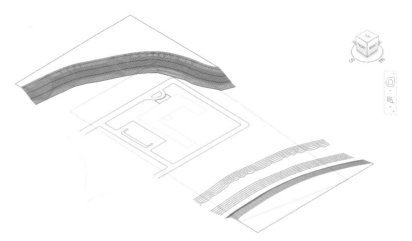

FIGURE 13.7 Linked CAD file as seen in a 3D view

6. From the Massing And Site tab in the ribbon, click the Toposurface button. In the Tools panel on the Modify | Edit Surface ribbon, select Create From Import and then Select Import Instance.

7. Pick the linked CAD file, and the Add Points From Selected Layers dialog box will appear (Figure 13.8). Click the Check None button and then select the layers C-TOPO-MAJR and C-TOPO-MINR.

FIGURE 13.8 Select only the layers containing 3D contour information.

8. Click OK to close the dialog box. It may take a few seconds to generate the points based on the contour polylines in the linked file, but they will appear as black squares when they have all been placed.

9. If you would like to use fewer points to define the toposurface, click the Simplify Surface button in the contextual ribbon and enter a larger value such as 1'-0" [250 mm].

10. Click the Finish Surface button in the contextual ribbon to complete the toposurface. Change the visual style of the view to Consistent Colors to examine your results.

Creating a Building Pad

A *building pad* in Revit is a unique model element that resembles a floor. It can have a thickness and compound structure, it is associated with a level, and it can be sloped using slope arrows while you're sketching its boundary. The building pad is different from a floor because it will automatically cut through a toposurface, defining the outline for your building's cellar or basement.

Certification
Objective

The process to create a building pad is virtually identical to that of creating a floor. Let's run through a quick exercise to create a building pad in a sample project:

1. Open the file c13-Site-Pad.rvt, which can be downloaded from this book's web page.

2. Activate the floor plan named Site in the Project Browser. You will see an existing topographic surface and property line. Notice that reference planes were created to demarcate the required zoning setbacks from the property line. Foundation walls have been created within these reference planes.

   Note that you don't have to create a property line and walls before creating a building pad. You might create a building pad before any other building elements. Just realize that you can utilize the Pick Walls mode to associate the boundary of the building pad with the foundation walls.

3. Activate the Cellar floor plan from the Project Browser.

4. Go to the Massing And Site tab in the ribbon and click the Building Pad button. In the Properties palette, change the Height Offset From Level value to 0.

5. Switch to Pick Walls mode in the Draw panel of the contextual ribbon and then pick the inside edges of the four foundation walls. You can use the Tab-Select method to place all four lines at once.

6. Click the Finish Edit Mode button in the contextual ribbon to complete the sketch and then double-click the section head in the plan view to examine your results. Notice the top of the building pad is at the Cellar level and the poche of the topographic surface has been removed in the space of the cellar (Figure 13.9).

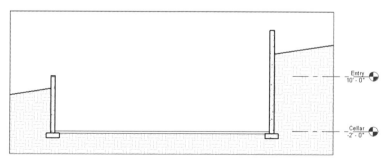

FIGURE 13.9 This section view illustrates how the building pad adjusts the extents of the topographic surface.

Adjusting the Section Poche for Topographic Surfaces

If you would like to customize the settings for the fill pattern and depth of poche, locate the small arrow at the bottom of the Model Site panel in the Massing And Site tab of the ribbon. Clicking on it will open the Site Settings dialog box as shown here:

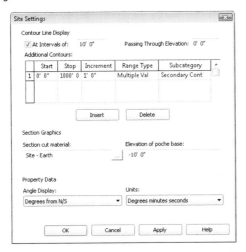

As you can see in this dialog box, you can change the Section Cut Material and the Elevation Of Poche Base settings. Note that the elevation value is in relation to the Revit project base point. You can also adjust the display format of contour lines shown on topographic surfaces as well as the units displayed by property lines.

Detailing in Revit

Since you can create the same details and sheet views using a few different methods, it becomes important to understand when to use each of these detail methodologies. Knowing when to use each will depend on how your model was constructed, the scale of your view, and ultimately your comfort level and experience with Revit. To choose the right type of workflow to use, ask yourself these three simple questions:

How many times will you see the detail in the model?

There are many detail conditions within the model environment that you will see a variety of times. Knowing how often you will see that condition will help you gauge whether it is worth taking the time to model in 3D or whether it will be better as a simple, 2D detail. As a general rule of thumb, if you are going to see the condition more than once, it will probably be worth your time to model it. If you will see the condition only once, it will probably be a good idea to simply draft it as a 2D detail. You will have many doorjamb conditions within the model, but you'll need to see the detail condition only once. In this case, it's probably better to simply draft that detail in 2D because you'll never see the exposed conditions within the doorjamb beyond this detail. As another example, if you are working on a window detail (the whole window, not the head or sill or jamb), you will see this window cut in several plan locations and several sectional location—so many times with the document set. Because of all these cuts, it makes more sense to model the window once and set the parametric conditions to reflect the level of detail needed for the scale of the drawing.

What scale are you drawing your detail in?

The scale you are drawing in will have a large impact on whether to model the elements or draft them. A good rule of thumb is to draft all your details 1″ = 1′-0″ [1:10] and larger. Obviously, the smaller the scale, the more likely you are to see the building elements within the context of the rest of the model and of other components. So, a wall section at ⅜″ = 1′-0″ [1:25] scale would include a lot of the modeled building context, while our doorjamb condition would show very little of the building context.

How good are you at using Revit?

This is a critical question for modeling and detailing. Using Revit is an iterative process—you cannot expect to master the entire application the first time you model a building. So, it's important to be honest with your skill level so you don't bite off more than you can chew in any phase of the project. If it is your first use of Revit and the deadline is short and modeling the detail is complicated, draft it. You'll still be able to take advantage of many other key elements of the application, like its ability to organize your sheet set, automatic section cuts, and detail flags, among other things. You can take on modeling the complex detail in the next project when you have more experience with the application.

Performing Quality Control on Your Revit Model

In any project process, you should always maintain a level of quality control to ensure a solid workflow. When working in a BIM environment, good model maintenance is an imperative part of the process. A well-maintained model will open quickly and be responsive when changing views or manipulating content. A model that is not well maintained can have a very large file size, take a long time to open or save, or even become corrupted. Letting the quality control of your model suffer can negatively impact the team's overall production and lead to frustration because team members cannot be as efficient as they'd like to be. The model size will grow, it will take a long time to save locally or synchronize with central (SWC), and the file can suffer corruption or crashes.

Maintaining a good, healthy model is not a hard thing to accomplish. Doing so takes about as much effort as regularly changing the oil in your car. The important thing, as with your car, is doing the regular maintenance so you don't have to fix a big problem that could have been avoided. In the following sections, we'll discuss simple things you can do and watch using tools already built into Revit that will help flag whether a problem exists.

Keeping an Eye on File Size

Watch the size of your file. The size of your file is a good metric for general file stability. A typical Revit file size for a project in construction documents will be between 100 MB and 250 MB—250 MB is on the high side of file sizes. Beyond that, you will find that the model will be slow to open and hard to rotate in 3D views, and other views, such as building elevations and overall plans, will also be slow to open.

Should your file become large or unwieldy, you have several ways you can trim your file down and get your model lean and responsive again.

Purging Unused Families and Groups

On the Manage tab is a command called Purge Unused. This command removes all the unused families and groups from your model by deleting them. There are many times within a design process when you will change window types or wall types or swap one set of families for another. Even if those elements are not being used in the project, they are being stored within the file, and therefore when the file is opened, they are being loaded into memory. Depending on the stage of your project, you should periodically delete these elements from the model to keep your file size down. Don't worry—if you find you need a family you've removed, you can always reload it.

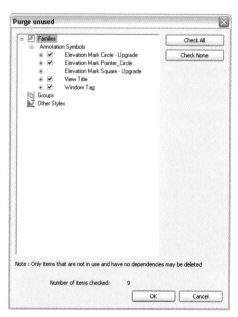

Select the Manage tab and choose Purge Unused from the Settings panel. Depending on the size of your model and how many families you have loaded, it might take Revit a few minutes to complete this command.

After Revit is done thinking, it will provide you with a list of all the families and groups in the file that are not actively within a view (Figure 13.10). At this point, you have the option to select the elements you want to delete or to keep and remove the rest.

FIGURE 13.10 The Purge Unused
dialog box

We don't recommend that you use this command in the early stages of design, mainly because your file size won't be that large early on and purging at this stage would eliminate any preloaded families that you might have included in your template. During schematic design and design development, you are typically going through design iteration and will likely be adding and removing content regularly. It can become a hassle to have to constantly load or reload families into the model. If your model is not suffering from performance issues or the file size isn't unruly, it's not necessary to perform a Purge Unused.

Cutting Down on the Number of Views

The ability to quickly create views within a model is one of the fast and easy benefits of using Revit. This ability can also be a detriment, though, if it is not managed. Beyond the hassle of having to sort through many views to find the one you need, having too many views in Revit can also impact your performance and file size.

Obviously, a number of views are needed within the model to create the construction documentation. Beyond those views, you will find yourself creating additional views to study the design, deal with model creation, or simply view the building or project from a new angle. These types of "working views" will never make it to the sheet set, and some will be used for only brief periods.

How Many Working Views Is too Many?

How many working views is too many to have in your model? The obvious answer is when performance begins to suffer, you need to start looking at ways to make the model lean and speed up response times. We had a project team new to Revit, and they were complaining about the file being slow to open and manipulate. When reviewing their model, we saw their file size was around 800 MB! We were surprised they were even able to do any work at all.

One of the first things we did to get the file size down was look at all the views that were not on sheets. We found they had more than 1,200 views not being used. Deleting those views, paired with a File ➢ Save (with the Compress box checked), brought the file size down to 500 MB. Although the result was still high, you can see the impact too many views has on your file size.

Finding Errors and Warnings

A seemingly obvious way to troubleshoot your model is to use the Errors And Warnings tool. Although this tool will do very little to affect your overall file size, the Errors And Warnings box will alert you to problems within the model that should regularly be addressed to ensure file stability. To locate this dialog box, on the Inquiry panel of the Manage tab, click the Errors And Warnings button.

Clicking this button opens the dialog box shown in Figure 13.11, which lists all errors and warnings still active in your project file.

FIGURE 13.11 The Errors And Warnings dialog box

Errors and warnings are essentially all types of issues Revit has resolving geometry, conflicts, or formulas that do not equate. Things that will appear in this dialog box are instances where you have multiple elements sitting directly on top of each other, thereby creating inaccurate schedule counts; wall joints that do not properly clean themselves up; wall and room separation lines overlapping; stairs that have the wrong number of risers between floors; and so on. This dialog box shows you all the times the yellow warning box appeared at the bottom-right corner of the screen and you ignored it. Errors that go unchecked not only can compound to create other errors but can lead to inaccurate reporting in schedules or even file corruption. Check the Errors And Warnings dialog box regularly as part of your periodic file maintenance and try to keep the number of instances to a minimum.

Notice that the Errors And Warnings dialog box has an Export feature. Use this feature to export your error list to an HTML file, so you can read it at your leisure outside the model environment (Figure 13.12). You can also pull this list into a Microsoft Word or Excel document so you can distribute the errors across the team for them to be resolved.

In the example shown in Figure 13.12, using the Jenkins model, we have 261 errors and warnings in the file. How many errors in a file are too many? Much of that depends on your model, computer capabilities, what the error types are, and your deliverable. For instance, if you are delivering a BIM model to your client or to the contractor, you might have a zero error requirement. In that case, no errors are acceptable. If you are still actively in the design phase of the project, however, you will always have some errors—it is an inescapable part of the process of iteration. As you refine the drawings, errors will be resolved, and as you add new content to the model that is in need of resolution, new errors will be created. If you are not worried about a model deliverable, you can get away with having fewer than 1,000 errors in the project without too much trouble. That said, the cleaner the model, the smoother it will run.

JenkinsMusicBldg-Cntrl-Eddy Error Report (1/3/2010 11:51:07 AM)

Error message	Elements
Highlighted walls are attached to, but miss, the highlighted targets.	Exterior and Structure : Floors : Floor : CIP Concrete : id 263090 Exterior and Structure : Walls : Basic Wall : 12" COATED CMU : id 613698
Highlighted walls are attached to, but miss, the highlighted targets.	Exterior and Structure : Floors : Floor : CIP Concrete : id 263090 Exterior and Structure : Walls : Basic Wall : Exterior - Brick 2 : id 693453
Highlighted walls are attached to, but miss, the highlighted targets.	Exterior and Structure : Floors : Floor : CIP Concrete : id 269226 Interiors : Walls : Basic Wall : Interior - Gyp 4 7/8" : id 605102
Highlighted walls are attached to, but miss, the highlighted targets.	Exterior and Structure : Walls : Basic Wall : Exterior - Brick 2 : id 325781 Exterior and Structure : Floors : Floor : CIP Concrete : id 334468
Highlighted walls are attached to, but miss, the highlighted targets.	Exterior and Structure : Walls : Basic Wall : Exterior - Brick 2 : id 325861 Exterior and Structure : Floors : Floor : CIP Concrete : id 334468

FIGURE 13.12 Exporting the errors and warnings

THE ESSENTIALS AND BEYOND

This chapter focused on understanding some essential but atypical things about Revit and a BIM workflow. We discussed how you can best transition from a 2D CAD environment to a Revit BIM workflow, how to incorporate some of the lesser used (but just as important) tools like site work and creating pads. We also discussed not only how to use the tools in Revit but how to make sure to manage the file itself. Good file management will help to ensure your Revit projects are quick and responsive. Using Revit means u nderstanding BIM as a workflow and process at all levels within your office and at all phases on your project. Being prepared for a process change as well as a software change will help you become successful as you move into BIM.

ADDITIONAL EXERCISES

▶ Diagram your project or office's historical workflow using CAD or hand drafting. Consider the hours used in each phase of the project and the number of staff needed to complete a given phase. Track your first Revit project so you can compare the two.

▶ Revit is a great tool, but it is also one of many that you will use in your projects. Discuss with your design teams how they would like to transition from design tools (like SketchUp or trace paper) to Revit.

CHAPTER 14

Tips, Tricks, and Troubleshooting

This chapter provides tips, tricks, and troubleshooting to help keep your project files running smoothly. Listed here are pointers to keep you from getting into trouble, as well as a peppering of time-savers and other great ideas.

In this chapter, you learn the following skills:

▶ **Optimizing performance**

▶ **Using best practices**

▶ **Fixing file corruption**

▶ **Learning tips and shortcuts**

▶ **Finding additional resources**

Optimizing Performance

It should make sense that a smaller file on a good network will run the fastest. There is no "typical" Revit file size, and they can range anywhere from 10 MB to over 300 MB. Much of that variation depends on the level of detail in the model itself, the presence of imported geometry (2D CAD files, SketchUp, and so on), the number of views you have, and the overall complexity. Obviously, your hardware configuration will also be a factor in determining the speed and operation of your models.

You can optimize your hardware in a number of ways to get the most out of the configuration you have. You should first look at the install specifications and recommended hardware specs for a computer running Revit. Autodesk has published those requirements on its website, and they are updated with each new version of Revit. You can find the current specs at **www.autodesk.com/revit**; choose System Requirements under the Product Information heading.

Beyond the default specifications, you can do a number of things to help keep your files nimble. Here are some other recommendations:

Use a 64-bit OS.   Revit likes RAM, and the more physical RAM it can use, the more model you can cache into active memory. Windows now offers several versions of a 64-bit OS. Windows XP, Windows Vista, and Windows 7 all have 64-bit capability. This allows you to bridge the 32-bit limit of Windows XP and earlier. The older operating systems were limited to only 2 GB of RAM per application. A 64-bit OS allows you to use as much as you can pack into your machine.

If you have a 32-bit OS, use the 3 GB switch.   If you have a 32-bit OS such as Windows XP, need to get your project done, and don't want to deal with the upgrade, use the 3 GB switch. This setting allows you to grab an extra gigabyte of RAM from your computer for a maximum of 3 GB. To take advantage of this switch, you'll need to load Windows XP Service Pack 2 and follow the instructions found on the Autodesk support site at **www.autodesk.com/support**; choose Revit Building from the menu, and read the support article on enabling the 3 GB switch. Of course, you need more than 2 GB of RAM in your workstation.

Figure out how much RAM your project will need.   Before you email your IT department requesting 12 GB of RAM, figure out how much you're actually going to use on your project. Your OS and other applications like Microsoft Outlook will use some of your RAM, but you can calculate how much RAM Revit will need to work effectively. The formula is as follows:

Model size in Explorer × 20 + Linked File Size(s) × 20 = Active RAM needed

Let's look at a couple examples of this to demonstrate how it works. You have a Revit file with no linked files and your file size on your server is 150 MB. So 150 × 20 = 3,000 or 3 GB of RAM to operate effectively. In another example, you have a 120 MB file, a 50 MB structural model linked in, and four CAD files at 1 MB each:

$(120 \times 20) + (50 \times 20) + (4 \times 20) = 3480$ MB, or 3.5 GB of RAM

Once you've put as much RAM into your workstation as is practical, your next recourse for improving model performance is to reduce your file size so you're not using as much RAM. Here are some tips to do that and thereby improve your file speed.

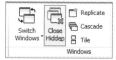

Manage your views.   There are two things you can do using views to help improve performance. First, the more views you open, the more information you will load into active RAM. Close windows you're not using to help minimize the drain on your resources. You can always close all the windows but your active one, using the Close Hidden Windows tool. Choose the View tab and click the Close Hidden button. It's easy to have many views open at once, even if you're concentrating on only a few views.

The other way to manage your views is to get rid of the ones you don't need. Revit allows you to make different views within your model quickly and easily. This feature can sometimes lead to having a lot of views (sometimes hundreds) that you aren't using in your document set and don't plan to use. Adding too many views can raise your overall file size even if you haven't added any geometry. Get rid of those unused views—typically views that are not on sheets—to help keep your file running smooth.

Delete or unload unused CAD files. There are many times in a project process when you'll want to load content from another source as a background. This could be a client's CAD as-built drawings or a consultant's MEP design. You might link or import these files into your drawing and, during the busy course of the project, forget about them. As you've seen from the earlier tips on RAM use, all these small files add up. Getting rid of them can speed up your file and is just good housekeeping. If the file is linked, you can unlink it using the Link CAD button on the Insert tab. If they are inserted, right-click an instance of the file and choose Select All Instances from the context menu. Clicking Delete now will delete all the instances in the entire model as opposed to only the active view.

Don't explode imported CAD files. A CAD file when imported into Revit is a collection of objects that is managed as single entity. If you explode a CAD file, the single object immediately becomes many objects—and these all take up space in the file, requiring more resources from Revit to track and coordinate.

If you're importing DWG files, leave them unexploded as much as possible. If you need to hide lines, use the Visibility/Graphic Overrides dialog box to turn layers on and off. Explode *only* when you need to change the imported geometry, and start with a partial explode to minimize the number of new entities. The margin illustration shows the tools available in the Options Bar when you select an imported or linked DWG file. Also note that lines smaller than $\frac{1}{32}''$ (1mm) are not retained with CAD files are exploded. You could wind up with unusable imports.

A better workflow than importing your CAD files directly into the project is to import them into a Revit family and then load that family into the project. This approach will also aid in keeping accidents from happening, such as a novice user exploding the file.

Turn on volume computation only as needed.   Calculating the volumes on a large file can slow down your model speed immensely. Volume calculations are typically turned on when exporting to gbXML, but sometimes teams forget to turn them back off again. Volumes will recalculate each time you edit a room, move a wall, or change any of the building geometry. Turn off this option using the Area & Volume Computations dialog box found on the Room & Area panel on the Home tab (Figure 14.1).

FIGURE 14.1 Choose the area calculations to minimize unneeded computations.

Using Best Practices

Good file maintenance is critical to keeping your files running smoothly and your file sizes low. Here are some best practices and workflows identified in other areas of the book but consolidated here as a quick reference.

Manage the amount of information shown in views.   Learn to manage the amount of information needed in a given view. Don't show more than you need to show in a view by working to minimize your view depth and level of detail. Here are some simple tips to keep your individual views working smoothly:

> **Minimize the level of detail.**   Set your detail level, found in the View Control Bar, relative to your drawing scale. For example, if you're working on a ⅟₃₂″ (1:100) plan, you probably don't need

Detail Level set to Fine. Doing so will cause the view to have a higher level of detail than the printed sheet can show, and you'll end up with not only black blobs on your sheets, but also views that are slow to open and print.

Minimize view detail.   Along with the amount of detail you turn on in the view using the Detail Level tool, make sure you're not showing more than you need to. For instance, if you have wall studs shown in a ¹⁄₁₆″ (1:200) scale plan or the extruded aluminum window section shown in a building section, chances are it will not represent correctly when printed. Turning off those elements in your view will keep things moving smoother as well as printing cleaner.

Minimize view depth.   View depth and crop regions are great tools to enhance performance. As an example, a typical building section is shown in Figure 14.2. The default behavior causes Revit to regenerate all of the model geometry the full depth of that view every time you open the view. To reduce the amount of geometry that needs to be redrawn, drag the section's far clip plane (the green dashed line when you highlight the section) in close to the cutting plane.

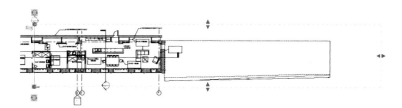

FIGURE 14.2 Minimizing the view depth

Model only what you need.   While it is possible to model to a very small level of detail, don't fall into the trap of overmodeling. Be smart about what you choose to model and how much detail you plan to show. If it's not conveying information about the project, maybe it's not really needed. The amount of information you do or do not model should be based on your project size and complexity, your timeframe, and your comfort level with the software.

How much to model: use these three rules of thumb. When trying to decide how much detail to put into a model or even a family, there are three very good rules of thumb to help you make the right decision for the element you're looking to create.

Scale What scale will this detail be seen in? If it's a very small-scale detail, it might be simpler to just draw it in 2D in a drafting view.

Repetition How many times will this detail appear in the drawing set? If it will appear only in one location or only one time, it might be easier to just draft it in 2D rather than try to model the element. If it will appear in several locations, modeling is probably the better solution. The more exposure an element has in the model (the more views it shows in), the more reason you have to model it. For example, doors are good to model. They show in elevations and plans all over the sheet set.

Quality How good at modeling families in Revit are you? Honestly? Don't bite off more than you can chew. If you're new to Revit, keep it simple and use 2D components. The more projects you complete in Revit, the better you'll understand the change to a BIM workflow.

Don't overconstrain. Embedding user-defined constraints into families and the model help keep important information constant. However, if you don't need to lock a relationship, don't do it. Overconstraining the model can cause problems later in the project process when you want to move or modify locked elements. Constrain only when necessary. Otherwise, let the model be free.

Watch out for imported geometry. While Revit has the ability to use geometry from several other file sources, use caution when doing so. Remember that everything you link into Revit takes up about 20 times the file size in your system's RAM. So, linking a 60 MB NURBS-based ceiling design will equal 2 GB of RAM and more than likely slow down your model. Deleting unused CAD files, using linking rather than importing, and cleaning up the CAD geometry before insertion will help keep the problems to a minimum.

Purge unused files. You will find that you won't use every family or every group you create in your model. Revit has a tool that will allow you to get rid of those unused elements to help keep your file sizes down to a reasonable level. This tool, Purge Unused, can be found on the Manage tab on the Settings panel. If your file is very large, it can take several minutes to run, but eventually you'll be presented with a list (Figure 14.3) of all the unused elements within your file.

FIGURE 14.3 Use the Purge Unused
dialog box to reduce file size.

Using this tool is typically not recommended at the beginning of a project while
you are still iterating various design solutions and file sizes tend to be fairly small.

Model correctly from the beginning.   As you refine your design, it's critical
to model correctly right from the beginning, not taking shortcuts, so you don't
have to fix things later. If you can begin by thinking about how your project will
be assembled, it will save you a lot of time later in the process. It's good practice
to plan ahead, but remember that Revit will allow you to make major changes at
any stage in the process and still maintain coordination. If you are still in early
phase of design and do not know the exact wall type, use generic walls to cap-
ture your design intent; changing them later will be simple.

Manage workshar files.   When employing worksharing on a project, there
are additional tools and tips you'll want to follow:

> **Make a new local copy once a week.**   In a workshared environ-
> ment, your local copy can begin to perform poorly or grow in file
> size while the central file remains small and nimble. If this is the
> case, it might be time to throw out the old local copy for a new
> one. As a general practice, if you're accessing a project on a daily
> basis, it's a good idea to make a new local copy once a week.

Divide your model.   For larger projects or campus-style projects, you can break up your model into smaller submodels that are linked together. You can also do this on a single, large building. Dividing up a model helps limit the amount of information you are loading into a project at one time.

If you decide to divide your project, make your cuts along lines that make sense from a holistic-building standpoint. Don't think of the cuts as you would in CAD, but think about how the actual assemblies will interact in the building. For example, don't cut between floors 2 and 3 on a multistory building unless you have a significant change in building form or program. Here's a list of some good places to split a model:

- ▶ At a significant change in building form or massing
- ▶ At a significant change in building program
- ▶ Between separate buildings on the site
- ▶ At the building site

Fixing File Corruption

From time to time your project files will begin to experience duress and possible corruption. This can happen for any number of reasons; network problems, file size, too many errors, gremlins. If your file begins crashing, don't panic. There are a few things you can do before calling Revit Support. Here are some suggestions to help get you back on track:

Review warnings.   Each time you create something that Revit considers a problem, a warning is issued. Warnings will accumulate if left unresolved. Think of all these errors as unresolved math calculations. The more there are, the more your computer will have to struggle to resolve them, and eventually you will have performance issues or file instability. To review the warnings, click the Warning button on the Manage tab. You'll get a dialog box like Figure 14.4, which will allow you to search for and resolve the problem objects.

Reduce your file size.   Sometimes when file corruption occurs it's due to a file that has grown beyond capacity of the machines using it. Reduce your file size using the previous tips to make the model more manageable and resolve some of the errors.

FIGURE 14.4 Resolving errors

Audit the file. Another way to deal with file corruption is to perform an audit on your file. You can find this tool in the lower-left corner of the File Open dialog box (Figure 14.5). Auditing a file will review the data structures and try to correct any problems that have occurred. When the audit is completed, ideally you will have a fully functioning file again.

FIGURE 14.5 Auditing a file

You can audit either a local file or the central file itself. Whenever you audit a file, you'll want to make a new central copy and have all of your project team create new local copies. The last thing you want is have someone with file corruption in a local copy synchronize those problems back to your newly fixed central file.

Learning Tips and Shortcuts

Beyond all the things you can do to hone your Revit skills, you will begin to learn a number of tips and shortcuts as your experience grows using Revit. Here is a compilation of some of those tips and tricks:

Let Revit do the math. Revit is like a big calculator and it's very good at doing math correctly. Don't want to spend the time trying to figure out what your room size is after you subtract a 3⅝″ and ⅝″ piece of gypsum board from an 11′–2″ room? Don't. If you need to modify a dimension, simply add an equal sign and a formula (Figure 14.6), and Revit will calculate the value for you.

Dimensions	
Thickness	=4' 5" - 2 13/16"
Height	7' 0"
Trim Projection Ext	0' 1"
Trim Projection Int	0' 1"

FIGURE 14.6
Performing calculations in Revit

Add a sloped ceiling. You want to add a gypsum soffit to the bottom of a stair or you want a sloped ceiling? Well, you can't do that with the Ceiling tool. But you can with a ramp. Make a gypsum board ramp and align it to the bottom of your stair or angle it to create your sloped ceiling plane.

Make elevators visible in your plans. You want to create a shaft that will penetrate all the floors of your building and put an elevator in it that will show in all your plans. You could do this with an elevator family and cut a series of holes in the floors by editing floor profiles, but sometimes those holes stop aligning on their own recognizance. Fortunately, you can do both things at once using the Shaft tool found on the Opening panel of the Home tab. Here, you can not only cut a vertical hole through multiple floors as a single object, but you can also insert 2D linework to represent your elevator in plan (Figure 14.7). Every time the shaft is cut, you're certain to see the elevator linework.

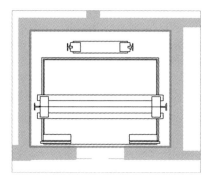

FIGURE 14.7 Adding elevators to a shaft

Orient to view. Creating perspective views of isolated design elements can be quick and easy in plan or section, but let's say you want to see that same element in 3D to be able to work out the details.

1. Create a plan region or section cut isolating the area in question. If you're using a section, make sure to set your view depth to something practical.

2. Open the default 3D view or any axon of the project.

3. Right-click the ViewCube, select Orient To View, and select your view from the context menu

4. Now your 3D view will look identical to your section or plan region, but by rotating the view, you'll be able to see that portion in 3D.

Tune your shortcuts. Revit now allows you to edit your keyboard shortcuts without the hassle of rooting through your hard drive looking for a TXT file. To edit your shortcuts, click the Application menu and select Options. Choose the User Interface tab and then the Customize button. The Keyboard Shortcuts dialog box (Figure 14.8) allows you to edit those shortcuts. Consider making common shortcuts the same letter. So, instead of pressing VG to get to your Visibility/ Graphic Overrides dialog box, make the shortcut VV for quicker access.

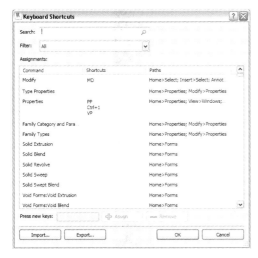

FIGURE 14.8 Editing your keyboard shortcuts

Drag and drop families.   You need to load a family into Revit, you have the Explorer window open, and you know where the family is, but you don't want to go through the laborious effort of navigating across your office's server environment to get there. No problem. You can drag and drop Revit families from Explorer directly into the project file.

Copy a 3D view.   You made the perfect 3D view in your last project, and you can't figure out how to get it into your current project. Fortunately, there's a way to copy views from one project to another. Open both files in the same instance of Revit.

1. In your perfect view, right-click the 3D view in the Project Browser and choose Show Camera from the context menu.

2. Press Ctrl+C to copy the selected camera.

3. In your new model, use Ctrl+V to paste the camera and your view and all its settings are now there.

Use a quick cut poche.   Want to change everything that's cut in a view without having to select every family and change its properties? A quick cut poche is, well, quick:

1. Open the view you want to modify.

2. Using a crossing window, select all the elements within the view.

3. Right-click and choose Override Graphics ➢ By View from the context menu. As shown in Figure 14.9, you can choose any filled region in the project and assign it to anything that is cut within your model.

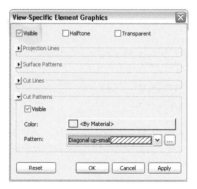

FIGURE 14.9 Using Override Graphics for a quick poche

Move your ribbon. Did you know that you can reorganize the tabs on the ribbon and place them in any order you'd like? Hold down the Ctrl key and select a tab (like Home). You can drag it left or right to change the order they appear in.

Finding Additional Resources

A number of resources are available to help you along the way and improve your Revit use, help you solve problems, or create new content. In our digital age, there is a wealth of information online to help you learn or communicate with users far and wide. So, before you spend hours trying to solve a particularly challenging problem on your own, you might check some of these tools:

Revit Help Menu Open the Revit Help menu by clicking the question mark icon in the upper-right corner of the application. This tool will give you a basic synopsis of all the tools, buttons, and commands available in the application.

Subscription Support If you have purchased Revit on subscription, Revit Subscription Support offers web-based support. Their responses are speedy, their advice top-notch, and chances are they've seen your problem before. Subscription Support can be accessed online at **subscription.autodesk.com**.

AUGI Autodesk User Group International (AUGI) is a source for tips and tricks as well as excellent user forums. The forums are free to participate in, and it's a great place where you can ask questions, find answers, or discuss project workflows. AUGI is located online at **www.augi.com**. Once you're there, look for Revit Architecture.

Revit City Looking for content or families? Revit City offers another free online resource and has a growing database of families posted by users. See **www.revitcity.com**.

YouTube Here's a great reason to tell your IT department you need access to YouTube. Autodesk has its own channel that has some great content, it's free, and it has hundreds of short videos showing you how to perform specific tasks in Revit. See **www.youtube.com/user/autodesk**.

AECbytes AECbytes is a website dedicated to following the trends in the AEC industry, with a strong focus on BIM, technology, and the direction of the industry, put together by Lachmi Khemlani. See **www.aecbytes.com**.

What Revit Wants Revit Professionals is an online resource put together by Luke Johnson that is peppered with great tips and workflows with everything from tips on creating graphics to dealing with crashes. See **www.whatrevitwants .blogspot.com**.

THE ESSENTIALS AND BEYOND

Whew! You made it to the end of what would be 3 days of Revit training. You should know enough by this point to be valuable to your project teams and ready to start your first Revit project. In this chapter you learned some of the tips and tricks seasoned users employ every day. High fives all around! While you bask in the glow of your new knowledge, you might be wondering, "Where do I go from here?" If you're looking for some additional resources beyond what is listed above, join the larger Revit community:

▶ Reading our blog, **http://www.architecture-tech.com/**, is a great place to start.

▶ Check out the AUGI forums. Many a Revit user has found helpful hints there.

▶ If you truly learned from what you read here and want to take the next step, we recommend the Mastering Revit book series, which you can find at **www.sybex.com**, **amazon.com**, or wherever fine Revit titles are sold.

Revit Certification

Autodesk certifications are industry-recognized credentials that can help you succeed in your design career—providing benefits to both you and your employer. Getting certified is a reliable validation of skills and knowledge, and it can lead to accelerated professional development, improved productivity, and enhanced credibility.

This Autodesk Official Training Guide can be an effective component of your exam preparation. Autodesk highly recommends (and we agree!) that you schedule regular time to prepare, review the most current exam preparation roadmap available at **www.autodesk.com/certification**, use Autodesk Official Training Guides, take a class at an Authorized Training Center (find ATCs near you here: **www.autodesk.com/atc**), take an Assessment test, and use a variety of resources to prepare for your certification—including plenty of actual hands-on experience.

To help you focus your studies on the skills you'll need for these exams, the following tables show the objective and in what chapter you can find information on that topic—and when you go to that chapter, you'll find certification icons like the one in the margin here.

Certification Objective

Table A.1 is for the Autodesk Certified Associate Exam and lists the topic, exam objectives, and chapter where the information is found. Table A.2 is for the Autodesk Certified Professional Exam. The topics and exam objectives listed in the table are from the Autodesk Certification Exam Guide.

These Autodesk exam objectives were accurate at press time; please refer to **www.autodesk.com/certification** for the most current exam roadmap and objectives.

Good luck preparing for your certification!

TABLE A.1   Certified Associate Exam Topics and Objectives

Topic	Exam Objectives	*Revit Essentials*
Collaboration	Use work sharing	Chapter 10
	Import DWG files into Revit	Chapter 13
Documentation	Create and modify filled regions	Chapter 11
	Place detail components and repeating details	Chapter 11
	Use dimension strings	Chapter 11
	Set the colors used in a color scheme legend	Chapter 9
Elements	Create a stacked wall	Chapter 3
	Differentiate system and component families	Chapter 6
	Modify an element's type parameters	Chapter 7
	Use Revit family templates	Chapter 6
Modeling	Create a building pad	Chapter 13
	Define floors for a mass	Chapter 2
	Create a stair with a landing	Chapter 5
	Generate a top surface	Chapter 13
	Model railings	Chapter 5
	Edit a model element's material (door, window, furniture)	Chapters 3, 7
	Change a generic floor/ceiling/roof to a specific type	Chapter 3
	Attach walls to a roof or ceiling	Chapter 3

TABLE A.1 Certified Associate Exam Topics and Objectives *(Continued)*

Topic	Exam Objectives	*Revit Essentials*
Views	Define element properties in a schedule	Chapter 12
	Control visibility	Chapters 1, 7
	Use levels	Chapter 2
	Create and manage legends	Chapter 12
	Manage view position on sheets	Chapter 12
	Move the view title independently of the view	Chapter 12
	Organize and sort items in a schedule	Chapter 12

TABLE A.2 Certified Professional Exam Topics and Objectives

Topic	Exam Objectives	*Revit Essentials*
Collaboration	Copy and monitor elements in a linked file	**Not Covered**
	Import DWG files into Revit	Chapter 13
Documentation	Tag elements (doors, windows, etc.) by category	Chapter 6
Elements	Change elements within a curtain wall (grids, panels, mullions)	Chapter 3
	Create compound walls	Chapter 3
	Create a stacked wall	Chapter 3
	Create and modify family categories	Chapters 6, 7
	Create a new family type	Chapter 7

(Continues)

TABLE A.2   Certified Professional Exam Topics and Objectives *(Continued)*

Topic	Exam Objectives	*Revit Essentials*
Modeling	Assess review warnings in Revit	Chapters 13, 14
	Define floors for a mass	Chapter 2
	Create a stair with a landing	Chapter 5
	Create elements such as floors, ceilings, or roofs	Chapters 3, 4
	Generate a top surface	Chapter 13
	Model railings	Chapter 5
	Work with phases	Chapter 8
	Attach walls to a roof or ceiling	Chapter 3
Views	Control visibility	Chapters 1, 7
	Use levels	Chapter 2
	Create a duplicate view for a plan, section, elevation, drafting view, etc.	Chapter 1
	Create and manage legends	Chapter 12

INDEX

Note to the Reader: Throughout this index **boldfaced** page numbers indicate primary discussions of a topic. *Italicized* page numbers indicate illustrations.

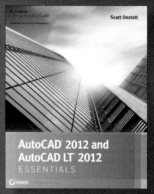